Praise for *The Grangaard Strategy:* *Invest Right During Retirement*

"... an excellent, comprehensive resource for both current retirees and investors concerned about the best ways to prepare for and thrive during retirement. If you are looking for a clear and well-reasoned plan to create dependable income while accounting for the effects of inflation and taxes, *The Grangaard Strategy*® is worth exploring."
— *Better Investing*

"A conventional wisdom–challenging work that explains in detail the 'income ladder' concept. . . . We like the idea behind *The Grangaard Strategy*® . . . The book walks readers through the process of determining how much income they need, and how to set up income ladders. It also discusses different ways to invest for growth, as well as the all-important strategies for determining when to sell growth investments."
— *Fort Lauderdale Sun-Sentinel*

"Grangaard likes to tell the story of two retirees. One is a conservative investor who lives on income from bonds and CDs. He's had to make big lifestyle adjustments lately because his income has withered. The other retiree has invested heavily in stocks and sells them periodically to support himself in retirement. He, too, has had to cut back as a vicious bear market sliced his portfolio's value. Both worry their money won't last long enough. If you share these concerns, then this book is for you. . . . With today's stocks still unsettled and yields at all-time lows, this book should have broad appeal."
— *Kiplinger's Retirement Report*

Continued on next page . . .

What people are saying about
Paul Grangaard . . .

"One of the best seminars I have seen in twenty-one years of financial planning. Great explanations of compounding, risk management and many other fundamental investment concepts."
>—Robert N. Prentiss, Jr.,
>President, Independent Service Company

"Paul Grangaard's seminar was a riveting, eye-opening experience. . . . Paul's ability to organize an immense amount of invaluable information and data, and then deliver it in a comprehensible manner was extremely impressive. The most important aspect of the seminar was that I left with the motivation to develop a lifelong financial plan that will assure the security of my family's future."
>—Shane A. Coen,
>President, Coen & Partners, Inc.

"In the most worthwhile and fundamental way, Grangaard demonstrates how to be well off when you retire and how imperative it is to save for retirement."
>—Robert W. Nemitz,
>Chairman, Rasmussen College

"Not only did Grangaard's seminar cover all the important points, but the content was easy to grasp and Paul's speaking presence and delivery kept the entire audience engaged all evening. It was the best seminar of its type that I have ever attended."
>—Michael J. Galvin, Jr.,
>Past President, Minnesota State Bar Association

Plan Right for
RETIREMENT

with The Grangaard Strategy®

PAUL A. GRANGAARD, CPA

A Perigee Book

A Perigee Book
Published by The Berkley Publishing Group
A division of Penguin Group (USA) Inc.
375 Hudson Street, New York, New York 10014

Copyright © 2004 by Paul A. Grangaard
Text design by Tiffany Estreicher
Cover design by Dorothy Wachtenheim

First Perigee trade paperback edition: January 2004

Visit our website at www.penguin.com

Library of Congress Cataloging-in-Publication Data

Grangaard, Paul A.
Plan right for retirement with the Grangaard strategy / Paul Grangaard.
p. cm.
Includes index.
ISBN 0-399-52944-6
1. Finance, Personal. 2. Retirement income. 3. Investments. 4. Retirement—Planning. I. Title.

HG179.G71873 2004
332.024'014—dc22   2003060935

PRINTED IN THE UNITED STATES OF AMERICA

10 9 8 7 6 5 4 3 2 1

For my family—again, and always.

DISCLAIMERS

The ideas presented in this book are based upon the application of a particular methodology of analyzing and managing investments for retirement planning. Other models and methods of analysis exist in the investment world and some of them may be more suitable for some people under certain circumstances. The methodology presented in this book is for analyzing individual situations and is not a guarantee of any particular investment strategy or result. Readers assume full responsibility for deciding whether the ideas in this book will help them achieve their desired results and for selecting all investments and investment strategies used in their own financial plans.

This publication is designed to provide accurate and authoritative information in regard to the subject matter covered. It is published with the understanding that the publisher and author are not engaged in rendering legal, financial, accounting, or other professional advice or services. If legal, financial, accounting, or other professional advice or services are required, you should consult with a competent professional.

The information provided in this book is for general and informational purposes only and should not be considered an individualized recommendation or personalized investment advice. Although all reasonable efforts have been made to ensure that the information contained in this book is accurate as of the date of publication, the author and the publisher disclaim any liability with respect to the accuracy or timeliness of the information.

Before you go any further there are a few important points you need to be aware of. First, the investment performance data we will be using is historical in nature and does not reflect sales or investment management charges. Second, you should always remember that past performance is not indicative of future results. We often use it to gain a sense of the reasonableness of our own assumptions, but there can never be any guarantee that the past will be able to predict the future. Third, as an investor, your investment returns and the value of your investments will fluctuate, so when redeemed, they may be worth more or less than original cost. Investments are always subject to investment risk, including the possible loss of principal invested. And finally, the equity, or stock market investments we will be talking about in this book are not insured by the FDIC and are not deposits or other obligations of, or guaranteed by, any depository institution. Please keep these points in mind as you read *Plan Right for Retirement*.

All financial organizations and software publishers include a disclaimer that tells users that there is no warranty that their method is correct, and that the work is presented "AS IS." I would like to caution you to read the disclaimer in the front of this book that says that we also present this material "AS IS" and make no warranties—implied or otherwise.

CONTENTS

PART ONE
Deciding When to Retire   9

1. TIMING IS EVERYTHING 11

Deciding when to retire ▪ Figuring out how much time you have to prepare ▪ The importance of timing ▪ Getting started as soon as possible ▪ Creating your own plan

2. THE POWER OF COMPOUNDING 14

The importance of compounding ▪ Compounding different rates of investment return ▪ The impact of longer and shorter compounding periods ▪ The importance of saving early ▪ The consequences of saving too late

3. RATES OF RETURN 21

Different asset classes and rates of investment return ▪ Using reasonable rate of return assumptions ▪ Using history as your guide ▪ Most recent stock market data ▪ The "Rule of 72"

PART TWO
Deciding How Much Income You'll Need

ACKNOWLEDGMENTS

I want to thank John Duff, my publisher and editor at Perigee, for his untiring support and assistance. Salvaging a writer from an inveterate seminar presenter is no mean feat. I only wish I could have made it easier. I also need to thank Beth Mellow, my publicist at Perigee, for her efforts in promoting my first book. She has made a real difference in our ability to get the message out.

Thank you also to Marc Hadley, CFP®. Marc and I have known each other for a long time, and he's the person I go to with my own questions. His intelligence, knowledge, experience, and overwhelming concern for his clients are an inspiration, and his constant willingness to discuss issues or take some time to probe a difficult question is greatly appreciated.

Special thanks go out to all the human resource managers who invited me into their companies over the years to educate their employees about personal financial planning. Their leadership, vision, and sincere concern for their employees have made a real difference in the lives of many. In particular, I want to thank W.F. "Duke" Fuhrer for believing in the importance of financial education way back when it wasn't nearly so trendy. He is one of the most forward-looking business executives I have ever had the pleasure of working with.

And finally, I owe a special debt of gratitude to Theresa Ochs for her gracious assistance in reviewing the book for regulatory compliance purposes. Her work was tireless and far beyond the call of duty.

INTRODUCTION

Do you have a financial plan? Will you be able to retire someday? Do you have any idea what it will take? Do you know how much you will get from your employer and how much you will need to take care of yourself? Many people don't.

I have been presenting seminars and financial planning workshops for the last seven or eight years, and I know from experience how much people still have to learn about managing their own financial affairs. I also know that it isn't that difficult to teach them what they need to understand—and that time is of the essence.

The Current Situation

Walk into any business today and ask someone at random if they participate in their company's 401(k) plan. They can usually give you a "yes" or a "no." Probe a little deeper, however, and you'll begin to get a sense for how little most people really understand about their own financial situation.

Ask the Important Questions

Ask what sort of lifestyle they plan to have when they retire, how much inflation-adjusted income they'll need, or how much they have to accumulate, and you'll probably get a blank, angst-ridden stare. Ask how much they need to save every month, how to invest it, what kind of mutual funds they own, what kind they should own, the risk of those funds, and the rates of return they should be expecting, and most people will give you an uneasy shrug. Ask how their investment strategies should change as they approach retirement and how their annuities and IRAs fit into the mix, and they might just look at you like you're from Mars. These are critical issues for people in control of their own financial destiny—and you need to know the answers.

The Future Isn't Looking So Good

A recent survey by the Consumer Federation of America found that two out of three households—an estimated 65 million families—will fail to realize their major life goals because they haven't developed any kind of broad financial plan. Study after study shows that Americans are not saving enough, that they are not investing properly, and that they are misusing their retirement plans at work. You can't pick up a newspaper or magazine or turn on the news without seeing something about the financial crisis we face in this country—and to make matters worse, it's being played out against the background of a fundamental change in the way we provide for retirement.

You're in Control of Your Own Destiny

For a variety of reasons, and for better or worse, more and more of us are being forced to manage our own retirement affairs. Not only are there more options, but over the last twenty years we've undertaken a huge transfer of responsibility from professional pension plan managers to everyday workers and employees. Unfortunately, we often haven't provided the training and education to go along with it.

You're the Expert Now

We have been moving rapidly away from the old-fashioned pension plans that require no input from participants, provide a guaranteed monthly income for life, and are managed by highly trained investment professionals. They're being replaced by a variety of self-directed retirement accounts like 401(k) and 403(b) plans that require you, the participant, to manage everything yourself. Essentially, we are turning every working American into a pension plan manager—but unfortunately, very few people really know how to do it.

Everyone Is Worried

In November of 1997, President Clinton signed the Savings Are Vital to Everyone's Retirement Act (SAVER Act) into law, which, among other things, called for a national summit on retirement savings. "Through the SAVER Act," said Secretary of Labor Alexis M. Herman, "we will encourage employers to provide pension plans and help teach workers to plan and save adequately for retirement." The prime sponsor of the act, Rep. Harris Fawell, R-Ill., warned that the nation faces "a ticking demographic time bomb that requires increased retirement savings," and that "educating the public about the problem is the first step in diffusing that retirement time bomb."

Education and Action

I couldn't agree more—but the emphasis should be on taking action. We certainly need better education, but we also need to provide tools that help people take control of their own lives. **That's why this book is set up to help you create your own financial plan,** while providing the information and understanding you need to make more informed investment decisions for the rest of your life. To the best of my knowledge, no other book provides the theory and concepts you need to understand, while at the same time giving you the immediate opportunity to apply everything in your own life in the fashion presented here.

Accepting Responsibility

You need to accept the fact that your financial future is in your own hands. In a world of IRAs, annuities, 401(k) and 403(b) plans, taxable accounts, and many other kinds of investments, you need to be able to take care of yourself—because no one is doing it for you. If you have any doubts, just look around. Your long-term financial security will overwhelmingly be a function of how well *you* manage your *own* financial affairs. For most people, step number one is a good education, and step number two is a good financial plan. This book will help to provide both.

Make Sure to Get the Help You Need

Many people have asked me if this is a do-it-yourself manual for financial planning, and the answer is both "yes" and "no." The Grangaard Strategy® has always been dedicated to the idea that everyone can understand what they need to know about creating their own financial plan—but that doesn't necessarily mean that you can do everything yourself. In fact, it's always a good idea to review your plan with a qualified professional and get their advice whenever you make important financial decisions. Selecting an advisor is one of the most important decisions you will ever make, and I hope the information in this book helps you make a better choice. You can also find additional resources to help you do that by going to my website at www.thegrangaardstrategy.com.

Paul A. Grangaard, CPA
Saint Paul, Minnesota

Twenty-five Steps to a Twenty-first-Century Retirement Plan

This book considers personal financial planning in a more logical manner than it's usually presented. Rather than starting out with a mishmash of information about retirement plans, rules, regulations, products, and all the other details that make up the gist of most other financial books, we go right back to the beginning and present everything in the context of your *own* retirement situation. Using twenty-five easy-to-follow steps, you will be able to create a comprehensive and sophisticated financial plan while learning most of what you need to know about saving and investing for retirement.

It's much easier to grasp important and sometimes complicated financial ideas, and to see how they all fit together, when you understand what they mean to *you*. The best way to gain that kind of perspective is to approach the whole topic in the same manner in which you would approach the creation of your own financial plan—and then deal with each individual item as it becomes relevant. Then, all of the important strategies, issues, and product discussions, which are frequently much too abstract and disconnected from the real world, can be understood in terms of how they impact *you*. Everything is much more relevant, compelling, and understandable that way.

Creating a Plan

As you read this book, keep in mind that creating a financial plan is a very linear process, which means that it proceeds in an orderly way from step to step and assumption to assumption, so it's important to be as accurate and realistic as you can. You'll notice that in the examples I use throughout the book I make fairly conservative assumptions and realistic decisions each step of the way.

However, you will also notice that in the illustrations I use every input field and include every kind of asset and source of retirement income, which isn't very realistic. Most people will use only a small number of the available options. I did it this way to show you how to use each of the input fields and lookup tables so you'll be prepared to deal with almost any scenario in your own life.

Don't worry if all the information you need to complete your plan isn't immediately available, or if you have to estimate a few rates of return or account balances. Just follow along and do your best. One of the most important parts of the process is to identify the places you need to do a better job the next time. Remember, planning is an ongoing process, not a one-time event.

The planning strategies we will be using throughout the book are rooted in what I've learned about financial planning education over the years by providing seminars and workshops for corporations, professional groups, non-profit organizations and others. They are being used successfully by thousands of people around the country—and I sincerely hope they will help you as well.

Financial Planning One Small Step at a Time

As you work through the planning process you may be surprised by some of the results. Don't panic. Many of the most important elements, like employer contributions into your retirement plans at work, don't come into play until late in the book. So be calm and patient until you finish. You'll also find that small changes in a rate of return or monthly savings amount are often all that's required to change what may look like a diffi-cult situation into an acceptable and much more readily achievable objective.

Another thing you need to know is that if you want to create a plan for you and a spouse you should each complete your own worksheets, and then pull them together into a combined plan. The only exception is if your spouse doesn't earn income outside the home. As you will see, the overall planning process deals with numerous assumptions and variables that are individually unique, like current salary, expected salary growth, and/or employer matching contributions, which should all be considered separately.

The Map Is Not the Territory

The only thing you can be sure of in financial planning is that your life will not unfold the way you expect—which isn't an indictment of finan-cial planning. You need to have a plan to know whether you are on or off course, and to be able to figure out how to make adjustments throughout your life. Without a plan, you probably won't quantify your goals and objectives, and if you don't do that, it's difficult to know where you're going—or how to get there. But don't make the mistake of taking your plan for reality. More than anything else, it's a map to steer by, and it should be reworked and reconsidered as often as necessary.

Have a Navigator with You at the Helm

Although the plan you create for yourself will be comprehensive and detailed, you should still visit with a financial professional. The time and money you spend getting to know a financial advisor is usually a very good investment. There are just too many elements in a well-managed financial strategy to cover them all in one short book, including income taxes, insurance, long-term care, estate planning, and many others. A qualified financial professional should be able to help you in these areas. You will find more information in the appendix about finding a qualified advisor.

Overview: The Book, the Process, and the Twenty-five Steps

The overall financial planning process is really quite logical. At the highest level, it boils down to six fundamental parts, each of which includes some of the twenty-five steps you need to know and understand.

Part One

First, you have to decide *when* you think you will want to retire. This decision probably has more impact on your plan than anything else, so following *Step #1: Decide When to Retire* is very important. It also leads directly to a discussion of some of the most important theoretical issues—so following the discussion of timing in Chapter 1, we move on to the power of compounding in Chapter 2, investigate rates of return in Chapter 3, dig into compound average annual returns in Chapter 4, discuss the concept of holding periods in Chapter 5, and talk about the importance of diversification in Chapter 6. Each of these concerns is closely related to questions about when you want to retire and how much time you have available to prepare, so we deal with them early on.

Part Two

After you decide when you want to retire, you have to figure out how much income, or lifestyle, you may need for the rest of your life—so we look next at *Step #2: Think About Your Lifestyle,* in Chapter 7. But you also have to consider inflation when you think about your future income needs, so Chapter 8 focuses on *Step #3: Adjust for Inflation.* After taking cost-of-living increases into account, you can move on to Chapter 9 to figure out how much total, inflation-adjusted income you may need in retirement.

Ultimately, you have to estimate how much of your retirement income is likely to come from sources other than your own savings—like traditional pension plans and Social Security. In Chapter 10, we'll consider *Step #4: Estimate Social Security, Step #5: Account for Protected*

Pensions, and *Step #6: Anticipate Other Income* to take all of them into account.

Once you know how much of your income you are likely to have to take care of yourself, you can use that information to figure out how much you may need to accumulate by the time you get to retirement.

Part Three

You can't figure out how much you might need to accumulate *for* retirement until you know how to manage your money *during* retirement, so we start this section with a comprehensive discussion of postretirement asset management in Chapter 11. After you understand *Step #7: Plan to Invest Right in Retirement,* you can use that information to follow *Step #8: Set a Good Accumulation Target* in Chapter 12. And finally, you need to think about the impact of taxes on your overall plan, so in Chapter 13 you will have a chance to consider *Step #9: Keep Taxes in Mind.*

Part Four

This section of the book is set up to help you determine the hypothetical value of your *existing* retirement assets, which may include retirement plans at work, IRAs, annuities, taxable investments, and so on. The hypothetical projected value of these accounts should take care of part of your overall accumulation needs, so you obviously have to include them in the analysis.

In Chapters 14 through 19, you will consider *Step #10: Put a Value on Pensions, Step #11: Project Retirement Plan Balances, Step #12: Project IRA Balances, Step #13: Project Roth IRA Balances, Step #14: Project Annuity Balances,* and *Step #15: Project Taxable Account Balances.* By considering the hypothetical future value of the assets you already have, you can determine how much more you should need to accumulate in the future. In Chapter 20, you will explore *Step #16: Measure the "Missing Money"* to help figure it out.

Part Five

Ultimately, you also need to anticipate the hypothetical value of *future* contributions you intend to make into your IRAs, annuities and taxable accounts. Although much of your future savings will probably go into your retirement plans at work, you may also want to take advantage of these other savings vehicles.

Chapters 21 through 25 consider *Step #17: Value IRA Contributions, Step #18: Value Roth IRA Contributions, Step #19: Value Annuity Contributions,* and *Step #20: Value Your Savings in Taxable Accounts.* By considering the hypothetical future value of the additional contributions you plan to make into these accounts, you should ultimately be able to determine how much more you may need to accumulate in your retirement plans at work. Then, in Chapter 26, you will have an opportunity to start figuring it out by following *Step #21: Establish a Retirement Plan Accumulation Target.*

Part Six

The last step in the planning process is to determine how much you may need to save in your retirement plans at work to accumulate the rest of the money you might need to retire. Before you can do that, you have to account for the contributions you hope to receive from your employer in the form of pension, profit sharing, or matching contributions. In Chapter 27, we follow *Step #22: Account for Employer Contributions* to build these amounts into your plan. Then, you should be able to figure out how much more **you** may need to put away yourself.

In Chapter 28, we implement *Step #23: Formulate a "Fixed-Amount" Savings Plan*, by developing a contribution strategy focused around the idea of saving a fixed amount each month in your retirement plans at work. This is the most conservative approach, because saving the same amount each month for the rest of your life requires you to save a larger percentage of your salary in the early years, and a smaller percentage later on—and can help you get off to a fairly quick start.

Then, to look at it another way, Chapter 29 brings us to *Step #24: Prepare a "Percent-of-Salary" Savings Plan*. Under this strategy, you put away a percentage of your income each month rather than a fixed dollar amount. This approach is less conservative because you tend to save smaller amounts in the early years and larger amounts as your salary increases. The benefit, however, is that you are likely to contribute less when you're making less, and more when you're making more. By putting away a consistent percentage of your lifestyle each year, you are often able to spread the pain of saving for retirement more equally over the years. Even though you may not get off to such a fast start, this is the approach used by many younger investors because it allows you to create a sound retirement plan that you should actually be able to afford to implement.

By the time you finish Chapters 28 and 29 you should have considered most of your current and future retirement assets and determined how much you and your employer may have to sock away in your retirement plans at work.

However, the first retirement plan you pull together is probably not going to be the one you actually use. The importance of your first time through is to give you a feel for how everything fits together. Once you understand that, you should be able to go back and do a better job the second or third time around.

That's why it's so important to follow *Step #25: Get Started Now!* You can't just sit back and hope everything turns out okay. You need to apply what you've learned by reconsidering your assumptions, reevaluating your planning decisions and trying out some different alternatives. With a little practice, you should be able to develop a sound retirement plan, gain a better understanding of your own financial situation and figure out what you need to do next to create the retirement of your dreams.

Finding a "Trained" Grangaard Strategy® Advisor

It's never too early and it's never too late to create a financial plan. If you're looking for a financial professional to help you develop, refine, and implement your plan, you will find resources in the appendix, along with the address of a website that has a list of advisors in your area who have been trained by my company in how to manage money before and during retirement.

PART ONE

Deciding When to Retire

In this section, we will cover:

Step #1: Decide When to Retire

We will also deal with the vitally important concepts of compounding, historical rates of return, compound average annual returns, holding periods, and diversification.

After completing this part of the book, you should have decided when you want to retire and have a good understanding of the importance of that decision.

Timing Is Everything

The first thing you should do when you start working on your financial plan is figure out when you think you will want to retire. Over time, you may want to consider a number of different ages, because it can make a big difference in your overall strategy.

How Much Time Do You Have?

You need to determine a retirement age because it's the only way you can calculate how many years you still have available to accumulate assets— and you do that by subtracting your current age from your retirement age. The result is the number of years still available until you plan to stop working, and it's one of the most important variables in the planning process—because it impacts virtually everything else.

Timing Affects Everything

Once you know the number of years until retirement, you can make some assumptions about your salary in the year before you stop working, which can then be used to determine the lifestyle you may want to carry with you into retirement. You should also know how many years you have available to ride out the ups and downs in the stock market if you plan to go after some of the higher rates of return which, while not guaranteed, have historically been available there. Additionally, you should be able to make forecasts about the hypothetical future value of your assets, because you will know how many years are left for your current and future savings to grow before you need them in retirement. As you can see, setting up a retirement timeline affects just about everything else you do.

Small Changes Can Make a Big Difference

Small changes in the number of years until retirement can have a dramatic effect on your plan. For example, if you're thirty-five years old and you want to retire at age sixty-two, you have about twenty-seven years to grow your assets. If you have a current balance of $40,000 in your retirement accounts, and plan to invest another $350 per month over the next twenty-seven years, you might end up with a balance of about $1,056,000 at retirement—if you earn a stock market rate of return of 10 percent per year.

However, if you decide to retire at age sixty-five, you have three more years to save and invest, so your retirement accounts might be worth about $1,420,000 in thirty years, or more than 34 percent more. Assuming you waited until your full-benefit Social Security age of sixty-seven, your accounts could grow to over $1,700,000 in thirty-two years, an increase of more than 60 percent. You should always remember how dramatic the effects of adding a few more years to your preretirement investment period can be, because it can make the difference between a gloomy retirement scenario and a financial future that could be really exciting and worth striving for.

Don't Wait

You will never have more time than you do right now—so don't wait. It's never too early and it's never too late to start saving for retirement. As the ancient Chinese saying goes, "Don't wait until you are thirsty to begin digging a well."

Create Your Own Plan

It's time to calculate how many years you think you have available until retirement. As you can see in Plan Aid 1a: Example, it's as simple as putting your planned *Retirement Age* into box (a), your *Current Age* into box (b), and then subtracting your *Current Age* from your *Retirement Age* to get the *Number of Years Until Retirement* in box (c).

Plan Aid 1a: Example
Number of Years Until Retirement

Retirement Age	(a)	**66**
Current Age	(b)	**44**
Number of Years Until Retirement	(c)	**22**
		(a) – (b)

For illustration purposes only. All assumptions and computational results are hypothetical in nature. There are no guarantees that you will achieve the results shown. You should consult with a financial professional.

After reviewing the example, fill in Plan Aid 1b: Your Plan now, and you will have taken the first step toward creating your own financial plan.

Plan Aid 1b: Your Plan
Number of Years Until Retirement

Retirement Age	(a)	
Current Age	(b)	
Number of Years Until Retirement	(c)	
		(a) – (b)

For illustration purposes only. All assumptions and computational results are hypothetical in nature. There are no guarantees that you will achieve the results shown. You should consult with a financial professional.

The Power of Compounding

Compounding is the process through which you earn investment returns each year on the investment returns from all prior years, as well as on the amounts you originally invest. If there was ever a good reason to seriously consider *Step #1: Decide When to Retire,* it's the power of compounding. In fact, one of the most important reasons for deciding how many years you have until retirement is to establish your preretirement compounding period.

Compounding can be considered the financial equivalent of a snowball rolling downhill. You start with a small amount of snow in the palm of your hand—which is like your original investment. As that little ball starts rolling downhill, it slowly begins to accumulate more snow—which is like the investment returns you earn in the early years. Then, as it picks up momentum, the original little snowball starts getting bigger and bigger at a faster and faster rate, accumulating more and more snow on top of the snow it has already accumulated—which is like the investment returns you earn on all the investment returns you earned in prior years.

An Example of Compounding

To understand how important compounding is, assume that you contribute $500 per month into your 401(k) plan for the next thirty years. If you earn an 11 percent rate of return each year, your account should grow to about $1,253,000 by the time you retire, with your contributions making up only $180,000, or about 14.4 percent. As you can see in Illustration 1, the other $1,073,000, or 85.6 percent of the total, is made up of compounded growth.

In other words, if you start early, invest wisely, and get a reasonable rate of return, most of the money you need to accumulate for retirement should come from the growth on your contributions, not from the contributions themselves.

Everyone's Life Is Different

Some people have thirty years until retirement, while other people have more or less, and not everyone is in a position to contribute $500 per month into a retirement plan. Illustration 2 presents many different combinations of investment time horizons and contribution amounts, and can help you get a better feel for what your own situation might look like.

For example, if you invest half as much, or $250 per month, at 11 percent for forty years, you should be able to accumulate about $1,832,000, or roughly 46 percent more. Alternatively, if you invest $100 per month and plan to retire in twenty years, your account may only grow to about $81,000. The thing to remember is that you need to start saving as soon as possible, because the longer the money can stay invested, the more compounded growth you are likely to get.

Start Saving Now!

One of the most important things about compounding is that the money you put away in the early years should take care of a much larger slice of the retirement pie than the money you contribute later on, because it has so much more time to grow. It's not that you won't need to keep investing, it's just that the early dollars have much more built-in growth potential.

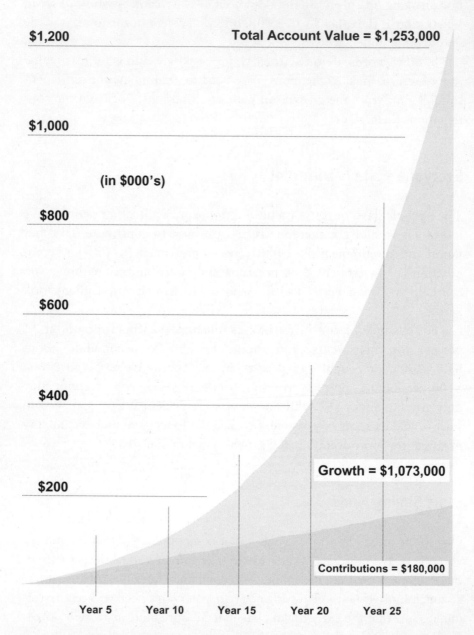

Illustration 1: Compounded Investment Growth
Value of Contributions and Growth on an
Investment of $500 per Month for 30 Years
at an Average Annual Rate of Return of 11%

$1,200   Total Account Value = $1,253,000

$1,000

(in $000's)

$800

$600

$400

$200   Growth = $1,073,000

Contributions = $180,000

Year 5   Year 10   Year 15   Year 20   Year 25

Illustration 2: The Power of Compounding
Value of Investments Growing at an Average Annual Rate of 11.0%

Years Invested	Amount Invested Each Month					
	$1	$25	$50	$100	$250	$500
1	13	315	630	1,259	3,148	6,297
2	27	664	1,329	2,657	6,643	13,286
3	42	1,052	2,104	4,209	10,522	21,045
4	59	1,483	2,966	5,931	14,828	29,656
5	78	1,961	3,922	7,843	19,608	39,215
6	100	2,491	4,983	9,965	24,913	49,826
7	123	3,080	6,160	12,321	30,802	61,603
8	149	3,734	7,468	14,935	37,338	74,676
9	178	4,459	8,919	17,838	44,594	89,188
10	211	5,265	10,530	21,059	52,648	105,295
11	246	6,159	12,317	24,635	61,587	123,174
12	286	7,151	14,302	28,604	71,510	143,020
13	330	8,252	16,505	33,010	82,525	165,049
14	379	9,475	18,950	37,900	94,751	189,502
15	433	10,832	21,664	43,329	108,322	216,644
16	494	12,339	24,677	49,354	123,386	246,771
17	560	14,011	28,021	56,043	140,106	280,213
18	635	15,867	31,733	63,467	158,667	317,333
19	717	17,927	35,854	71,707	179,268	358,537
20	809	20,214	40,427	80,854	202,136	404,272
21	910	22,752	45,504	91,008	227,520	455,039
22	1,023	25,570	51,139	102,278	255,695	511,390
23	1,148	28,697	57,394	114,788	286,970	573,940
24	1,287	32,169	64,337	128,674	321,685	643,370
25	1,441	36,022	72,044	144,088	360,219	720,438
26	1,612	40,299	80,598	161,197	402,991	805,983
27	1,802	45,047	90,094	180,188	450,469	900,938
28	2,013	50,317	100,634	201,268	503,169	1,006,338
29	2,247	56,167	112,333	224,666	561,666	1,123,332
30	2,506	62,660	125,319	250,639	626,597	1,253,195
31	2,795	69,867	139,734	279,469	698,672	1,397,343
32	3,115	77,867	155,735	311,470	778,674	1,557,348
33	3,470	86,748	173,495	346,991	867,476	1,734,953
34	3,864	96,605	193,209	386,419	966,047	1,932,094
35	4,302	107,546	215,092	430,184	1,075,461	2,150,921
36	4,788	119,691	239,382	478,764	1,196,910	2,393,820
37	5,327	133,172	266,344	532,687	1,331,718	2,663,437
38	5,925	148,136	296,271	592,542	1,481,356	2,962,711
39	6,590	164,745	329,491	658,981	1,647,453	3,294,906
40	7,327	183,182	366,364	732,729	1,831,822	3,663,643
41	8,146	203,647	407,294	814,588	2,036,470	4,072,941
42	9,055	226,363	452,726	905,452	2,263,630	4,527,261
43	10,063	251,578	503,156	1,006,311	2,515,778	5,031,556
44	11,183	279,566	559,132	1,118,265	2,795,662	5,591,324
45	12,425	310,633	621,267	1,242,533	3,106,333	6,212,667
46	13,805	345,118	690,236	1,380,471	3,451,178	6,902,357
47	15,336	383,396	766,791	1,533,583	3,833,956	7,667,913
48	17,035	425,884	851,768	1,703,536	4,258,840	8,517,680
49	18,922	473,046	946,092	1,892,184	4,730,461	9,460,922
50	21,016	525,396	1,050,792	2,101,584	5,253,960	10,507,920

For example, if you want to accumulate $1,253,000 in thirty years, and plan to earn an 11 percent rate of return on your money, you need to put away about $500 a month, or $6,000 per year, to reach the target. What's so amazing is that the $30,000 you put away in the first five years of that thirty-year period should grow to over $530,000 by the time you get to retirement.

As you can see in Illustration 3, the $30,000 saved in each subsequent five-year period accumulates to progressively smaller amounts. In fact, the $30,000 you put away in the last five years only accumulates to about $39,000—because it has so much less time to grow.

Waiting Too Long Can Be Costly

The longer you wait to start saving, the more you will probably have to contribute each month, and the smaller will be the share of your total retirement assets taken care of by growth through compounding.

For example, you know that if you save $500 per month at 11 percent for thirty years, you should accumulate about $1,253,000, and that about 85.6 percent of it is likely to come from compounded growth. However, if you wait ten years to get started, and still want to accumulate the same $1,253,000, you will have to put away about $1,550 per month, or three times as much, to be able to reach your target in twenty years. As a result, only about 70% of your total retirement assets will come from growth, and you will probably have to fund a much larger portion yourself.

Illustration 4 shows how dramatically your monthly savings would have to increase if you postpone saving for retirement, and how much less growth you are likely to get. At a certain point, it's probably not even possible to save enough to reach your goal, and you may end up having to reduce your retirement expectations altogether. When it comes to compounding, time can be either your best friend or your worst enemy.

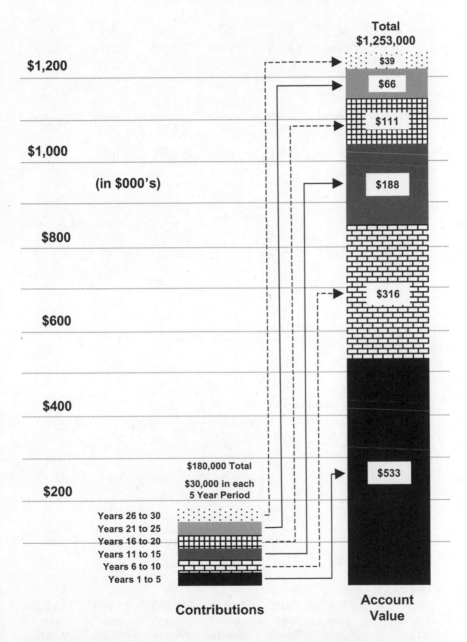

Illustration 3: The Power of Time
$500 per Month Compounding
at 11% Rate of Return for 30 Years

Total
$1,253,000

$1,200

$39

$66

$111

$1,000

(in $000's)

$188

$800

$316

$600

$400

$180,000 Total

$30,000 in each
5 Year Period

$533

$200

Years 26 to 30
Years 21 to 25
Years 16 to 20
Years 11 to 15
Years 6 to 10
Years 1 to 5

Contributions

**Account
Value**

For illustration purposes only. Not representative of an actual investment. Past performance is not a guarantee of future results. Rates of return are hypothetical, and an investor's results may vary. Investments with the potential to earn higher rates of return are generally offset with a higher degree of risk.

Illustration 4: The Importance of Saving Early
Required Monthly Savings Amounts
to Accumulate $1,253,000 at an 11% Rate of Return
over Various Accumulation Periods

	30 Years	25 Years	20 Years	15 Years	10 Years	5 Years
$1,200						
	Growth $1,073	Growth $992	Growth $881	Growth $732	Growth $539	Growth $294
	85.6%	79.2%	70.3%	58.5%	43.0%	23.5%
$1,000						
$800						
$600						
$400						
$200						
	Invest $180	Invest $261	Invest $372	Invest $521	Invest $714	Invest $959
	14.4%	20.8%	29.7%	41.5%	57.0%	76.5%

(In $000's)

$500 per Month	$870 per Month	$1,550 per Month	$2,893 per Month	$5,950 per Month	$15,980 per Month

For illustration purposes only. Not representative of an actual investment. Past performance is not a guarantee of future results. Rates of return are hypothetical, and an investor's results may vary. Investments with the potential to earn higher rates of return are generally offset with a higher degree of risk.

3

Rates of Return

In the compounding examples in Chapter 2, you achieved substantial increases in your account values because you invested in assets like the stock market, which, based on historical averages, might reasonably be expected to earn average annual rates of return in the range of 11 percent per year. If you get lower rates of return you won't be able to accumulate nearly as much, which will most likely have a negative effect on your lifestyle in retirement.

The Twin Pillars of Investing Success

To figure out how much you might expect to accumulate for retirement you have to consider two things. The first is how much you plan to save each month, and the other is the rate of return you hope to earn on those savings. You obviously have to decide for yourself how much to save, and although you can never be sure how much you will earn, you can use history as your guide to making "reasonable" assumptions about future rates of return.

Asset Classes

The returns you are likely to earn in the future will be based substantially on the kinds of investments into which you put your money. Financial professionals often refer to the alternatives as "asset classes," and studies have shown that the "asset class" in which you invest is probably responsible for more than 90 percent of the total return you are likely to get.

For example, if you invest $500 per month in small company stocks, and earn an historical average annual rate of return of 12.4 percent, you should accumulate almost $1,652,000 over a thirty-year investment period. 12.4 percent is the seventy-five-year average annual rate of return for small company stocks between 1926 and 2000, as reported by Ibbotson Associates. Small company stocks are represented by the smallest one-fifth of all stocks listed on the New York Stock Exchange.

However, if you decide instead to put your money into large company stocks for the same thirty-year period, you should accumulate about $1,253,000 at an historical average annual rate of 11 percent, while the same investment in intermediate-term government bonds may only grow to about $430,000 at an historical return of 5.3 percent. Large company stock returns, also reported by Ibbotson Associates, are based on the total return of the S&P Composite Index, which includes five hundred of the largest stocks in the United States from 1957 to the present, and ninety of the largest stocks between 1926 and 1957. Intermediate-term government bond returns are based on data from the *Wall Street Journal* and the CRSP Government Bond File, and are also reported by Ibbotson Associates.

You Will Never Have a Crystal Ball

The past can never infallibly predict the future, and there are always risks involved in using history as your guide in anticipating future investment performance. But you don't really have much else to go on, and it's usually helpful to reflect on past experience when making these kinds of investment decisions and predictions.

Investing for Higher Rates of Return: Creating Larger Accumulations

Illustration 5 shows the hypothetical investment of $500 per month growing in a variety of accounts and at different rates of return, including small company stocks, large company stocks, and intermediate-term government bonds. Shown alongside the actual historical asset class results are hypothetical rates of return from 2 to 12 percent for comparison purposes. Notice the dramatic differences in accumulated values as you increase your return percentages.

Historical Returns as a Guide to "Reasonable" Expectations

When it comes to retirement planning you have little choice but to develop personal expectations about future investment results. The challenge is to reduce the possibility that your expectations will be different from what actually occurs. The historical average annual returns for each asset class shown in Illustration 5 provide a good benchmark for you to use in determining the reasonableness of the rates of return you use in your own retirement plans. As always, there are no guarantees about future performance based upon past performance, but you probably shouldn't stray too far from what history has shown is reasonable.

Most Recent Stock Market Return Data

In the short run, throughout 2001 and 2002, the stock market has continued to slide. According to Ibbotson Associates in *Stocks, Bonds, Bills and Inflation*™ *2003 Yearbook*, the impact has been to reduce the long-term average annual rate of return from 12.4 percent to 12.1 percent for small company stocks, and from 11 percent to 10.2 percent for large company stocks. You should keep this in mind when deciding on reasonable rates of return to use in your own financial plan.

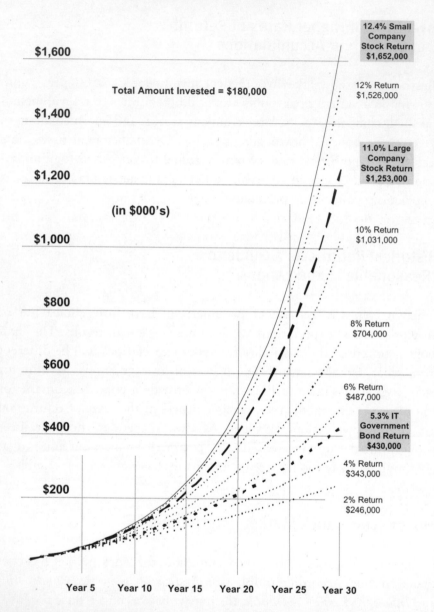

Illustration 5: Investment Returns
Compounded Growth of an Investment
of $500 per Month for 30 Years at a
Variety of Average Annual Rates of Return

Total Amount Invested = $180,000

(in $000's)

12.4% Small Company Stock Return $1,652,000

12% Return $1,526,000

11.0% Large Company Stock Return $1,253,000

10% Return $1,031,000

8% Return $704,000

6% Return $487,000

5.3% IT Government Bond Return $430,000

4% Return $343,000

2% Return $246,000

$1,600
$1,400
$1,200
$1,000
$800
$600
$400
$200

Year 5   Year 10   Year 15   Year 20   Year 25   Year 30

Source: Calculated by Paul Grangaard using data presented in *Stocks, Bonds, Bills and Inflation®
2001 Yearbook*, © 2001 Ibbotson Associates, Inc. Based on copyrighted works by Ibbotson and Sinquefield. All
rights reserved. Used with permission. Large Company Stocks are based on the S&P Composite Index which
includes 500 of the largest stocks in the United States from 1957 to the present and 90 of the largest stocks prior
to 1957. Small Company Stocks are based on the historical series developed by Professor Rolf W. Banz for 1926
through 1981, and on the Dimensional Fund Advisors (DFA) Small Company 9/10 Fund from 1982 to the present.
Intermediate-Term Government Bonds are based on data from The Wall Street Journal and the CRSP Government
Bond File. For illustration purposes only. Not representative of an actual investment. Past performance is not a
guarantee of future results. An investment cannot be made directly in an index. Rates of return are hypothetical,
and an investor's results may vary. Investments with the potential to earn higher rates of return are generally offset with a higher degree of risk. Government bonds are guaranteed by the US Government and if held to maturity,
offer a fixed rate of return and fixed principal value.

The "Rule of 72"

People are often looking for an easy way to assess the consequences of their investment decisions. One of the simplest is the "Rule of 72," which allows you to get a quick feel for the effect of different rates of return on your investments.

The Rule of 72 says that by dividing the number 72 by the rate of return you expect to earn on an investment, you can determine how many years it may take to double in value. For example, if you expect to get a return of 6 percent per year, it should take approximately twelve years for the account to double in value. On the other hand, if you expect to earn 12 percent per year, it should take only about six years for the same account to double.

You need to understand that the Rule of 72 does not guarantee investment results or serve as a prediction of how your investments will perform. It's just an approximation of the impact a targeted rate of return may have over time. Since investments are subject to fluctuating returns, there can never be a guarantee that any investment will double in value. You should also keep in mind that higher rates of return are offset by higher volatility and higher degrees of risk.

4

Average Annual Returns

One of the most important things about investing for retirement is the concept of average annual returns. People in the financial community often refer to them as "geometric returns" and/or "compound average annual returns." However, to keep it simple, I usually just refer to them as "average annual returns."

Average Annual Returns Defined

An average annual return is simply the rate of return, applied on a consistent, year-to-year basis, which is required to grow an investment from a given starting value to a given ending value over a stated period of time. For example, if you invest $1,000 at the beginning of a ten-year period, and at the end of that period have $2,595, you can easily determine the average annual rate of return for the investment. It's simply the one single rate of return, applied consistently, year after year, which would grow the $1,000 investment to $2,595 in ten years. In this example, that one single rate of return is exactly 10 percent per year.

The Importance of Average Annual Returns

The reason average annual returns are so important in financial planning is that you can use them to compare the historical performance of similar investments over different time periods, and of different investments over the same time period. Your ability to compare historical investment results is very important, because having a sense of what's happened in the past can help give you the perspective you may need to develop better expectations about what might happen in the future.

An Example of Average Annual Returns

Using actual historical performance data for large company stocks, the example in Illustration 6 shows an actual ten-year investment period from the beginning of 1959 to the end of 1968, in which large company stock returns and investment values fluctuated rather dramatically. The best year returned 26.9 percent in 1961 while the worst year lost 10.1 percent in 1966. Over the entire ten-year period however, an initial investment of $1,000 would have grown to an ending balance of $2,595. Although the value of the account went up and down as the annual returns fluctuated from year to year, overall it was a pretty good ten-year period, with the initial investment more than doubling in value.

Average Annual Returns: The Order Within the Chaos

Despite typical market fluctuations, there is generally a fair degree of order underlying the chaos in the stock market; the $1,000 growing to $2,595 in the ten years between 1959 and 1968 is actually the same as earning 10 percent per year over the same period. The random pattern of ups and downs and the calculated average annual rate of 10 percent are mathematically the same. As different as they may at first appear, they get us to exactly the same place. So from an overall investment perspective, the two patterns are essentially interchangeable.

Illustration 6: Actual Average Returns vs Average Annual Returns

10-Year Investment Period from 1959 to 1968
$1,000 Invested in Large Company Stocks

Year	Actual Return %	Actual Balance	Average Return %	Average Balance
Balance		$1,000		$1,000
1959	12.0%	$1,120	10.0%	$1,100
1960	0.5%	$1,125	10.0%	$1,210
1961	26.9%	$1,427	10.0%	$1,331
1962	-8.7%	$1,303	10.0%	$1,464
1963	22.8%	$1,600	10.0%	$1,611
1964	16.5%	$1,863	10.0%	$1,772
1965	12.5%	$2,095	10.0%	$1,949
1966	-10.1%	$1,885	10.0%	$2,144
1967	24.0%	$2,336	10.0%	$2,358
1968	11.1%	$2,595	10.0%	$2,595

Source: Calculated by Paul Grangaard using data presented in *Stocks, Bonds, Bills and Inflation®*
2001 Yearbook, © 2001 Ibbotson Associates, Inc. Based on copyrighted works by Ibbotson and Sinquefield. All rights reserved. Used with permission. Large Company Stocks are based on the S&P Composite Index which includes 500 of the largest stocks in the United States from 1957 to the present and 90 of the largest stocks prior to 1957. For illustration purposes only. Not representative of an actual investment. Past performance is not a guarantee of future results. An investment cannot be made directly in an index. Rates of return are hypothetical, and an investor's results may vary. Investments with the potential to earn higher rates of return are generally off-set with a higher degree of risk.

Visualizing Average Annual Returns

A good way to visualize average annual returns is to look at a graph of actual annual values compared to average annual values. The graph in Illustration 7 shows actual account balances compared to average account balances for the same ten-year period between 1959 and 1968. The actual value of the investment jumped around all over the place from year to year, but ultimately arrived at an ending balance of $2,595.

However, underlying the apparent chaos is a smooth 10 percent average annual return line sloping upward and to the right. It illustrates how the average annual rate of return would ultimately get you to the same place, but without all the ups and downs, and that lurking behind the random fluctuations in the stock market is a generally more predictable pattern of returns. In fact, over longer investment periods, like the ten years in the example, there is usually more predictability in the market than most people think.

Making Comparisons with Average Annual Returns

You can use average annual returns to compare investment results during this ten-year period with investment results during any other ten-year period. You can also use them to compare this kind of investment—large company stocks in this case—with other kinds of investments over the same period. The actual pattern of ups and downs is generally much less important and certainly less helpful than the equivalent average annual return for use in making comparisons—at least in terms of your ability to use historical data to anticipate hypothetical future returns for planning purposes.

Using History as Your Guide

Understanding average annual returns and how they're calculated can give you a better appreciation for the importance of maintaining a long-term historical investment perspective, because you will often use long-term historical return data as the basis for making "reasonable"

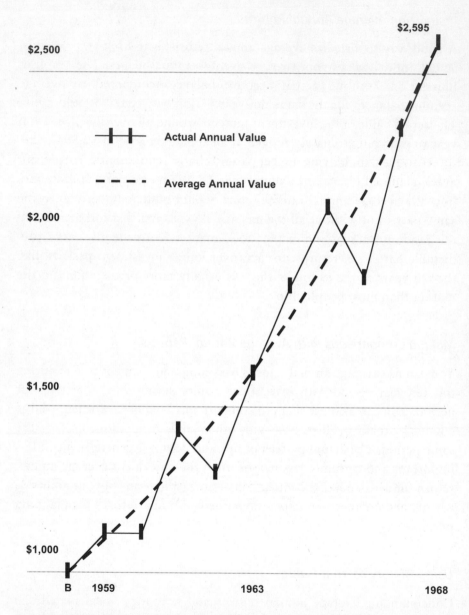

Illustration 7: Actual vs Average Annual Returns
Graph of $1,000 Invested in Large Company Stocks
During the 10 Years Between 1959 and 1968

$2,595

$2,500

— ┨ ┠ — Actual Annual Value

– – – – Average Annual Value

$2,000

$1,500

$1,000

B   1959   1963   1968

Source: Calculated by Paul Grangaard using data presented in *Stocks, Bonds, Bills and Inflation*®
2001 Yearbook, © 2001 Ibbotson Associates, Inc. Based on copyrighted works by Ibbotson and Sinquefield. All
rights reserved. Used with permission. Large Company Stocks are based on the S&P Composite Index which
includes 500 of the largest stocks in the United States from 1957 to the present. For illustration purposes only.
Not representative of an actual investment. Past performance is not a guarantee of future results. An investment
cannot be made directly in an index. Rates of return are hypothetical, and an investor's results may vary.
Investments with the potential to earn higher rates of return are generally offset with a higher degree of risk.

assumptions about the hypothetical rates of return you build into your own financial plans.

Illustration 8 shows the overall pattern of actual returns, and the average annual return for large company stocks for all seventy-five years between 1926 and 2000. The actual annual returns bounced around all over the place, just like you would expect—between a high of 54 percent in 1933 and a low of negative 43.3 percent in 1931.

But notice that large company stocks produced an average annual rate of return of 11 percent per year over the entire seventy-five-year period. This simply means that earning 11 percent per year in each and every year between 1926 and 2000 would have gotten you to exactly the same place as earning the actual rates of return over the same period.

For example, if you invested $10 at the beginning of 1926, you would have accumulated $25,865 by the end of 2000 if you earned the actual rates of return each year and held the investment for the entire period. If you invested the same $10 at the beginning of 1926 and earned instead the average annual rate of 11 percent each year, again, holding for the entire period, you would have accumulated exactly the same $25,865 by the end of 2000. In other words, the two patterns of returns are essentially the same. They get you to the same place.

A Picture of Large Company Stocks

Illustration 9 shows what the long-term historical pattern of annual returns actually looks like for large company stocks, with the steady 11 percent average annual values underlying the significantly fluctuating actual amounts. Of course, they both get you to the same $25,865. So while it may have been a roller-coaster ride of ups and downs, it had a strong and easily discernable bias toward positive long-run growth—11 percent per year to be exact.

A History of Small Company Stocks

The same average annual return calculations can be made for other segments of the stock market too, as well as for the bond market. In fact,

Illustration 8: Actual Annual Returns vs Average Annual Returns
75-Year Investment Period from 1926 to 2000
Large Company Stocks

$10 Earning Actual Returns Would Have Grown to $25,865
$10 Earning Average Returns Would Have Grown to $25,865

+ = 0% to 6%	"++" = 6% to 16%	"+++" = 16% to 26%	"++++" = > 26%
"-" = 0% to -6%	"--" = -6% to -16%	"---" = -16% to -26%	"----" = < -26%

Year	Actual Return	Average Return	Year	Actual Return	Average Return	Year	Actual Return	Average Return
1926	++	11.0%	1951	+++	11.0%	1976	+++	11.0%
1927	++++	11.0%	1952	+++	11.0%	1977	--	11.0%
1928	++++	11.0%	1953	-	11.0%	1978	++	11.0%
1929	--	11.0%	1954	++++	11.0%	1979	+++	11.0%
1930	+++	11.0%	1955	++++	11.0%	1980	++++	11.0%
1931	----	11.0%	1956	++	11.0%	1981	-	11.0%
1932	--	11.0%	1957	--	11.0%	1982	+++	11.0%
1933	++++	11.0%	1958	++++	11.0%	1983	+++	11.0%
1934	-	11.0%	1959	++	11.0%	1984	++	11.0%
1935	++++	11.0%	1960	+	11.0%	1985	++++	11.0%
1936	++++	11.0%	1961	++++	11.0%	1986	+++	11.0%
1937	++++	11.0%	1962	--	11.0%	1987	+	11.0%
1938	++++	11.0%	1963	+++	11.0%	1988	+++	11.0%
1939	-	11.0%	1964	++	11.0%	1989	++++	11.0%
1940	--	11.0%	1965	++	11.0%	1990	-	11.0%
1941	++	11.0%	1966	--	11.0%	1991	++++	11.0%
1942	+++	11.0%	1967	+++	11.0%	1992	++	11.0%
1943	+++	11.0%	1968	++	11.0%	1993	++	11.0%
1944	+++	11.0%	1969	--	11.0%	1994	+	11.0%
1945	++++	11.0%	1970	+	11.0%	1995	++++	11.0%
1946	--	11.0%	1971	++	11.0%	1996	+++	11.0%
1947	+	11.0%	1972	+++	11.0%	1997	++++	11.0%
1948	+	11.0%	1973	--	11.0%	1998	++++	11.0%
1949	+++	11.0%	1974	----	11.0%	1999	+++	11.0%
1950	++++	11.0%	1975	++++	11.0%	2000	--	11.0%

Source: Calculated by Paul Grangaard using data presented in *Stocks, Bonds, Bills and Inflation®
2001 Yearbook*, © 2001 Ibbotson Associates, Inc. Based on copyrighted works by Ibbotson and Sinquefield. All
rights reserved. Used with permission. Large Company Stocks are based on the S&P Composite Index which
includes 500 of the largest stocks in the United States from 1957 to the present and 90 of the largest stocks prior
to 1957. For illustration purposes only. Not representative of an actual investment. Past performance is not a
guarantee of future results. An investment cannot be made directly in an index. Rates of return are hypothetical,
and an investor's results may vary. Investments with the potential to earn higher rates of return are generally offset with a higher degree of risk.

Illustration 9: Cumulative Large Company Stock Values
Actual vs Average Returns From 1926 to 2000
$10 Invested at the Beginning of 1926

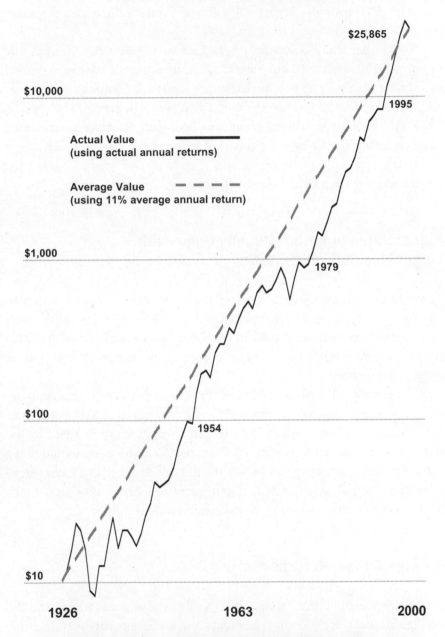

$25,865

$10,000

1995

Actual Value
(using actual annual returns)

Average Value
(using 11% average annual return)

$1,000

1979

$100

1954

$10

1926   1963   2000

Illustration 10 provides actual and average annual return data for small company stocks between 1926 and 2000.

Notice that small company stocks generated an average annual rate of return of 12.4 percent, but with much more dramatic swings in annual investment results. The best performance for small company stocks was 142.9 percent in 1933, while the worst year was a negative 58 percent in 1937. Although over the long-term, small company stocks outperformed large company stocks by 1.4 percent, it came at the cost of much larger fluctuations in value. The highs and lows were far more extreme for small company stocks than they were for large company stocks.

Higher Rates of Return Usually Come with Larger Fluctuations in Value

To get higher average annual rates of return over the long run, you usually have to accept more uncertainty and be willing to invest in markets that fluctuate more dramatically in the short run. However, you may also be able to increase your earnings potential by accepting that higher degree of uncertainty.

Although the 1.4 percent per year difference between large company and small company stocks may seem insignificant, your $10 invested in small company stocks back in 1926 would have grown to $64,022 by the end of 2000—substantially more than the $25,865 you would have earned in large company stocks. That's the difference a small change in your hypothetical average annual rate of return can make—and that's why it's so important to select your investments carefully.

Average Annual Returns for Bonds

Finally, it's worth looking at the pattern of actual annual returns and the average annual return for intermediate-term government bonds. Illustration 11 shows that intermediate-term government bonds don't fluctuate nearly as much as either stock market investment, but that their seventy-five-year average annual return is only about 5.3 percent. At this lower

Illustration 10: Actual Annual Returns vs Average Annual Returns

75-Year Investment Period from 1926 to 2000
Small Company Stocks

$10 Earning Actual Returns Would Have Grown to $64,022
$10 Earning Average Returns Would Have Grown to $64,022

"+" = 0% to 6%	"++" = 6% to 16%	"+++" = 16% to 26%	"++++" = > 26%
"-" = 0% to -6%	"--" = -6% to -16%	"---" = -16% to -26%	"----" = < -26%

Year	Actual Return	Average Return	Year	Actual Return	Average Return	Year	Actual Return	Average Return
1926	+	12.4%	1951	++	12.4%	1976	++++	12.4%
1927	+++	12.4%	1952	+	12.4%	1977	+++	12.4%
1928	++++	12.4%	1953	--	12.4%	1978	+++	12.4%
1929	----	12.4%	1954	++++	12.4%	1979	++++	12.4%
1930	----	12.4%	1955	+++	12.4%	1980	++++	12.4%
1931	----	12.4%	1956	+	12.4%	1981	++	12.4%
1932	-	12.4%	1957	--	12.4%	1982	++++	12.4%
1933	++++	12.4%	1958	++++	12.4%	1983	++++	12.4%
1934	+++	12.4%	1959	+++	12.4%	1984	--	12.4%
1935	++++	12.4%	1960	-	12.4%	1985	+++	12.4%
1936	++++	12.4%	1961	++++	12.4%	1986	++	12.4%
1937	----	12.4%	1962	--	12.4%	1987	--	12.4%
1938	++++	12.4%	1963	+++	12.4%	1988	+++	12.4%
1939	+	12.4%	1964	+++	12.4%	1989	++	12.4%
1940	-	12.4%	1965	++++	12.4%	1990	---	12.4%
1941	--	12.4%	1966	--	12.4%	1991	++++	12.4%
1942	++++	12.4%	1967	++++	12.4%	1992	+++	12.4%
1943	++++	12.4%	1968	++++	12.4%	1993	+++	12.4%
1944	++++	12.4%	1969	---	12.4%	1994	+	12.4%
1945	++++	12.4%	1970	---	12.4%	1995	++++	12.4%
1946	--	12.4%	1971	+++	12.4%	1996	+++	12.4%
1947	+	12.4%	1972	+	12.4%	1997	+++	12.4%
1948	-	12.4%	1973	----	12.4%	1998	--	12.4%
1949	+++	12.4%	1974	---	12.4%	1999	++++	12.4%
1950	++++	12.4%	1975	++++	12.4%	2000	-	12.4%

Source: Calculated by Paul Grangaard using data presented in *Stocks, Bonds, Bills and Inflation®* *2001 Yearbook*, © 2001 Ibbotson Associates, Inc. Based on copyrighted works by Ibbotson and Sinquefield. All rights reserved. Used with permission. Small Company Stocks are based on the historical series developed by Professor Rolf W. Banz for 1926 through 1981, and on the Dimensional Fund Advisors (DFA) Small Company 9/10 Fund from 1982 to the present. For illustration purposes only. Not representative of an actual investment. Past performance is not a guarantee of future results. An investment cannot be made directly in an index. Rates of return are hypothetical, and an investor's results may vary. Investments with the potential to earn higher rates of return are generally offset with a higher degree of risk.

Illustration 11: Actual Annual Returns vs Average Annual Returns
75-Year Investment Period from 1926 to 2000
Intermediate-Term Government Bonds

$10 Earning Actual Returns Would Have Grown to $486
$10 Earning Average Returns Would Have Grown to $486

+ = 0% to 6%	"++" = 6% to 16%	"+++" = 16% to 26%	"++++" = > 26%
"-" = 0% to -6%	"--" = -6% to -16%	"---" = -16% to -26%	"----" = < -26%

Year	Actual Return	Average Return	Year	Actual Return	Average Return	Year	Actual Return	Average Return
1926	+	5.3%	1951	+	5.3%	1976	++	5.3%
1927	+	5.3%	1952	+	5.3%	1977	+	5.3%
1928	+	5.3%	1953	+	5.3%	1978	+	5.3%
1929	++	5.3%	1954	+	5.3%	1979	+	5.3%
1930	++	5.3%	1955	-	5.3%	1980	+	5.3%
1931	-	5.3%	1956	-	5.3%	1981	++	5.3%
1932	++	5.3%	1957	++	5.3%	1982	++++	5.3%
1933	+	5.3%	1958	-	5.3%	1983	++	5.3%
1934	++	5.3%	1959	-	5.3%	1984	++	5.3%
1935	++	5.3%	1960	++	5.3%	1985	+++	5.3%
1936	+	5.3%	1961	+	5.3%	1986	++	5.3%
1937	+	5.3%	1962	+	5.3%	1987	+	5.3%
1938	++	5.3%	1963	+	5.3%	1988	++	5.3%
1939	+	5.3%	1964	+	5.3%	1989	++	5.3%
1940	+	5.3%	1965	+	5.3%	1990	++	5.3%
1941	+	5.3%	1966	+	5.3%	1991	++	5.3%
1942	+	5.3%	1967	+	5.3%	1992	++	5.3%
1943	+	5.3%	1968	+	5.3%	1993	++	5.3%
1944	+	5.3%	1969	-	5.3%	1994	-	5.3%
1945	+	5.3%	1970	+++	5.3%	1995	+++	5.3%
1946	+	5.3%	1971	++	5.3%	1996	+	5.3%
1947	+	5.3%	1972	+	5.3%	1997	++	5.3%
1948	+	5.3%	1973	+	5.3%	1998	++	5.3%
1949	+	5.3%	1974	+	5.3%	1999	-	5.3%
1950	+	5.3%	1975	++	5.3%	2000	++	5.3%

Source: Calculated by Paul Grangaard using data presented in *Stocks, Bonds, Bills and Inflation®*
2001 Yearbook, © 2001 Ibbotson Associates, Inc. Based on copyrighted works by Ibbotson and Sinquefield.
All rights reserved. Used with permission. Intermediate-Term Government Bonds are based on data from the
Wall Street Journal and the CRSP Government Bond File. For illustration purposes only. Not representative
of an actual investment. Past performance is not a guarantee of future results. An investment cannot be
made directly in an index. Rates of return are hypothetical, and an investor's results may vary. Investments
with the potential to earn higher rates of return are generally offset with a higher degree of risk.

average annual rate, your $10 investment would only have grown to about $486 between 1926 and 2000, compared with $25,865 for large company stocks and $64,022 for small company stocks. You would have had a much smoother ride to a much smaller balance if you put your money into bonds rather than stocks back in 1926.

Historical Returns as a Guide to "Reasonable" Expectations

You should now have a better understanding of the concept of average annual returns and a better feel for how the markets have actually behaved over the last seventy-five years. Your understanding of long-term average annual returns is the starting point in deciding what level of hypothetical return expectations to build into your own plan. The bottom line is that you will probably have to save more or earn higher rates of return to get the accumulated values you need and want for retirement. The choice is yours and should be weighed against your tolerance for risk, investment horizon, and ability to invest.

5

Holding Periods

Two sides of the same coin in financial planning are establishing "reasonable" rates of return for your investments and then reducing the likelihood that you will earn anything other than those "reasonable" rates. You need to reduce the possibility of getting rates of return other than what you're hoping for because you will most likely be building your financial security around the assets you plan to accumulate at those rates.

Using "Reasonable" Rates of Return

Of course you should always use "reasonable" hypothetical rates of return in your financial plans. Reasonable rates of return have to make sense given the historical long-run averages for the markets you plan to invest in. Hoping for higher rates of return because they make you feel better doesn't make them any more reasonable. Wishful thinking won't get you very far in retirement. You have to ground your investment decisions in real experience—and that means using long-term history as your guide.

Investing in the Stock Market

During the accumulation phase of life, while you're working and saving for retirement, you often buy stock market investments, or equities, and then stay invested to go after the higher rates of return they have historically provided. In fact, the higher rates of return that are typically available in the stock market are what make it possible for many people to accumulate enough to retire in the first place.

Stock Market Holding Periods

Throughout your working career you need to manage your retirement assets in large part based upon what you think you may earn in the stock market. If you don't achieve the hypothetical rates of return you are planning for you may not be able to accumulate enough to retire. So the big question is how to stay invested in the stock market for the growth you might need, while reducing the possibility of getting rates of return that are lower than you are hoping for—especially when you know that the stock market is almost certain to be bouncing around all over the place from year to year.

One of the most important answers to this dilemma is stock market holding periods. They are a crucial element in reducing the likelihood of getting rates of return other than the "reasonable" hypothetical rates you build into your plan. Understanding how to use holding periods will probably change the way you think about investing and owning stocks for retirement.

Stock Market Holding Periods Defined

A stock market holding period is simply the length of time you can stay invested in the stock market for growth before needing to sell some of your equities (or stocks) to get the money you may need to live on in retirement. In essence, it's the amount of time you have to ride out the inevitable ups and downs in the stock market while waiting for the reasonable rates of return you are hoping for and building into your plan. That's why it's so important to know how many years you have until retirement—because it establishes your preretirement holding period.

Reasonable Return Expectations: Longer and Shorter Holding Periods

Long-run historical stock-market performance provides a fairly good benchmark for establishing "reasonable" hypothetical return expectations. But you have to ask: can long-run, seventy-five-year historical average annual rates of return really be used to anticipate what you are likely to earn over investment periods which are often much shorter than that? The answer is yes and no.

Clearly, most of us don't have seventy-five-year stock-market holding periods. At age twenty-five, even if you don't plan to retire until you're seventy, you only have a forty-five-year preretirement holding period, and if you're fifty-five and plan to retire at sixty-five, you only have ten years. So you need a way to use long-term historical stock market returns to draw meaningful conclusions about much shorter and more realistic investment periods.

Anticipating Short-Term Stock Market Performance

Is it really reasonable to expect an 11 percent average annual rate of return for large company stocks next year just because they produced an 11 percent average annual rate of return over the last seventy-five years? The answer is no.

Although it's true that an 11 percent rate of return is probably the best guess you can make about what will happen next year, it's also true that over one-year investment periods it isn't a very good guess. The truth is, long-run average annual returns are a very poor predictor of what will actually happen in any future one-year period.

A Picture of Short-Term Stock Market Performance

Illustration 12 shows the actual annual returns for every year between 1926 and 2000 for large company stocks. Each dot on the graph represents the rate of return for one year. The shaded line running across the graph at 11 percent is the average annual return for the entire seventy-five-year period.

The highest rate of return for any single year was 54 percent in 1933, while the lowest rate was negative 43.3 percent in 1931—and of course the market produced just about everything else in-between. On a yearly basis, large company stock returns jumped around all over the place, so although the 11 percent long-run average might be a good estimate for long-range planning purposes, it certainly isn't a very good predictor of what will happen next year.

Obviously, one-year holding periods are very unpredictable, because the stock market itself is very unpredictable over such short investment horizons. If you think you might need your money in a year or two you would be foolish to put it in the stock market, because it's virtually impossible to predict your return over such a short holding period. It's like gambling—it could be very good or it could be very bad, and there is no way to know in advance.

Longer-Term Investment Performance: Five-Year Holding Periods

Longer holding periods, however, can lead to more predictability. The upper chart in Illustration 13 shows what happens when you consider the average annual rates of return for all five-year holding periods. Although the long-run average of 11 percent doesn't change—since we are still dealing with the same seventy-five years—the overall range of five-year returns compared to one-year returns changes quite a bit. Not only are the highs and lows much less dramatic, but all the five-year periods also tend to cluster much closer to the 11 percent long-run average,

Illustration 12: Large Company Stock Returns
Individual Years (1926 through 2000)

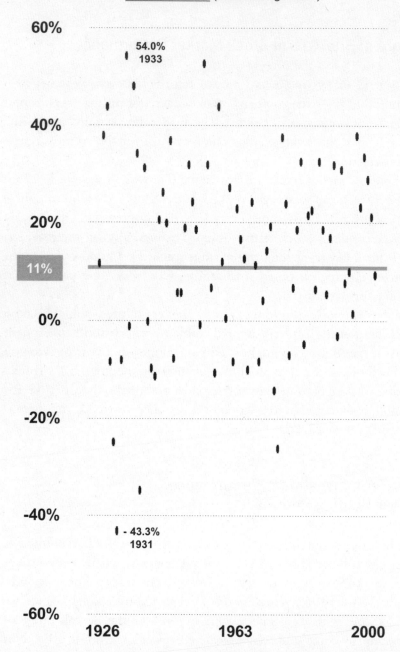

Source: Calculated by Paul Grangaard using data presented in *Stocks, Bonds, Bills and Inflation*®
2001 Yearbook, © 2001 Ibbotson Associates, Inc. Based on copyrighted works by Ibbotson and Sinquefield.
All rights reserved. Used with permission. Large Company Stocks are based on the S&P Composite Index
which includes 500 of the largest stocks in the United States from 1957 to the present and 90 of the largest
stocks prior to 1957. For illustration purposes only. Not representative of an actual investment. Past
performance is not a guarantee of future results. An investment cannot be made directly in an index.

indicating that it is a better predictor of what you might actually get over any future five-year period.

The best five years, between 1995 and 1999, provided an average annual return of 28.6 percent, while the worst five years, between 1928 and 1932, lost 12.5 percent per year. Obviously, if you are going to plan to get an 11 percent rate of return on your stock market investments, your odds are much better if you can stay invested for at least five years rather than having to sell after just one.

Five-Year Holding Periods: Good But Not Good Enough

The predictive accuracy of the 11 percent long-run average annual return improves a lot as you increase your holding period from one year to five years. But even with such a big improvement there is still a fairly wide range of returns between the best and the worst five-year period, which might leave some people feeling a little uncomfortable using the 11 percent long-run average as an estimate in their retirement plans. In other words, if you are going to use long-run historical average annual returns as a basis for determining "reasonable" planning estimates, you might not have a lot of confidence in those estimates if you can only stay invested for five years, because—as good as they are—they may not be good enough.

Ten-Year Holding Periods

If five-year holding periods don't give you the confidence you need, how about ten-year holding periods? Can they improve the accuracy of the long-run averages you may want to use in your plan? The answer is yes. The bottom chart in Illustration 13 shows why. The best average annual rate of return for all ten-year periods was 20.1 percent between 1949 and 1958. The worst ten-year average annual return was negative .9 percent between 1929 and 1938. So the range of returns has come down a lot. In fact, there were only two ten-year periods in history in which large company stocks lost money—1929 to 1938 and 1930 to 1939.

It's also important to notice that over ten-year investment periods the returns tend to cluster ever more tightly around the long-run average of

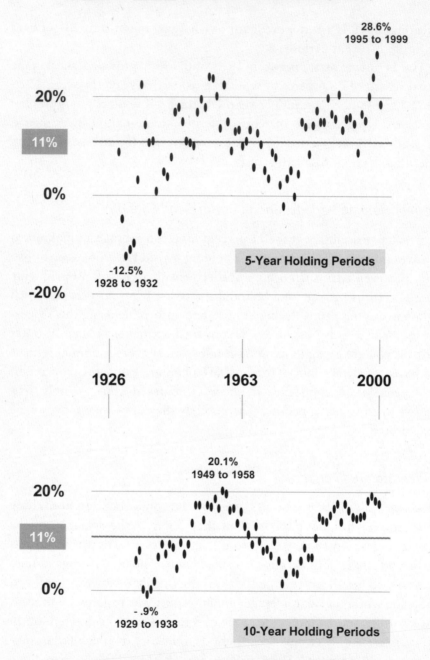

Illustration 13: Large Company Stock Returns
5-Year and 10-Year Holding Periods (1926 through 2000)

28.6%
1995 to 1999

20%

11%

0%

-12.5%
1928 to 1932

-20%

5-Year Holding Periods

1926   1963   2000

20.1%
1949 to 1958

20%

11%

0%

- .9%
1929 to 1938

10-Year Holding Periods

11 percent. So the predictive power of the long-run average improves quite a bit as compared to either one- or five-year holding periods.

All the Way Out to Twenty-Year Holding Periods

The upper chart in Illustration 14 shows what happens to investment returns when they are considered over even longer twenty-year holding periods—and as preretirement investors, many people have holding periods at least that long.

As you can see, there continues to be a reduction in the variation from the best to the worst twenty-year period, as well as a tighter clustering around the long-term average. In fact, there has never been a twenty-year period in which you would have lost money in large company stocks. The worst it has ever been is 3.1 percent between 1929 and 1948—a period that started in the depression and runs straight into World War II.

A Look at Thirty-Year Holding Periods

The bottom chart in Illustration 14 shows what happens to the range of returns for all thirty-year holding periods between 1926 and 2000. The best thirty-year period delivered a 13.7 percent average annual rate of return between 1970 and 1999, while the worst thirty-year period delivered an average annual rate of 8.5 percent between 1929 and 1958. The rest of the thirty-year periods cluster very close to the long-run average of 11 percent. So when you consider thirty-year stock-market holding periods, the odds of getting anything other than what you are reasonably expecting start to get pretty small.

Think of the historical risk. There has never been a thirty-year period in which you would have earned less than 8.5 percent in large company stocks—which is more than 3 percent above the long-run average annual return for intermediate-term government bonds. And you know how big an impact a 3 percent difference can make over a thirty-year investment horizon. A $500 per month investment should grow to about $705,000 at 8 percent over thirty years, and only $408,000 at 5 percent.

Illustration 14: Large Company Stock Returns
20-Year and 30-Year Holding Periods (1926 through 2000)

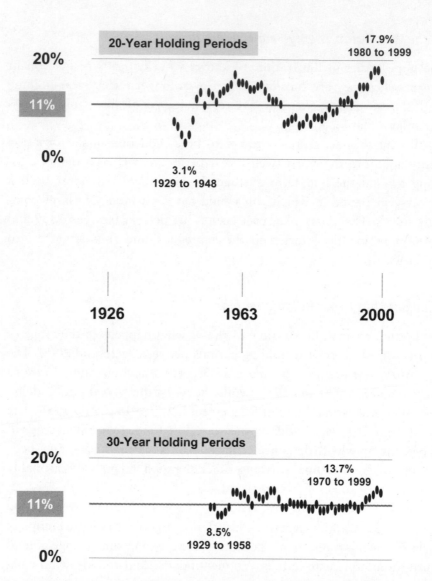

Why Most People Like Longer Holding Periods

What the illustrations make clear is that the longer you can stay invested in the stock market, or in other words, the longer your stock-market holding periods, the more likely you are to actually get the long-run historical average annual rates of return that you are reasonably expecting and building into your financial plans. As a result, most investors want the longest possible holding periods to get as much comfort as they can in their ability to earn the rates of return they are expecting. That's why it's so important to start saving early—because you will never have longer holding periods than you do right now.

Holding Periods During Retirement

Not only are the years prior to retirement part of your equity-holding periods, but you also have the years during retirement too. As you approach retirement, you may begin to sell stock market investments to get income to live on—but you probably won't sell them all at once. Many of the stock market investments you bring with you into retirement won't be sold for ten, twenty, or even thirty years after you stop working—so you may have much longer holding periods than you initially think.

Reducing Variability with Longer Holding Periods

Illustration 15 shows how longer holding periods tend to reduce the odds of getting rates of return other than what you are expecting. Each of the previous illustrations for one-year, five-year, ten-year, twenty-year, and thirty-year holding periods have been squeezed down into individual bars for comparison purposes. The top and bottom of each bar represent the range of average annual returns for each holding period, and the dots represent the individual holding periods within each bar. As always, the 11 percent long-run average annual return is the straight line running down the middle.

Illustration 15: Large Company Stock Returns
Various Holding Periods (1926 through 2000)

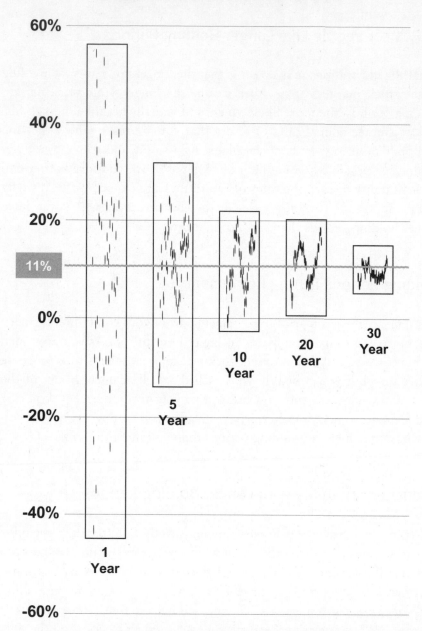

As holding periods increase, you achieve fairly dramatic reductions in the variability of historical returns around the long-run average. The reduction in variability is significant as you move from one-year to five-year holding periods, from five-year to ten-year holding periods, and then ultimately out to thirty years.

But remember, you can only reduce variability around the long-run average up to a point. You can never get rid of market fluctuations altogether. But you are able to squeeze a great deal of the variation and unpredictability out of the stock market by the time you get out to about ten-year holding periods, and a whole lot more as you move out to thirty years and beyond.

The Costs and Benefits of Being Overly Conservative

If you are willing to accept historical rates of return in the range of 5.3 percent per year for an investment such as intermediate-term government bonds, you will find that there has never been a five-year period in which you would have lost money. But remember, you also won't be getting nearly as much compounded growth—so bonds may not be the best choice, even if they do appear less risky.

Historical Stock Market Data

You will find that there have only been seven five-year periods—out of a total of seventy-one—and only two ten-year periods—out of a total of sixty-six—in which you would have lost money in large company stocks over the last seventy-five years. And remember, all the while, you would have been much more likely to compound your money at higher rates of return in the stock market than in bonds.

Stocks and Bonds Revealed

Illustration 16 provides some interesting historical information about large company stocks, small company stocks, and intermediate-term

Illustration 16: Rates of Return
Holding Periods From 1 to 30 Years
75-Year Investment History from 1926 to 2000

Holding Period	Large Company Stocks		Small Company Stocks		Intermediate-Term Treasury Bonds	
1 Year (75 periods)	worst -43.3%	best 54.0%	worst -58.0%	best 142.9%	worst -5.1%	best 29.1%
	average 11.0%	negative 21	average 12.4%	negative 23	average 5.3%	negative 8
5 Years (71 periods)	worst -12.5%	best 28.6%	worst -27.5%	best 45.9%	worst 1.0%	best 17.0%
	average 11.0%	negative 7	average 12.4%	negative 9	average 5.3%	negative 0
10 Years (66 periods)	worst -0.9%	best 20.1%	worst -5.7%	best 30.4%	worst 1.3%	best 13.1%
	average 11.0%	negative 2	average 12.4%	negative 2	average 5.3%	negative 0
15 Years (61 periods)	worst 0.6%	best 18.9%	worst -1.3%	best 23.3%	worst 1.5%	best 11.3%
	average 11.0%	negative 0	average 12.4%	negative 3	average 5.3%	negative 0
20 Years (56 periods)	worst 3.1%	best 17.9%	worst 5.7%	best 21.1%	worst 1.6%	best 10.0%
	average 11.0%	negative 0	average 12.4%	negative 0	average 5.3%	negative 0
25 Years (51 periods)	worst 5.9%	best 17.2%	worst 6.9%	best 20.4%	worst 2.2%	best 9.2%
	average 11.0%	negative 0	average 12.4%	negative 0	average 5.3%	negative 0
30 Years (46 periods)	worst 8.5%	best 13.7%	worst 8.8%	best 18.8%	worst 2.2%	best 8.7%
	average 11.0%	negative 0	average 12.4%	negative 0	average 5.3%	negative 0

Source: Calculated by Paul Grangaard using data presented in *Stocks, Bonds, Bills and Inflation*®
2001 Yearbook, © 2001 Ibbotson Associates, Inc. Based on copyrighted works by Ibbotson and Sinquefield.
All rights reserved. Used with permission. Large Company Stocks are based on the S&P Composite Index which
includes 500 of the largest stocks in the United States from 1957 to the present and 90 of the largest stocks prior
to 1957. Small Company Stocks are based on the historical series developed by Professor Rolf W. Banz for 1926
through 1981, and on the Dimensional Fund Advisors (DFA) Small Company 9/10 Fund from 1982 to the present.
Intermediate-Term Government Bonds are based on data from The Wall Street Journal and the CRSP Government
Bond File. For illustration purposes only. Not representative of an actual investment. Past performance is not a
guarantee of future results. An investment cannot be made directly in an index.

government bonds for different-length holding periods. It shows the best, the worst, and the average rates of return for each period, as well as the number of times you would have lost money.

Over longer holding periods you can see that you would have been able to increase your expected rates of return by investing in the stock market, while also reducing your downside risk. As a younger investor, this can provide a great deal of comfort as you face the inevitable ups and downs in the market.

6

Diversification

Barron's *Finance & Investment Handbook* defines diversification as the "spreading of risk by putting assets in several categories of investments—stocks, bonds, money market instruments, and precious metals, for instance, or several industries, or a mutual fund, with its broad range of stocks in one portfolio."

The Winners Can Offset the Losers

The above is a pretty good definition because it points out that diversification can be achieved in many ways and that it can help you manage risk by spreading it over a number of different investments. The general concept is that because you never know which markets will be up and which will be down at any given time, it's usually a good idea to own a variety of different assets—so the winners can offset the losers.

Keep in mind that diversification, while potentially reducing risk, can never guarantee a profit or protect against a loss—but it can certainly help. Diversification tends to reduce investment risk by offsetting the performance of one investment with another, so that by diversifying your portfolio you should be able to get a smoother ride and a more consistent rate of return. Traditional diversification is an attempt to be sure that you will always have at least a few investments that have done well enough for you to be comfortable selling them if you have to get some money.

Holding Periods Reduce Risk Too

As a preretirement investor, however, you're typically not expecting to need your money for a long time, so you're probably not planning to sell—at least any time soon. And, as a long-term investor, you know that you're reducing risk by having longer holding periods in the first place. So even if you invest in only one asset, say a large-company stock mutual fund, you're still reducing risk because of your holding periods—and therefore you don't necessarily need to rely as much on a diversified combination of other assets to do it for you.

If you have longer holding periods, and don't plan to sell your investments any time soon, traditional diversification between stocks and bonds is somewhat less important—so you should be able to be more comfortable skewing your assets toward the stock market if you need to get higher rates of return. One of the best things about stock market mutual funds is that most of them invest in a large number of individual securities anyway, so you gain a very important kind of diversification right off the bat.

Of course when you are considering mutual funds you need to remember that they are available by prospectus only and do involve risk. Investment returns and principal value will fluctuate, so when redeemed, your shares may be worth more or less than their original cost. You should always read the prospectus carefully before investing or sending money.

A Smoother Ride to a Smaller Balance?

Because of the perceived benefits of traditional diversification, investors are often advised to own a diversified portfolio of stocks and bonds. There is little doubt that such a strategy will lead to smoother overall investment performance since stocks and bonds tend to perform differently over time.

But there is something else you need to consider: Let's say that you plan to retire in twenty-five years, and decide to diversify by putting half of your retirement funds into bonds—assuming an aggressive 6 percent rate of return, and the other half into large company stocks—assuming a conservative 10 percent rate of return. If you have confidence that twenty-five-year holding periods will get you close to the hypothetical rates of return you're expecting, you should probably be able to plan for a combined rate of return of about 8 percent—6 percent in bonds, plus 10 percent in stocks, divided by two. So an investment of $400 per month should grow to about $364,000 over the next twenty-five years.

Do You Need to Be More Aggressive?

Alternatively, you could put the entire $400 per month into the stock market, and diversify it evenly between small company stocks, which you might expect to grow at a hypothetical rate of about 12 percent per year, and large company stocks, growing at the same hypothetical 10 percent. Then, you could probably expect an overall average hypothetical rate of return of about 11 percent, in which case the $400 per month should grow to about $576,000, or almost 59 percent more.

Is the "All-Stock" Portfolio Really that Much More Risky?

In conventional terms you would have to admit that the "all-stock" portfolio is technically a more "risky" portfolio, because it will be jumping around all over the place from year to year. But your twenty-five-year stock-market holding period should mitigate much of that risk. Remember, you're not planning to sell your investments anytime soon because you need to keep them growing for retirement. In other words, you're a long-term investor.

In fact, one of the most important questions you need to ask yourself if you want to be more conservative with bonds, is whether you can even afford to retire with $364,000—because it may not be enough to provide the lifestyle you're looking for. If not, bonds may not even be an option.

You always have to consider your preretirement investment decisions, including how much risk you can tolerate, after evaluating their impact on your retirement lifestyle. These kinds of decisions simply cannot be made in a vacuum.

You have to define risk much more broadly. You can't simply focus on the risk that your investments will fluctuate up and down over time, because you know they'll do that—that's what stocks do, and that's why you use holding periods in the first place. The risk you really need to be concerned about is the risk that you may not have the lifestyle you want during the last third of your life.

Diversifying Within the Stock Market

For these reasons, investors with longer holding periods and reasonably high retirement lifestyle expectations may need to think of diversification more in terms of diversifying *within* the stock market, rather than across traditional asset classes like stocks and bonds. Although some people may be able to save enough to invest more conservatively, many can't. And for them, the diversification they get within mutual funds and across various segments of the stock market, combined with longer holding periods, will probably have to suffice.

The Different Segments of the Stock Market

There are many different components making up what we generally refer to as the "stock market." For analytical purposes the equity markets consist of a variety of different segments that are often referred to as small company stocks, large company stocks, international stocks, growth stocks, value stocks, mid-caps, and a variety of combinations— such as small company growth stocks or large company value stocks.

The reason the market is broken up into these various segments is because each of them tends to perform differently over time. So while one segment is doing poorly another may be doing better. There can be significant benefits for investors who understand this phenomenon and know how to use it to their advantage.

A Look at Some Enlightening Historical Information

Illustration 17 can help you understand more about the performance of various segments of the stock market by showing annual rankings for a number of different categories between 1981 and 2000. Notice that the market as a whole is broken into seven different segments, each of which is defined by an index used by professional financial managers to chart the performance of the market:

- *large company stocks*, represented by the S&P 500® Index;

- *large company growth stocks*, represented by the S&P 500®/BARRA Growth Index;

- *large company value stocks*, represented by the S&P 500®/BARRA Value Index;

- *midsize stocks*, represented by the S&P 400® Midcap Index;

- *small company growth stocks*, represented by the Russell 2000® Growth Index;

- *small company value stocks*, represented by the Russell 2000® Value Index; and

- *international stocks,* represented by the MSCI® EAFE® Index.

Keep in mind that an investment cannot be made directly in an index. We use this data for informational purposes only.

The S&P 500® is an unmanaged index consisting of five hundred of the most commonly held stocks. The S&P 500®/Barra Growth Index is an unmanaged index generally representative of the U.S. market for growth stocks. The S&P 500®/Barra Value Index is an unmanaged index generally representative of the U.S. market for value stocks. The S&P 400® Midcap Index is an unmanaged index consisting of four-hundred stocks with medium capitalization. The Russell 2000® Growth Index is an unmanaged index generally representative of the U.S. market for small capitalization stocks. It contains securities that growth managers typically select from the Russell 2000® index. The Russell 2000® Value

Illustration 17: Diversification
Annual Winners and Losers in the Stock Market
Performance of Various Investment Markets from 1981 to 2000

		Best	Worst	Ave.
SP500 =	S&P 500 (Large Company) Stocks	37.6%	-4.9%	16.5%
LCV =	Large Company Value Stocks	37.0%	-6.9%	15.8%
LCG =	Large Company Growth Stocks	42.2%	-9.8%	16.7%
SP400 =	S&P 400 (Mid-Size) Stocks	50.1%	-5.1%	17.4%
SCV =	Small Company Value Stocks	41.7%	-21.8%	14.4%
SCG =	Small Company Growth Stocks	51.2%	-17.4%	10.3%
INT =	International Stocks	69.5%	-23.5%	12.7%

Year	Ave	Best Performers > ... > ... > ... > ... > Worst Performers						
1981	-1.4%	SCV 14.9%	SP400 1.8%	LCV 0.0%	INT -2.3%	SP500 -4.9%	SCG -9.2%	LCG -9.8%
1982	19.3%	SCV 28.5%	SP400 22.7%	LCG 22.0%	SP500 21.6%	LCV 21.0%	SCG 21.0%	INT -1.9%
1983	25.2%	SCV 38.6%	LCV 28.9%	SP400 26.1%	INT 23.7%	SP500 22.6%	SCG 20.1%	LCG 16.2%
1984	2.0%	LCV 10.5%	INT 7.4%	SP500 6.3%	LCG 2.3%	SCV 2.3%	SP400 1.2%	SCG -15.8%
1985	35.5%	INT 56.1%	SP400 35.6%	LCG 33.3%	SP500 31.7%	SCV 31.0%	SCG 31.0%	LCV 29.7%
1986	21.6%	INT 69.5%	LCV 21.7%	SP500 18.7%	SP400 16.2%	LCG 14.5%	SCV 7.4%	SCG 3.6%
1987	2.9%	INT 24.6%	LCG 6.5%	SP500 5.3%	LCV 3.7%	SP400 -2.0%	SCV -7.1%	SCG -10.5%
1988	21.3%	SCV 29.5%	INT 28.3%	LCV 21.7%	SP400 20.9%	SCG 20.4%	SP500 16.6%	LCG 12.0%
1989	24.7%	LCG 36.4%	SP400 35.6%	SP500 31.7%	LCV 26.1%	SCG 20.2%	SCV 12.4%	INT 10.5%
1990	-11.1%	LCG 0.2%	SP500 -3.1%	SP400 -5.1%	LCV -6.9%	SCG -17.4%	SCV -21.8%	INT -23.5%
1991	35.2%	SCG 51.2%	SP400 50.1%	SCV 41.7%	LCG 38.4%	SP500 30.5%	LCV 22.6%	INT 12.1%
1992	8.6%	SCV 29.2%	SP400 11.9%	LCV 10.5%	SCG 7.8%	SP500 7.6%	LCG 5.1%	INT -12.2%
1993	16.3%	INT 32.6%	SCV 23.9%	LCV 18.6%	SP400 14.0%	SCG 13.4%	SP500 10.1%	LCG 1.7%
1994	0.7%	INT 7.8%	LCG 3.1%	SP500 1.3%	LCV -0.6%	SCV -1.6%	SCG -2.4%	SP400 -2.9%
1995	30.2%	LCG 38.1%	SP500 37.6%	LCV 37.0%	SCG 31.0%	SP400 30.9%	SCV 25.8%	INT 11.2%
1996	18.1%	LCG 24.0%	SP500 23.0%	LCV 22.0%	SCV 21.4%	SP400 19.2%	SCG 11.3%	INT 6.1%
1997	25.5%	LCG 36.5%	SP500 33.4%	SP400 32.3%	SCV 31.8%	LCV 30.0%	SCG 12.9%	INT 1.8%
1998	17.0%	LCG 42.2%	SP500 28.6%	INT 20.0%	SP400 19.1%	LCV 14.7%	SCG 1.2%	SCV -6.5%
1999	20.8%	SCG 43.1%	LCG 28.3%	INT 27.0%	SP500 21.0%	SP400 14.7%	LCV 12.7%	SCV -1.5%
8-31 2000	6.4%	SP400 23.1%	SCV 14.3%	LCV 4.4%	SP500 4.1%	LCG 3.7%	SCG 2.3%	INT -7.3%

Index is an unmanaged index generally representative of the U.S. market for small capitalization stocks. It contains securities that value managers typically select from the Russell 2000® Index. The MSCI® EAFE® Index tracks the stocks of about one thousand companies in Europe, Australia, and the Far East (EAFE®).

Notice that large and small company stocks are broken into separate value and growth components. Value stocks tend to pay higher dividends and often sell at lower prices than comparable companies. They often consist of businesses that are temporarily out of favor with investors and have had their stock prices beaten down to levels that may suggest better "values." Growth stocks, on the other hand, tend to offer lower dividends because they retain most of their earnings for new business opportunities. They are often growing much faster than the competition and therefore attract more attention and command higher share prices.

There are certainly other ways to break up the stock market for analytical purposes, but don't worry about other categorization schemes or about all the names and acronyms. These are just standard, time-tested categories used by a majority of investment and financial advisors, and we are only using them to make a point.

When you look at this kind of information, you should also keep in mind that international markets are subject to special risks such as currency fluctuations, political instability, differing securities regulations, and periods of illiquidity.

Twenty Years' Worth of Experience to Rely On

Twenty years of market data is enough to give you a feel for the potential value of diversification. As you go from left to right across the chart you move from the best performing segment to the worst performing segment of the market. In most years the differences between the rates of return of the best performers and the worst performers are substantial.

For example, in 1992, *small company value stocks*, the best performing segment of the market that year, returned approximately 29.2 percent, while *international stocks,* the worst performing segment of the market, lost over 12.2 percent. All of the other segments of the market were somewhere in between. By contrast, in 1998, *large company growth stocks* returned about 42.2 percent as the best performing segment of the market, while *small company value stocks* lost about 6.5 percent as the worst performing segment.

Reasons to Diversify Before Retirement

No matter how strong your psychological constitution may be, it's always a good idea to diversify your investments across different segments of the market. For example, in 1987, the overall return from the entire stock market (if you had the same amount invested in each segment) was a measly 2.9 percent. But imagine if you didn't have some of your money invested in international and large company stocks that year. If all of your assets were in small and midsize stocks, you would have had a year of significant losses. If that happens too often, even the most stalwart investor can begin to lose confidence in the market and start drifting away from their original plan—which is one of the worst things that can happen.

Consider International Stocks

Notice that in 1987 international stocks would have been your saving grace, earning over 24 percent and pulling up the entire portfolio, while all the other segments of the market either lost money or were in single digits. However, in many years, including 1989, 1990, 1991, and 1992 international stocks were by far the worst performing segment of the market. In fact, international stock returns varied from a high of 69.5 percent in 1986, their best year, to a loss of 23.5 percent in 1990, their worst year. And yet, over the entire twenty years, they averaged about 12.7 percent.

Diversification May Help You Sleep Better at Night

Similar patterns emerge for other segments of the market too. They have their good years, their bad years, and their average years—and none of them resulted in an average annual return over the entire twenty-year period of less than 10.3 percent. Had you been diversified among all of the various categories, you would have had a much less harrowing ride to a successful twenty-year stock market investment period.

Managing Your Stock Portfolio

Once you decide on hypothetical rates of return and holding periods for each segment of the market in which you plan to invest, the overall process of using historical average annual rates of return, reasonable length holding periods, and intelligent savings strategies come together in a way that should help you achieve your overall long-term retirement planning objectives.

Diversification During Retirement

There is another reason you should be a diversified investor during your working years. When you get closer to retirement you may eventually have to start selling some of your equities to get the money you need to support your lifestyle when you stop working. When you have a diversified portfolio of stock market investments, you should be in a much better position to sell the ones that have done well up until that time. If you are not diversified as you approach retirement, and if all of your investments happen to be down at the same time, it can make the transition into your later years much more risky and much more stressful than if you had a variety of assets to choose from.

Managing Money During Retirement

The big thing during retirement is to increase the odds that you always have a few investments that will have achieved their expected rates of return, or hit their expected values, by the time you need to sell them to get more income to live on. Bringing a variety of investments with you into retirement, because you are diversified all along, should help you do that.

Calculating Rates of Return for Your Own Diversified Investment Accounts

You need to know how to compute hypothetical rates of return for *your own* diversified investment portfolios. If your accounts are invested in more than one kind of asset, like they probably should be, you need to be able to determine combined hypothetical rates of return. In fact, you will have to do this for all of your investment accounts—your IRAs, 401(k) plans, annuities, etc. As you can see in Plan Aid 2: Example, calculating a hypothetical average rate of return for your own accounts is really pretty easy.

Types of Assets and the Percentage of Your Account Invested in Each

The first step in figuring out the hypothetical average rate of return for an investment account is to list each type of asset. Then, you need to determine the percentage of the account invested in each of them. You do this by totaling up the amounts invested in all categories and then dividing each of them by that total. For example, if your total account value is $50,000 and you have $7,500 invested in bonds, then 15 percent of your account is in bonds—$7,500 divided by $50,000 equals 0.15 or 15 percent. On the other hand, if you have $17,500 invested in large company value stocks, then 35 percent of your account is invested in that type of asset—$17,500 divided by $50,000 equals 0.35 or 35 percent. You do the same calculation for each asset in the account, and when you're done, they should all add up to 100 percent.

A Quick Review of Percentages and Decimals

Many people haven't had to use percentages and decimals for a long time—so I want to go over it briefly. As you know, percentages and decimals are really the same thing—they're completely interchangeable. A decimal can be converted into a percentage and a percentage can be converted into a decimal. For example, 25 percent is the same as 0.25, while 80 percent is the same as 0.80 and 3.5 percent is the same as 0.035. On the other hand, 0.37 is the same as 37 percent, while 0.68 is the same as

Plan Aid 2: Example
Weighted Average Rate of Return

Type of Asset	Asset Value	% of Assets	Expect. Ret.	Wtd. Ret.
Treasury Bonds	$7,500	15.0%	5.5%	0.8%
Large Company Value Stocks	$17,500	35.0%	10.0%	3.5%
International Stocks	$5,000	10.0%	9.0%	0.9%
Small Company Growth Stocks	$10,000	20.0%	12.0%	2.4%
Mid-Cap Stocks	$10,000	20.0%	10.5%	2.1%
Tot. Assets & Wtd. Ave. Return	$50,000	100.0%		9.7%

For illustration purposes only. Not representative of an actual investment. An individual investor's results may vary. All assumptions and computational results are hypothetical in nature. There are no guarantees that you will achieve the results shown. Higher volatility has historically been associated with higher rates of return, and average returns have had a tendency to fluctuate from year to year. The prices of large company, small company, international, and mid-cap stocks will fluctuate. Investing in international stocks may carry additional risks such as differing securities regulations and more volatile political and economic environments. Treasury Bonds are guaranteed by the U.S. government and, if held to maturity, offer a fixed rate of return and principal value. You should consult with a financial professional.

68 percent and .009 is the same as .9 percent—I'm sure it's all coming back to you.

The reason I digress at this point is to save you any confusion, because we will be talking a lot about percentages, while always making calculations with their decimal equivalents. For example, if we need to multiply 20 percent by 10.5 percent, we will do so by multiplying 0.20 by 0.105, to get .021, and then we'll convert it back to 2.1 percent. It's really pretty simple—but it might get a little confusing until you get used to it again.

You probably remember back in high school when you learned that converting a decimal to a percentage is as simple as moving the decimal point two places to the right, while converting from a percentage to a decimal simply requires you to move it two places to the left—and it *is* that easy. So .009 becomes .9 percent and .015 becomes 1.5 percent, while 65.6 percent becomes .656 and 15.3 percent becomes .153.

Just take your time when you do the conversions and you shouldn't have any trouble—especially if you follow the examples.

Hypothetical Returns

After you determine the percentage of your account invested in each type of asset, you also need to estimate the hypothetical rate of return you expect to earn on each part of the account. Think back to our discussions in Chapters 3 and 4 about historical rates of return to get an idea of what you might reasonably expect, and talk to your financial advisors about what they think you should use. At any rate, you need to come up with hypothetical rates of return that you and your advisors think are "reasonable" in light of historical data and your own expectations about the future.

Computing the Hypothetical Average Rate of Return

The final step in the process is to compute what is called a *weighted average rate of return* for the whole account. You do this by multiplying the percentage of total assets in each category by the hypothetical rate of return for that category, and then adding them all up.

For example, if you have 10 percent of your account in international stocks and expect to earn a hypothetical average of 9 percent per year, the return for that part of the account is .9 percent (.10 multiplied by .09 equals .009, which converts back to .9 percent). By making the same calculation for each type of asset, and adding up all the results, you will find that the entire account is expected to grow at a hypothetical weighted average rate of return of about 9.7 percent per year. This is the rate we're looking for. Ultimately, you need to round it up or down to the nearest whole percentage for planning purposes. You can round it up to be a little more aggressive and you can round it down to be a little more conservative, keeping in mind that higher rates of return are also associated with higher risk and volatility.

PART TWO

Deciding How Much Income You'll Need

In this section, we will cover:

Step #2: Think About Your Lifestyle;

Step #3: Adjust for Inflation;

Step #4: Estimate Social Security;

Step #5: Account for Protected Pensions; and

Step #6: Anticipate Other Income.

After completing this part of the book, you should know how much income you need to support your lifestyle in retirement, how much of that income will come from outside sources, and how much you may need to provide for yourself.

7

Forecasting Your
Preretirement Lifestyle

To create your own retirement plan you need to have an idea of what kind of lifestyle you want in retirement. This is what *Step #2: Think About Your Lifestyle* is all about. It's like planning a trip—you don't pull out of the driveway until you know where you're going, how much it's going to cost, and who you intend to visit along the way. While you can't predict *exactly* how much income you'll need for retirement, there are a few simple steps you can take to develop a better estimate.

Start with Where You Are Today

One of the best ways to estimate the kind of lifestyle you'll want in retirement is to start with your current salary. Then, by assuming a reasonable rate of growth for the rest of your career, you can estimate your standard of living at the time you think you may quit working. It won't be perfect, and your plans and expectations will probably change many times along the way, but with a little consideration you should be able to develop a pretty good estimate of your lifestyle prior to retirement. Then, you can use that preretirement lifestyle to anticipate what your income needs might be for the rest of your life.

You Can't Just Consider Inflation

One of the mistakes people make when doing their financial planning is to use an inflation rate as their salary growth rate assumption. Unfortunately, many software programs and workbooks also do it this way. But while you absolutely must consider inflation in the overall planning process, it's probably a mistake to limit your expected salary growth to that amount. Most people expect to get cost of living increases every year, but they also expect to get something beyond that—unless of course they're just waiting around to get fired.

Your Standard of Living Will Probably Improve Over Time

If you don't assume that your income will increase faster than inflation, you are essentially planning to lock in your current standard of living for the rest of your life—which may not make a lot of sense. Most people don't expect to have the same lifestyle at age sixty-five as they have at age thirty—so it's a good idea not to plan that way either.

You should consider all of your future salary growth—both cost of living increases and real improvements in your standard of living—to get a sense for the lifestyle you'll want in retirement.

Why Do We All Work So Hard?

Most people go to school, get additional training, acquire new job skills and apply themselves at work to improve their overall standard of living. Let's face it, you don't go back to school to get an MBA to protect your current salary against inflation—you do it to increase your real standard of living. A cost of living increase is the baseline in most people's annual salary expectations.

On top of the inflationary adjustments, however, most people also expect to be rewarded for their extra effort—or they'll just take their talents somewhere else. That's the way the system works. So you don't want to create financial plans that fail to take into account that "extra effort." You should consider your total salary expectations when planning for retirement, not just what you expect to get because of inflation.

Breaking Things Down into Bite-Size Chunks

One of the best ways to consider the whole salary issue is to break it down into smaller pieces that are easier to understand and work with. It's usually best to start with your expectations about *real* salary growth— the amount you think you will be paid for your "extra effort"—and then add inflation back in later. This approach has the added benefit of making it easier to analyze the reasonableness of your overall expectations.

Consider Everything on a Pretax Basis

When you do your long-range planning, it's usually best to plan for the amount of *pretax* income you need in retirement. Not only is it difficult to determine what your tax situation will be next year, let alone for the rest of your working career, but it's even more difficult to anticipate what it will be during retirement. As a result, you should plan in terms of the amount of *pretax* retirement income you think you'll need, and make the reasonable assumption that your postretirement tax situation won't be that much different than your preretirement situation. It's not perfect, but it's really about the best you can do.

Always Think in Terms of Pretax Income

If you are making $50,000 per year, and someone asks you how much you make, you say "$50,000 per year"—not "$38,600 on a net after-tax basis." Most people don't have any idea about how much tax they paid last year. If someone asks you how much it costs to support your current lifestyle, you would probably say "about $50,000 per year"—not "$38,600 in net after-tax cash flow."

You should plan the same way. You have to make the reasonable assumption that if you're able to live on your *pretax* income the year before you retire—knowing that some of it will be used to pay taxes— you should also be able to live on that *pretax* income during retirement, knowing of course that some of it will continue to be used for taxes. This makes the planning process much simpler, easier, and more understandable, because using your *pretax* income prior to retirement to estimate your *pretax* income during retirement is much easier than trying to take all of the possible tax considerations into account.

Projecting Your Preretirement Income

To estimate your income in the year prior to retirement, you start with your current gross annual salary, or pretax earnings. You shouldn't include irregular or unpredictable bonuses, unusually high commissions, or other amounts of income that you don't reasonably expect to continue into the future. You anticipate your need for retirement income based upon a projection of your current salary, so you want the current amount to be as normal or typical as possible. If you make the calculation using total income from a year in which you get an unusually high bonus or earn abnormally high commissions, you will probably project an unrealistically high preretirement lifestyle—which can really throw off your planning.

For example, let's say you have a base salary this year of $60,000 and an exceptionally high bonus of $30,000, and that you expect real salary increases, over and above inflation, of about 2 percent per year until you retire in thirty years. If you don't include the bonus, your projected income at retirement would be about $108,600 in today's purchasing power—that is, before adjusting for inflation.

However, if you add the $30,000 bonus to your base salary and project the $90,000 total at 2 percent for thirty years, you will project a preretirement lifestyle of almost $162,900, or over $54,000 more. This will obviously have a tremendous impact on your overall financial plan because you will have to figure out how to accumulate all of the additional assets needed to replace a much higher amount of income during retirement. As a result, you would probably choose to ignore the $30,000 bonus for projection purposes, or at least scale it back to a more typical amount. You have to make these kinds of adjustments when considering your own situation, because the quality of your financial plan will only be as good as the assumptions you make.

Establishing Your Own Real Salary Growth Rate

In the above example, we chose 2 percent as your expected salary growth rate. The amount you actually use may be more or less, depending upon your goals and expectations. You have to use an amount that makes sense in your own circumstances, and you should probably be a little on the conservative side with your estimates.

The *real* salary growth rate you decide to use for planning purposes will be the annual percentage by which you expect the *real* value, or purchasing power, of your current salary to grow until retirement. It's the amount of increase you are expecting over and above the rate of inflation. For instance, if you assume a *total* salary growth rate of 4 percent per year, including inflation, and expect annual inflation of 3 percent, your *real* salary growth rate would be 1 percent—your total salary growth less the amount of inflation.

A Little Guidance Concerning Salary Growth Expectations

The raises you get each year can generally be thought of as consisting of two parts—a "cost of living" increase that helps you keep up with inflation, and a "merit" increase that adds to your *real* standard of living. It's the merit increase that reflects your effort to enhance your value in the labor market, and it's the merit increase that you need to consider at this stage in the planning process.

For guidance in making this decision, consider data provided in the *2001/2002 US Compensation Planning Survey* from the human resource consulting firm of William M. Mercer, Inc., which covers more than 1,500 organizations representing pay practices affecting more than 14 million U.S. workers. According to that survey, the average *real* increase in wages for the ten years between 1993 and 2002 was approximately 1.6 percent.

But remember, that's just an average, and it doesn't necessarily relate to you or me, so consider your own goals and objectives, your own work experience, and your own employer's projections about the future to get a handle on your salary growth expectations. You need to make a good decision in this area because it affects everything else in the planning pro-cess—so take your time and consider it carefully.

An Example of Salary Growth Rate Assumptions

If you use a base income of $50,000 and anticipate a 1 percent *real* salary growth rate for thirty years, you will project a preretirement lifestyle of about $67,500. However, if you start with the same $50,000, but expect it to increase by 2.5 percent per year, you will estimate a preretirement lifestyle of about $105,000. Obviously, you would need significantly more income during retirement to sustain that higher lifestyle, and you would therefore have to save a lot more money, or invest your savings more aggressively, to accumulate the additional assets you may need to make it work.

Income Projections Are Never Perfect

Keep in mind that your salary probably won't actually increase by the same percent each year—you just need to look at it that way for planning purposes.

Most people experience salary increases a bit more randomly, and in more of a steplike fashion, with a few larger increases, a bunch of fairly average years, and perhaps an occasional period of lower growth or even temporary unemployment. Other people may be self-employed, starting businesses, or getting involved in other ventures that could lead to rap-idly changing income scenarios. It's impossible to know in advance what will actually happen. However, establishing an average annual growth rate that results in a preretirement income amount that makes sense from an overall planning perspective should help you make better decisions in the long run.

Deciding How Much Retirement Income You Need

After establishing your current base income and estimating a *real* salary growth rate, you should be able to compute your projected preretirement lifestyle. This is the standard of living you hope to have during the last year of your working career, and it provides the foundation upon which you should be able to determine how much income you may need to maintain that standard of living throughout retirement.

Is the Amount Reasonable?

The preretirement lifestyle you determine for planning purposes will be the income you project for the year prior to retirement, stated in terms of current purchasing power, or *real* dollars. Once you calculate this amount, you need to evaluate its reasonableness before moving on to the next step in the process.

A good way to perform this "smell test" is to ask yourself how much you think you would be earning *today*, if you were at the end of your working career, and if you had achieved all of the job success that you are hoping and working for. In other words, think of someone you know who is in a position today that is similar to the one that you think you will be in *at the end of your career*—and then find out how much that person is making *right now*. That will give you a reasonable approximation of the "current value" of the lifestyle you may be expecting to have at the end of your career.

Of course it's not always as simple as marching into the vice president's office and demanding to know how much he makes. Instead, you may need to talk with friends or relatives or perhaps your human resource department. You might also want to refer to some of the salary surveys that are available online and/or through various trade associations and industry groups. But however you do it, the bottom line is that you need to come up with a reasonable estimate of that comparative salary to use in evaluating your own projections.

Next, ask yourself whether the amount you compute as your own expected preretirement salary is reasonable compared with that amount. For some people, the comparison will make sense right away, while others will find it necessary to make an adjustment because they over- or underestimated their final salary relative to the comparative benchmark.

You May Need to Consider a Few Different Alternatives

Assume that your current salary is $75,000 and that you initially expect it to grow at a *real* rate of about 2 percent per year for twenty-five years. That's 2 percent over and above the rate of inflation you're expecting. After doing the computations, you find that you expect to be earning about $123,000 per year in current purchasing power prior to retirement. However, after a little investigation, you find out that your boss's boss, the person who holds a position today similar to what you think you will have at the end of your career, is only making about $105,000.

It appears that you might have overestimated your salary growth rate—so you would probably go back and reduce it a little bit. In fact, if you drop the rate of expected salary growth to 1.5 percent, the resulting final annual salary of $108,750 makes more sense given your overall expectations—so you would probably want to use 1.5 percent *real* salary growth in your retirement plan.

However, perhaps your boss's boss is making more—say $140,000 per year. In that case, you might want to increase your salary growth rate to 2.5 percent, which would bring you to a closer projection of about $138,750.

Get As Close As You Can

You may need to go through this process a few times to come up with a reasonable preretirement lifestyle expectation. At this point, it's easy to make changes before going on to the rest of your plan. Since everything else we talk about will be directed toward helping you achieve the retirement lifestyle you want, it's very important to get it right.

Create Your Own Plan

Take a moment now to see how to project your hypothetical final salary in the year prior to retirement. Using Plan Aid 3a: Example, you can see how easy it is to project your own preretirement income. Start with a "normal" or "typical" amount for your *Current Annual Salary* in box (d), and then divide it by twelve to compute your *Current Monthly Salary* in box (e), which will be used in later calculations.

Plan Aid 3a: Example
Preretirement Lifestyle

Current Annual Salary .... (d) $ **75,000**

Current Monthly Salary .... (e) $ **6,250**

  (d) ÷ 12

Real Salary Growth Rate Assumption .... (f)   **1.5** %
  (Select 0.0% or 0.5% or 1.0% or 1.5% or 2.0% or 2.5%)

Real Salary Growth Factor .... (g)   **1.39**

  Look Up on Plan Aid Table 3, Using Number of Years Until Retirement and (f) above

Hypothetical Final Salary (current dollars) .... (h) $ **104,250**

  (d) x (g)

  Evaluate item (h) for reasonableness and redo items (f), (g), and (h) if necessary

For illustration purposes only. All assumptions and computational results are hypothetical in nature. There are no guarantees that you will achieve the results shown. You should consult with a financial professional.

Next, considering what we just said about establishing a reasonable rate of salary growth, decide on a rate to use in your own plan, and enter it as your *Real Salary Growth Rate Assumption* in box (f). Then, turning to Plan Aid Table 3: Real Salary Growth Rate Factors, find the column related to your salary growth rate and move down to the row relating to the number of years until retirement. If you don't remember what it is, you can find it in box (c), *Number of Years Until Retirement* in Plan Aid 1a: Example on page 13.

After using the table to find the salary growth factor for your number of years until retirement and your real salary growth rate, enter it as the *Real Salary Growth Factor* in box (g). And finally, multiply it by the *Current Annual Salary* in box (d) to establish your own *Hypothetical Final Salary (current dollars)* in box (h). This is the amount we're looking for. It represents the lifestyle that you think you will have in the year prior to retirement, and it will ultimately be used to help project your retirement income needs.

Plan Aid Table 3: Real Salary Growth Rate Factors

Years to Retirement	Real Salary Growth Rate Assumption				
	.5%	1.0%	1.5%	2.0%	2.5%
1	1.01	1.01	1.02	1.02	1.03
2	1.01	1.02	1.03	1.04	1.05
3	1.02	1.03	1.05	1.06	1.08
4	1.02	1.04	1.06	1.08	1.10
5	1.03	1.05	1.08	1.10	1.13
6	1.03	1.06	1.09	1.13	1.16
7	1.04	1.07	1.11	1.15	1.19
8	1.04	1.08	1.13	1.17	1.22
9	1.05	1.09	1.14	1.20	1.25
10	1.05	1.10	1.16	1.22	1.28
11	1.06	1.12	1.18	1.24	1.31
12	1.06	1.13	1.20	1.27	1.34
13	1.07	1.14	1.21	1.29	1.38
14	1.07	1.15	1.23	1.32	1.41
15	1.08	1.16	1.25	1.35	1.45
16	1.08	1.17	1.27	1.37	1.48
17	1.09	1.18	1.29	1.40	1.52
18	1.09	1.20	1.31	1.43	1.56
19	1.10	1.21	1.33	1.46	1.60
20	1.10	1.22	1.35	1.49	1.64
21	1.11	1.23	1.37	1.52	1.68
22	1.12	1.24	1.39	1.55	1.72
23	1.12	1.26	1.41	1.58	1.76
24	1.13	1.27	1.43	1.61	1.81
25	1.13	1.28	1.45	1.64	1.85
26	1.14	1.30	1.47	1.67	1.90
27	1.14	1.31	1.49	1.71	1.95
28	1.15	1.32	1.52	1.74	2.00
29	1.16	1.33	1.54	1.78	2.05
30	1.16	1.35	1.56	1.81	2.10
31	1.17	1.36	1.59	1.85	2.15
32	1.17	1.37	1.61	1.88	2.20
33	1.18	1.39	1.63	1.92	2.26
34	1.18	1.40	1.66	1.96	2.32
35	1.19	1.42	1.68	2.00	2.37
36	1.20	1.43	1.71	2.04	2.43
37	1.20	1.45	1.73	2.08	2.49
38	1.21	1.46	1.76	2.12	2.56
39	1.21	1.47	1.79	2.16	2.62
40	1.22	1.49	1.81	2.21	2.69
41	1.23	1.50	1.84	2.25	2.75
42	1.23	1.52	1.87	2.30	2.82
43	1.24	1.53	1.90	2.34	2.89
44	1.25	1.55	1.93	2.39	2.96
45	1.25	1.56	1.95	2.44	3.04
46	1.26	1.58	1.98	2.49	3.11
47	1.26	1.60	2.01	2.54	3.19
48	1.27	1.61	2.04	2.59	3.27
49	1.28	1.63	2.07	2.64	3.35
50	1.28	1.64	2.11	2.69	3.44

We're Not Quite Finished

At this point you have to do one more thing. You need to do the "smell test" analysis we talked about previously to determine if this is a reasonable final salary amount. If not, you will have to increase or decrease your *Real Salary Growth Rate Assumption* in box (f), use the lookup table again to determine a new *Real Salary Growth Factor* for box (g), and then use that new factor to compute a revised *Hypothetical Final Salary (current dollars)* amount in box (h). You shouldn't have to do this more than once or twice to come up with a reasonable amount.

After reviewing the example, fill in Plan Aid 3b: Your Plan now, to determine your own hypothetical preretirement lifestyle. In looking up your *Real Salary Growth Factor* in Plan Aid Table 3, be sure to use your number of years until retirement from Plan Aid 1b: Your Plan, on page 13. Remember this number for future reference. You will use it a lot.

Plan Aid 3b: Your Plan
Preretirement Lifestyle

Current Annual Salary .... (d) $

Current Monthly Salary .... (e) $

(d) ÷ 12

Real Salary Growth Rate Assumption .... (f)   %
(Select 0.0% or 0.5% or 1.0% or 1.5% or 2.0% or 2.5%)

Real Salary Growth Factor .... (g)
Look Up on Plan Aid Table 3, Using Number of Years Until Retirement and (f) above

Hypothetical Final Salary (current dollars) .... (h) $
(d) x (g)

Evaluate item (h) for reasonableness and redo items (f), (g) and (h) if necessary

8

Inflation

One of the biggest concerns you have to deal with in retirement planning is the problem of inflation. Unfortunately, too many people don't understand how bad it can be—and failing to take inflation into account can jeopardize your entire financial future. That's why it's so important to follow *Step #3: Adjust for Inflation.*

Accounting for Inflation *Before* and *After* Retirement

Although some people neglect to account for inflation altogether, those who do think about it tend to make the equally fatal mistake of considering it only in terms of how it impacts their income and lifestyle before retirement, forgetting that there will be inflation during retirement too. Inflation doesn't go away just because you retire—it has nothing to do with your work status. So you have to anticipate its impact on your financial life both *before* and *during* retirement.

Historical Inflation Rates

The examples in Illustration 18 use historical rates of inflation to illustrate the potential effect of rising prices. It's important to get a feel for how inflation rates have varied over the years because you have to decide for yourself what rate to use in your own plan—and small changes can have a dramatic impact. Many people tend to stick close to the long-run seventy-five-year average of about 3.1 percent, but you should have a feel for the consequences of using different rates as well.

Based upon data constructed by the U.S. Department of Labor, Bureau of Labor Statistics, concerning the Consumer Price Index for All Urban Consumers (CPI-U), in the twenty-five years between 1976 and 2000, inflation averaged 4.7 percent—which is extremely high for such a long period of time. Some of you may remember the oil embargoes, wage and price controls, stagflation, unemployment, high interest rates, and all the other problems that plagued us in the '70s and '80s. All combined, they lead to a twenty-five-year average annual rate of inflation well above the long-run average of 3.1 percent, and a fifty-year rate that reached as high as 4.0 percent.

In the ten years between 1991 and 2000, inflation moderated substantially, averaging only 2.7 percent, while during the five years between 1996 and 2000 it actually came down as low as 2.5 percent. In fact, over the last few years, we have seen some of the lowest rates of inflation we've had in a very long time. Keep in mind that this is historical data, and as I caution many times throughout the book, past performance is never a guarantee of future results. But the lessons of the past are all we really have to go on, as imperfect a predictor as they may be.

Effects of Inflation on the Cost of a Loaf of Bread

The first example in Illustration 18 uses historical inflation rates to explore what could happen to the cost of a loaf of bread over a sixty-year period. This may seem like a very long time, but just think about it: If you're thirty-five, plan to retire at sixty-five, and expect to live to ninety-five—you're looking at sixty years. You'll be working for thirty and retired for thirty but inflation will be hammering away at your lifestyle the entire time.

Consider what could happen to the price of a $2.50 loaf of bread over the first thirty years, while you're still working, at a fifty-year historical average inflation rate of 4.0 percent. After ten years, the price would go up to $3.70. After twenty years it would more than double to

Illustration 18: The Impact of Inflation
Before and During Retirement
Using Historical Inflation Rate Assumptions

Projected Cost of a Loaf of Bread that Costs $2.50 Today

Historical Information	Projected Amounts					
	Before Retirement			During Retirement		
	Cost in 10 Yrs	Cost in 20 Yrs	Cost in 30 Yrs	Cost in 40 Yrs	Cost in 50 Yrs	Cost in 60 Yrs
75 Years 1926 to 2000 3.10%	$3.39	$4.60	$6.25	$8.48	$11.50	$15.61
50 Years 1951 to 2000 4.00%	$3.70	$5.48	$8.11	$12.00	$17.77	$26.30
25 Years 1976 to 2000 4.70%	$3.96	$6.26	$9.92	$15.70	$24.85	$39.33
10 Years 1991 to 2000 2.70%	$3.26	$4.26	$5.56	$7.26	$9.47	$12.36
5 Years 1996 to 2000 2.50%	$3.20	$4.10	$5.24	$6.71	$8.59	$11.00

Projected Cost of a Current $50,000 Lifestyle

Historical Information	Projected Amounts					
	Before Retirement			During Retirement		
	Cost in 10 Yrs	Cost in 20 Yrs	Cost in 30 Yrs	Cost in 40 Yrs	Cost in 50 Yrs	Cost in 60 Yrs
75 Years 1926 to 2000 3.10%	$67,851	$92,075	$124,948	$169,557	$230,093	$312,241
50 Years 1951 to 2000 4.00%	$74,012	$109,556	$162,170	$240,051	$355,334	$525,981
25 Years 1976 to 2000 4.70%	$79,147	$125,286	$198,322	$313,933	$496,940	$786,631
10 Years 1991 to 2000 2.70%	$65,264	$85,188	$111,195	$145,140	$189,449	$247,284
5 Years 1996 to 2000 2.50%	$64,004	$81,931	$104,878	$134,253	$171,855	$219,989

Source: Calculated by Paul Grangaard using data presented in *Stocks, Bonds, Bills and Inflation*®
2001 Yearbook, © 2001 Ibbotson Associates, Inc. Based on copyrighted works by Ibbotson and
Sinquefield. All rights reserved. Used with permission. Based upon U.S. Department of Labor, Bureau of
Labor Statistics, Consumer Price Index for All Urban Consumers (CPI-U). For illustration purposes only.
Past performance is not a guarantee of future results.

$5.48, and by the time you retire at age sixty-five, it would have more than tripled to $8.11.

Inflation Protection While You're Working

While you're working, you are usually protected against inflation in a variety of ways. Most people expect annual cost of living increases at work, and those who are self-employed may be able to raise their prices, work more hours, increase their billing rates, or find other ways to offset the inevitable impact of inflation. Although for all these reasons you probably don't have to worry too much about inflation while you're working, you *do* have to consider it when projecting your preretirement income, or you may end up underestimating the amount of money you'll need to support your lifestyle in retirement.

You Also Have to Be Prepared for Inflation During Retirement

You have to be prepared to deal with inflation *during* retirement too. Anticipating inflation when you project your preretirement income is the first step, but you also have to plan to protect yourself against inflation after you stop working.

LIVING LONGER IN RETIREMENT

People are living a lot longer today. Obviously, living longer is a good thing, but it can be a real financial challenge for you and your family, because the longer you live, the greater your exposure will be to inflation. So you need to make your money last a lot longer during retirement while also overcoming the significant drag of inflation.

PRICES JUST KEEP GOING UP DURING RETIREMENT

As you can see in the first example in Illustration 18, at both the five- and ten-year average annual inflation rates, the cost of a loaf of bread would more than double during the thirty years you plan to be retired. At 2.5 percent, the lowest rate in the table for the five years between 1996 and 2000, the cost would go up from $5.24 the day you stop working to $11.00 in the last year of retirement. The increase would be slightly larger for the ten-year inflation rate of 2.7 percent, and far more dramatic if you consider some of the higher rates in the table. At the twenty-five-year average of 4.7 percent, the price of a loaf of bread would increase from $9.92 to over $39.00 during a typical thirty-year retirement period.

Maintaining a Lifestyle

Remember, inflation simply increases the price of everything—it forces you to have more money to purchase the same quantity of goods and services. The second example in Illustration 18 shows that to maintain any given lifestyle, you need more and more income each year just to stay in the same place—*before* and *after* retirement.

Using the long-run, seventy-five-year average annual inflation rate of 3.1 percent, a $50,000 current lifestyle would require an income of about $124,948 by the time you quit working. Then, ten years later, you would need about $169,557 to maintain the same lifestyle you brought with you into retirement. Ten years after that, or twenty years after you stop working, you would need $230,093 to maintain your preretirement purchasing power, and by the end of retirement you would need about $312,241 of income to give you the same lifestyle that $50,000 provides today—an increase of over 500 percent. During retirement alone your income would have to go up from $124,948 to $312,241—an increase of almost 150 percent.

Maintaining a Lifestyle During Retirement

If you calculate your income needs during retirement using different rates of inflation, you'll find that at a 4 percent average annual rate you would need to increase your income by more than 200 percent over a typical thirty-year period, from $162,170 all the way up to $525,981—just to maintain the same lifestyle. At the twenty-five-year average annual rate of 4.7 percent, your need for income would increase by almost 300 percent, from $198,322 in the first year to $786,631 in the last year. And of course, you wouldn't need nearly as much income over the last thirty years of your life if you assume one of the lower average annual rates of inflation for the five- or ten-year periods.

YOU WILL NOT BE WORKING OVERTIME IN RETIREMENT

But realize that even at the lower five-year historical inflation rate of 2.5 percent, you would still need to double your income over a typical thirty-year retirement period—just to maintain the same lifestyle. And think about this. During retirement, you will not be getting cost of living increases or merit raises at work, because you'll be retired. You will not be increasing your billing rate, working more overtime, taking on additional jobs, or doing any of the other things you did, or that were done for you, to offset rising prices while you're working. The only way you will be able to protect yourself against inflation while you're retired is to be much better at managing your money during retirement.

You Have to Anticipate Inflation for the Rest of Your Life

The most important thing to remember is that your retirement plans *today* have to anticipate *all* of the inflation that you are likely to experience over the rest of your life. You have to make sure that you accumulate enough money to provide the lifestyle you want the day you quit working—and then for the next thirty years. You have to accumulate sufficient resources by the time you retire to protect yourself against all the inflation that you will incur before you retire, as well as all the inflation you will incur after you retire. You do this by making an accurate projection of your inflation-adjusted, preretirement income needs, and then managing your assets properly during retirement.

Create Your Own Plan

The next step in the planning process is to adjust the preretirement lifestyle you calculated in the last chapter for inflation. To determine how much money you may ultimately need to accumulate for retirement, you have to know how much income you're going to need when you stop working. To do that, you have to estimate how much you think you will be making the year before you retire. It's not enough to know what kind of lifestyle you're expecting—you also have to convert that lifestyle into future income needs. You do this by adjusting your anticipated lifestyle for inflation.

Using Plan Aid 4a: Example, you can compute the amount of inflation-adjusted income you might expect to earn the year before retirement. You start with box (i) and enter the same *Real Salary Growth Rate Assumption* that you used for item (f) in Plan Aid 3a: Example on page 75. Next, you decide on a rate of inflation to use in your plan, and enter it as the *Inflation Rate Assumption* in box (j). Then, you simply add the two together to come up with a *Total Salary Growth Rate Assumption* in box (k)—which includes both inflation and the "real" salary growth you may be expecting for the rest of your working career.

Plan Aid 4a: Example
Preretirement Income

Real Salary Growth Rate Assumption ....…........... (i)   **1.5** %
   (From item (f), Plan Aid 3a: Example, on page 75)

Inflation Rate Assumption ....…...…........ (j)   **3.0** %
   (Select 2.0%, 2.5%, 3.0%, 3.5% or 4.0%)

Total Salary Growth Rate Assumption ...…............. (k)   **4.5** %
                                                          (i) + (j)

Total Salary Growth Factor ....…............. (l)   **2.63**
   Look Up on Plan Aid Table 4, Using Number of Years Until Retirement and (k) above

Current Annual Salary ....…................ (m) $ **75,000**
   (From item (d), Plan Aid 3a: Example, on page 75)

Hypothetical Final Salary ...…............................. (n) $ **197,250**
   Future Value Dollars in Year 1 of Retirement   *(l) x (m)*

For illustration purposes only. All assumptions and computational results are hypothetical in nature. There are no guarantees that you will achieve the results shown. You should consult with a financial professional.

The next step is to turn to Plan Aid Table 4: Total Salary Growth Rate Factors, find the column related to your total salary growth rate and move down to the row relating to the number of years until retirement, which you can find in box (c), *Number of Years Until Retirement* in Plan Aid 1a: Example on page 13.

After using the table to find the total salary growth factor at the point where the number of years until retirement and your total salary growth rate intersect, enter it as the *Total Salary Growth Factor* in box (l). Then

Plan Aid Table 4: Total Salary Growth Rate Factors

Years to Retire	Total Salary Growth Rate Assumption									
	2.0%	2.5%	3.0%	3.5%	4.0%	4.5%	5.0%	5.5%	6.0%	6.5%
1	1.02	1.03	1.03	1.04	1.04	1.05	1.05	1.06	1.06	1.07
2	1.04	1.05	1.06	1.07	1.08	1.09	1.10	1.11	1.12	1.13
3	1.06	1.08	1.09	1.11	1.12	1.14	1.16	1.17	1.19	1.21
4	1.08	1.10	1.13	1.15	1.17	1.19	1.22	1.24	1.26	1.29
5	1.10	1.13	1.16	1.19	1.22	1.25	1.28	1.31	1.34	1.37
6	1.13	1.16	1.19	1.23	1.27	1.30	1.34	1.38	1.42	1.46
7	1.15	1.19	1.23	1.27	1.32	1.36	1.41	1.45	1.50	1.55
8	1.17	1.22	1.27	1.32	1.37	1.42	1.48	1.53	1.59	1.65
9	1.20	1.25	1.30	1.36	1.42	1.49	1.55	1.62	1.69	1.76
10	1.22	1.28	1.34	1.41	1.48	1.55	1.63	1.71	1.79	1.88
11	1.24	1.31	1.38	1.46	1.54	1.62	1.71	1.80	1.90	2.00
12	1.27	1.34	1.43	1.51	1.60	1.70	1.80	1.90	2.01	2.13
13	1.29	1.38	1.47	1.56	1.67	1.77	1.89	2.01	2.13	2.27
14	1.32	1.41	1.51	1.62	1.73	1.85	1.98	2.12	2.26	2.41
15	1.35	1.45	1.56	1.68	1.80	1.94	2.08	2.23	2.40	2.57
16	1.37	1.48	1.60	1.73	1.87	2.02	2.18	2.36	2.54	2.74
17	1.40	1.52	1.65	1.79	1.95	2.11	2.29	2.48	2.69	2.92
18	1.43	1.56	1.70	1.86	2.03	2.21	2.41	2.62	2.85	3.11
19	1.46	1.60	1.75	1.92	2.11	2.31	2.53	2.77	3.03	3.31
20	1.49	1.64	1.81	1.99	2.19	2.41	2.65	2.92	3.21	3.52
21	1.52	1.68	1.86	2.06	2.28	2.52	2.79	3.08	3.40	3.75
22	1.55	1.72	1.92	2.13	2.37	**2.63**	2.93	3.25	3.60	4.00
23	1.58	1.76	1.97	2.21	2.46	2.75	3.07	3.43	3.82	4.26
24	1.61	1.81	2.03	2.28	2.56	2.88	3.23	3.61	4.05	4.53
25	1.64	1.85	2.09	2.36	2.67	3.01	3.39	3.81	4.29	4.83
26	1.67	1.90	2.16	2.45	2.77	3.14	3.56	4.02	4.55	5.14
27	1.71	1.95	2.22	2.53	2.88	3.28	3.73	4.24	4.82	5.48
28	1.74	2.00	2.29	2.62	3.00	3.43	3.92	4.48	5.11	5.83
29	1.78	2.05	2.36	2.71	3.12	3.58	4.12	4.72	5.42	6.21
30	1.81	2.10	2.43	2.81	3.24	3.75	4.32	4.98	5.74	6.61
31	1.85	2.15	2.50	2.91	3.37	3.91	4.54	5.26	6.09	7.04
32	1.88	2.20	2.58	3.01	3.51	4.09	4.76	5.55	6.45	7.50
33	1.92	2.26	2.65	3.11	3.65	4.27	5.00	5.85	6.84	7.99
34	1.96	2.32	2.73	3.22	3.79	4.47	5.25	6.17	7.25	8.51
35	2.00	2.37	2.81	3.33	3.95	4.67	5.52	6.51	7.69	9.06
36	2.04	2.43	2.90	3.45	4.10	4.88	5.79	6.87	8.15	9.65
37	2.08	2.49	2.99	3.57	4.27	5.10	6.08	7.25	8.64	10.28
38	2.12	2.56	3.07	3.70	4.44	5.33	6.39	7.65	9.15	10.95
39	2.16	2.62	3.17	3.83	4.62	5.57	6.70	8.07	9.70	11.66
40	2.21	2.69	3.26	3.96	4.80	5.82	7.04	8.51	10.29	12.42
41	2.25	2.75	3.36	4.10	4.99	6.08	7.39	8.98	10.90	13.22
42	2.30	2.82	3.46	4.24	5.19	6.35	7.76	9.48	11.56	14.08
43	2.34	2.89	3.56	4.39	5.40	6.64	8.15	10.00	12.25	15.00
44	2.39	2.96	3.67	4.54	5.62	6.94	8.56	10.55	12.99	15.97
45	2.44	3.04	3.78	4.70	5.84	7.25	8.99	11.13	13.76	17.01
46	2.49	3.11	3.90	4.87	6.07	7.57	9.43	11.74	14.59	18.12
47	2.54	3.19	4.01	5.04	6.32	7.92	9.91	12.38	15.47	19.29
48	2.59	3.27	4.13	5.21	6.57	8.27	10.40	13.07	16.39	20.55
49	2.64	3.35	4.26	5.40	6.83	8.64	10.92	13.78	17.38	21.88
50	2.69	3.44	4.38	5.58	7.11	9.03	11.47	14.54	18.42	23.31

in box (m), enter your *Current Annual Salary*, which is the same amount you used in item (d), Plan Aid 3a: Example, on page 75. The final step is to multiply your *Current Annual Salary* in box (m) by your *Total Salary Growth Factor* in box (l), to determine your inflation-adjusted *Hypothetical Final Salary* in box (n).

This is an estimate of your projected inflation-adjusted income in the year before you retire, and it gives you a feel for what your lifestyle will actually cost, in inflation-adjusted dollars, as you move into retirement. You will ultimately be able to use this amount to help project your income needs during retirement.

After reviewing the example, fill in Plan Aid 4b: Your Plan now, to determine your own hypothetical preretirement income. In looking up your *Total Salary Growth Factor* in Plan Aid Table 4, be sure to use your number of years until retirement from Plan Aid 1b: Your Plan, on page 13.

Plan Aid 4b: Your Plan
Preretirement Income

Real Salary Growth Rate Assumption .... (i)   %
(From item (f), Plan Aid 3b: Your Plan on page 77)

Inflation Rate Assumption .... (j)   %
(Select 2.0%, 2.5%, 3.0%, 3.5% or 4.0%)

Total Salary Growth Rate Assumption .... (k)   %
                                                                        (i) + (j)

Total Salary Growth Factor .... (l)
    Look Up on Plan Aid Table 4, Using Number of Years Until Retirement and (k) above

Current Annual Salary .... (m) $
(From item (d), Plan Aid 3b: Your Plan on page 77)

Hypothetical Final Salary .... (n) $
    Future Value Dollars in Year 1 of Retirement   *(l) x (m)*

For illustration purposes only. All assumptions and computational results are hypothetical in nature. There are no guarantees that you will achieve the results shown. You should consult with a financial professional.

Computing Your Total
Retirement Income Need

Once you know how much you are likely to be making prior to retirement, you should be able to come up with a reasonable estimate of how much you will need during retirement. This is a big milestone in the planning process—because many people don't have any idea about how much income they'll need to maintain their lifestyle when they stop working.

How Much of Your Preretirement Income
Will You Need During Retirement?

There are lots of rules of thumb concerning how much of your preretirement income you might need during retirement. While I'm generally against rules of thumb, this is one area where they can be helpful. As you get closer to retirement, you will probably need to get more specific about the actual details of your spending plans, but for long-range planning purposes you can generally come up with a pretty good estimate by using what I call the "percent-of-salary" method.

Using the "Percent-of-Salary" Method

The "percent-of-salary" method of forecasting your retirement income needs simply requires you to determine how much of your preretirement income will be necessary to maintain your lifestyle during retirement.

What Do the Experts Say?

Professionals often say that 80 percent of your preretirement income should be sufficient to maintain your lifestyle when you stop working, although estimates have been going up in recent years. Eighty percent is thought to be reasonable in light of the fact that most people will no longer be saving for retirement, won't be paying Social Security taxes on much of their retirement income, and may be getting their mortgages and other debts paid off.

If you're putting 10 percent of your salary into a retirement plan at work, you're already living on 90 percent of your preretirement income anyway. The employee portion of the Social Security tax eats up another 7 or 8 percent, which gets you down pretty close to 80 percent. Considering that you will probably get your mortgage paid off, and that some of your other expenses may also go down after you stop working, you can see why 80 percent is often thought to be a pretty good estimate.

Expenses Could Also Go Up

However, on the flip side, you could also argue that other costs may actually go up. For example, you may want to travel more in the early years or you might want to help a child or grandchild with college expenses later on. In addition, health insurance and drug and medical expenses are likely to go up, and many people will decide to purchase long-term care insurance. For everyone who thinks that living expenses will go down in retirement you can probably find someone else who thinks they will actually go up.

Nevertheless, you need to think through your own situation and ask yourself what percentage of *your* preretirement income may be needed to maintain *your* lifestyle in retirement. A good rule of thumb is probably somewhere between 70 and 100 percent.

How Much Will You Need?

Using the percent-of-salary method you can ultimately project the amount of income you may need to support your lifestyle *in the first year of retirement*. Then, to maintain that lifestyle throughout retirement, you need to be sure that your income goes up with inflation every year. The asset management approach I talk about in my first book, *The Grangaard Strategy®: Invest Right During Retirement*, which is summarized in Chapter 11, takes this important issue into account.

Remember What We Said About Taxes

It's also important to remember that we are always dealing with *pretax* income. The current salary data we've been using, the projected future salary amounts we're working with, the hypothetical income need we establish for the first year of retirement, and all the other sources of income we will talk about in Chapter 10, are always stated in terms of *pretax* income.

Create Your Own Plan

To determine the amount of pretax income you need after you stop working, assuming that you want to maintain a fairly consistent standard of living throughout retirement, use Plan Aid 5a: Example.

The first step is to remember the hypothetical final salary you calculated for item (n) in Plan Aid 4a: Example on page 84, and enter it in box (o), *Hypothetical Final Salary*. Then, you need to decide what percentage of your final salary you want to maintain during retirement, and enter it as your *Percent of Final Salary Wanted in Retirement* in box (p). The final step is to multiply them together to determine your *Hypothetical Retirement Income Need—Year 1*, and enter it in box (q). This is the amount of inflation-adjusted income you should need in the first year of retirement—and of course, you will have to protect it against inflation for the rest of your life.

Plan Aid 5a: Example
Retirement Income Need

Hypothetical Final Salary .... (o) $ **197,250**
    (From item (n), Plan Aid 4a: Example, on page 84)

Percent of Final Salary Wanted in Retirement .... (p) **80** %

Hypothetical Retirement Income Need — Year 1 ..... (q) $ **157,800**
    Future Value Dollars in Year 1 of Retirement   *(o) x (p)*

For illustration purposes only. All assumptions and computational results are hypothetical in nature. There are no guarantees that you will achieve the results shown. You should consult with a financial professional.

After reviewing the example, fill in Plan Aid 5b: Your Plan now, to help determine your own anticipated income for the first year of retirement. As surprising as it may seem, this is the amount of income that you should need from all available sources to provide the lifestyle you are looking for in the first year of retirement—and again, you will need to protect it against inflation for the rest of your life.

Plan Aid 5b: Your Plan
Retirement Income Need

Hypothetical Final Salary .... (o) $
    (From item (n), Plan Aid 4b: Your Plan, on page 86)

Percent of Final Salary Wanted in Retirement .... (p) %

Hypothetical Retirement Income Need — Year 1 ..... (q) $
    Future Value Dollars in Year 1 of Retirement   *(o) x (p)*

For illustration purposes only. All assumptions and computational results are hypothetical in nature. There are no guarantees that you will achieve the results shown. You should consult with a financial professional.

The Income You Will Get from Outside Sources

In the previous chapter you calculated how much income you may need to support your lifestyle when you stop working. But you don't necessarily need to get all of it from your own retirement investments. Some of your income will probably be taken care of by Social Security, some of it may come from pension plans at work, and some might be provided by other sources of income like rents or royalties. Of course it will be different for everyone, but ultimately, these other amounts must be subtracted from the total income you need to help determine how much *you* may have to provide for *yourself* out of your own retirement assets.

Considering Other Sources of Inflation-Adjusted Income

This chapter only deals with other sources of income that you are confident will *go up with inflation* every year in retirement. This is very important at this stage in the process because you always have to compare apples to apples and oranges to oranges.

The retirement income you estimated in the previous chapter is the amount you should need in the first year of retirement—and the expectation is that you will manage your affairs in a way that keeps it growing with inflation each year after that. In other words, we are assuming that the total retirement income you are planning for is completely inflation-adjusted.

The important thing to remember about the other sources of income we discuss in this chapter is that if you want to subtract them from the total amount you need in retirement, they also have to be inflation-adjusted. Otherwise, you'll be fooling yourself into believing that you can provide inflation-adjusted income with annual amounts that are *not* adjusted for inflation. Not only is this illogical, but it can get you into a lot of financial trouble as well.

Apples and Oranges in Retirement

For example, let's say that you need $50,000 per year of inflation-adjusted income over a thirty-year retirement period. Assuming an inflation rate of 3.5 percent, your income would have to grow to about $140,500 over that thirty-year period to maintain $50,000 of purchasing power.

Now, let's say you have a source of retirement income that provides $30,000 per year for thirty years—but it's *not* inflation-adjusted. You just keep getting $30,000 each year. It would be a big mistake to subtract that $30,000 from your total inflation-adjusted income need of $50,000, and then just assume that you only need to come up with the other $20,000 yourself.

Here's why: The whole $50,000 obviously needs to increase with inflation each year. If you decide to break it into two pieces—a $30,000 piece and a $20,000 piece—nothing changes. The $30,000 still needs to increase at 3.5 percent per year to $84,300, and the $20,000 still needs to grow to $56,200, in order to provide the necessary inflation-adjusted total income of $140,500 in the last year of retirement.

However, if the $30,000 is *not* adjusted for inflation each year, you would start falling short of what you need to maintain your lifestyle right from the start. After only ten years, you would need that portion of your income to go up from $30,000 to about $42,300 to maintain your lifestyle. Instead, because it remains fixed at $30,000, you'd be about $12,300 short. After twenty years, you'd be falling behind by about $29,700 per year, and after thirty years you'd be missing out on over

$54,000 per year of annual income. As you can see, things just don't add up this way.

Comparing Apples to Apples

The bottom line is that you can't subtract amounts of income that are *not* inflation-adjusted from amounts that *are*—because they're simply not worth as much. Just think about it—would you rather have $100 per month for the rest of your life, or $100 per month going up at 3 percent per year for the rest of your life? The answer is obvious, because they add up to very different amounts.

You May Have Income That Is *Not* Adjusted for Inflation

This doesn't mean that you won't include income amounts that are *not* adjusted for inflation in your financial plan. In fact, most corporate pension plans are *not* inflation-adjusted, and you certainly will want to consider them if you're lucky enough to have one. It's just that you need to think about them in a slightly different way. You have to build these sources of income into your financial plan—but you don't do it by subtracting them from your overall income needs. We'll look at how to do it in a little while. But until then, we'll just stay focused on sources of income that *are* adjusted for inflation.

Social Security

One source of retirement income that most people need to take into account is Social Security. Whether you expect to receive everything you've been promised, think the system is going to change by the time you're eligible, or don't expect to get anything at all, the fact remains that you should at least consider it.

ESTIMATING YOUR SOCIAL SECURITY BENEFITS

This is not the time or place for an essay on the economics of Social Security or the politics of fixing whatever its problems may be. We only consider it for the purpose of estimating the benefits you can reasonably build into your own financial plan—given the way the system currently works. When all is said and done, you can reduce the benefits you decide to build into your own plan by any amount you want if you have lingering concerns about the likelihood of collecting the full amount. You can even eliminate Social Security altogether—the choice is completely yours.

ANNUAL SOCIAL SECURITY REPORT

Most people receive an annual report about their projected benefits from the Social Security Administration (SSA) each year around the time of their birthday. This is a better estimate of the benefits you can expect to receive than the amounts you will be able to calculate using the tables in this chapter, so feel free to use it if you prefer. The good thing about the SSA report is that it uses your own historical earnings data to project your benefits, and it's updated annually—so it provides the best estimate you can get prior to actually applying for benefits.

SOCIAL SECURITY PROVIDES INFLATION-ADJUSTED INCOME

The Social Security benefits projected in the SSA report, as well as the amounts you calculate for yourself, are reported in terms of "current value" dollars, which means that they provide an estimate of the amount of current purchasing power you are being promised—not the actual future dollar amount.

For example, if you are told you will receive, or if you calculate, a monthly benefit of $1,200, that's not the actual dollar amount you will start receiving when you retire. Instead, it's the amount of today's purchasing power you will start receiving. When you adjust it for thirty years of inflation, that $1,200 of purchasing power is equivalent to getting about $2,916 per month in the first year of retirement, assuming an inflation rate of 3 percent. Under current law, Social Security benefits also increase with inflation after you retire, so they should keep going up each year for the rest of your life.

SOCIAL SECURITY CAN GET RATHER COMPLICATED

We can't possibly get into all the details about Social Security. We're simply trying to come up with a decent estimate of the amount you can build into your financial plan. There are lots of issues that can impact the benefits you actually receive, including when you start collecting, whether you and a spouse collect on one or both work histories, if you work while collecting benefits, and a number of other considerations that are well beyond the scope of this book. The tax issues alone surrounding Social Security can get very complicated, and we can't possibly get into them at this time. Just keep in mind that the amounts we come up with are estimates for planning purposes only.

KEEPING IT SIMPLE

In this book we try to keep everything as simple as possible by assuming that you retire at your full Social Security retirement age and that all of your benefits are taxable. Either or both of these assumptions may ultimately prove to be right or wrong, but you have to start somewhere. As you get closer to retirement you can incorporate more and more accurate assumptions about these matters into your plan.

CREATE YOUR OWN PLAN — SOCIAL SECURITY

Plan Aid 6a: Example shows how to estimate your projected Social Security benefits. You start by entering your *Current Annual Salary* in box (a), which is the same amount used in box (d), Plan Aid 3a: Example on page 75. Then, you simply enter the *Year You Were Born* in box (b).

Next, look up your estimated *Social Security Average Earnings* in Plan Aid Table 6a. Using the column for the year you were born and the row for your current annual salary, locate your *Social Security Average Earnings* in the table, and enter it in box (c). Then, turning to Plan Aid Table 6b, round your *Social Security Average Earnings* up or down to the nearest twenty-five dollars, find that amount in one of the five shaded columns, and select the monthly benefit just to the right of it in the unshaded box. Enter this amount as your *Hypothetical Monthly Benefit (current dollars)* in box (d). To convert this monthly Social Security benefit to an annual amount, simply multiply it by twelve and enter the new amount as the *Hypothetical Annual Benefit (current dollars)* in box (e).

The amount in box (e) is stated in terms of current purchasing power. So the next step is to adjust it for all the inflation you are expecting prior to retirement. To do that, input the *Number of Years Until*

Plan Aid 6a: Example
Social Security Benefits

Current Annual Salary .... (a) $ **75,000**
(From item (d), Plan Aid 3a: Example, on page 75)

Year You Were Born .... (b) **1958**

Social Security Average Earnings .... (c) $ **5,851**
Look Up on Plan Aid Table 6a, Using Items (a) and (b) above

Hypothetical <u>Monthly</u> Benefit (current dollars) .... (d) $ **1,827**
Look Up on Plan Aid Table 6b, Using Item (c) above

Hypothetical <u>Annual</u> Benefit (current dollars) .... (e) $ **21,924**
(d) x 12

Number of Years Until Retirement .... (f) **22**
(From item (c), Plan Aid 1a: Example, on page 13)

Inflation Rate Assumption .... (g) **3.0** %
(From item (j), Plan Aid 4a: Example, on page 84)

Inflation Factor .... (h) **1.92**
Look Up on Plan Aid Table 6c, Using Items (f) and (g) above

Hypothetical <u>Annual</u> Social Security Benefit .... (i) $ **42,094**
Future Value Dollars in Year 1 of Retirement   (e) x (h)

For illustration purposes only. All assumptions and computational results are hypothetical in
nature. There are no guarantees that you will achieve the results shown. You should consult
with a financial professional.

Retirement from box (c), Plan Aid 1a: Example on page 13, into box (f).
Next, input your *Inflation Rate Assumption* from item (j), Plan Aid 4a:
Example on page 84, into box (g). Then, using Plan Aid Table 6c, look
up your *Inflation Factor*, and enter it in box (h). You do this by using the
column related to your inflation rate assumption and the row related to
the number of years until retirement, and finding the place where they
intersect.

The last thing you have to do to follow *Step #4: Estimate Social
Security*, is to multiply your *Hypothetical <u>Annual</u> Benefit* in box (e),
which is still reported in current value dollars, by the *Inflation Factor* in
box (h), to calculate your *Hypothetical <u>Annual</u> Social Security Benefit* in

Plan Aid Table 6a: Social Security Average Earnings

Current Annual Salary	Year You Were Born							
	1940 or earlier	1941 to 1945	1946 to 1950	1951 to 1955	1956 to 1960	1961 to 1965	1966 to 1970	1971 to 1975
$5,000 to $10,000	513	531	549	567	593	611	622	625
$11,000 to $16,000	923	955	987	1,021	1,067	1,100	1,120	1,125
$17,000 to $22,000	1,332	1,380	1,426	1,474	1,542	1,589	1,617	1,625
$23,000 to $28,000	1,743	1,804	1,865	1,928	2,016	2,078	2,115	2,125
$29,000 to $35,000	2,187	2,264	2,341	2,419	2,530	2,607	2,654	2,667
$36,000 to $42,000	2,665	2,759	2,853	2,948	3,084	3,177	3,235	3,250
$43,000 to $49,000	3,132	3,247	3,365	3,478	3,637	3,748	3,815	3,833
$50,000 to $56,000	3,578	3,719	3,859	4,007	4,191	4,318	4,396	4,417
$57,000 to $63,000	3,980	4,156	4,356	4,536	4,744	4,888	4,976	5,000
$64,000 to $70,000	4,396	4,614	4,856	5,065	5,298	5,459	5,557	5,583
$71,000 to $77,000	4,770	5,055	5,322	5,571	5,851	6,029	6,137	6,167
$78,000 to $84,000 & >	5,121	5,473	5,802	6,094	6,405	6,599	6,718	6,750

Source: *National Underwriter Social Security Manual, 2002 Edition.*

Plan Aid Table 6b: Social Security Monthly Benefit

Ave. Earn.	Mon. Ben.	Ave. Earn.	Mon. Ben.	Ave. Earn.	Mon. Ben.	Ave. Earn.	Mon. Ben.	Ave. Earn.	Mon. Ben.
7,075	2,011	5,775	1,816	4,475	1,621	3,175	1,359	1,875	943
7,050	2,007	5,750	1,812	4,450	1,617	3,150	1,351	1,850	935
7,025	2,003	5,725	1,808	4,425	1,613	3,125	1,343	1,825	927
7,000	1,999	5,700	1,804	4,400	1,609	3,100	1,335	1,800	919
6,975	1,996	5,675	1,801	4,375	1,606	3,075	1,327	1,775	911
6,950	1,992	5,650	1,797	4,350	1,602	3,050	1,319	1,750	903
6,925	1,988	5,625	1,793	4,325	1,598	3,025	1,311	1,725	895
6,900	1,984	5,600	1,789	4,300	1,594	3,000	1,303	1,700	887
6,875	1,981	5,575	1,786	4,275	1,591	2,975	1,295	1,675	879
6,850	1,977	5,550	1,782	4,250	1,587	2,950	1,287	1,650	871
6,825	1,973	5,525	1,778	4,225	1,583	2,925	1,279	1,625	863
6,800	1,969	5,500	1,774	4,200	1,579	2,900	1,271	1,600	855
6,775	1,966	5,475	1,771	4,175	1,576	2,875	1,263	1,575	847
6,750	1,962	5,450	1,767	4,150	1,572	2,850	1,255	1,550	839
6,725	1,958	5,425	1,763	4,125	1,568	2,825	1,247	1,525	831
6,700	1,954	5,400	1,759	4,100	1,564	2,800	1,239	1,500	823
6,675	1,951	5,375	1,756	4,075	1,561	2,775	1,231	1,475	815
6,650	1,947	5,350	1,752	4,050	1,557	2,750	1,223	1,450	807
6,625	1,943	5,325	1,748	4,025	1,553	2,725	1,215	1,425	799
6,600	1,939	5,300	1,744	4,000	1,549	2,700	1,207	1,400	791
6,575	1,936	5,275	1,741	3,975	1,546	2,675	1,199	1,375	783
6,550	1,932	5,250	1,737	3,950	1,542	2,650	1,191	1,350	775
6,525	1,928	5,225	1,733	3,925	1,538	2,625	1,183	1,325	767
6,500	1,924	5,200	1,729	3,900	1,534	2,600	1,175	1,300	759
6,475	1,921	5,175	1,726	3,875	1,531	2,575	1,167	1,275	751
6,450	1,917	5,150	1,722	3,850	1,527	2,550	1,159	1,250	743
6,425	1,913	5,125	1,718	3,825	1,523	2,525	1,151	1,225	735
6,400	1,909	5,100	1,714	3,800	1,519	2,500	1,143	1,200	727
6,375	1,906	5,075	1,711	3,775	1,516	2,475	1,135	1,175	719
6,350	1,902	5,050	1,707	3,750	1,512	2,450	1,127	1,150	711
6,325	1,898	5,025	1,703	3,725	1,508	2,425	1,119	1,125	703
6,300	1,894	5,000	1,699	3,700	1,504	2,400	1,111	1,100	695
6,275	1,891	4,975	1,696	3,675	1,501	2,375	1,103	1,075	687
6,250	1,887	4,950	1,692	3,650	1,497	2,350	1,095	1,050	679
6,225	1,883	4,925	1,688	3,625	1,493	2,325	1,087	1,025	671
6,200	1,879	4,900	1,684	3,600	1,489	2,300	1,079	1,000	663
6,175	1,876	4,875	1,681	3,575	1,486	2,275	1,071	975	655
6,150	1,872	4,850	1,677	3,550	1,479	2,250	1,063	950	647
6,125	1,868	4,825	1,673	3,525	1,471	2,225	1,055	925	639
6,100	1,864	4,800	1,669	3,500	1,463	2,200	1,047	900	631
6,075	1,861	4,775	1,666	3,475	1,455	2,175	1,039	875	623
6,050	1,857	4,750	1,662	3,450	1,447	2,150	1,031	850	615
6,025	1,853	4,725	1,658	3,425	1,439	2,125	1,023	825	607
6,000	1,849	4,700	1,654	3,400	1,431	2,100	1,015	800	599
5,975	1,846	4,675	1,651	3,375	1,423	2,075	1,007	775	591
5,950	1,842	4,650	1,647	3,350	1,415	2,050	999	750	583
5,925	1,838	4,625	1,643	3,325	1,407	2,025	991	725	575
5,900	1,834	4,600	1,639	3,300	1,399	2,000	983	700	567
5,875	1,831	4,575	1,636	3,275	1,391	1,975	975	675	559
5,850	1,827	4,550	1,632	3,250	1,383	1,950	967	650	551
5,825	1,823	4,525	1,628	3,225	1,375	1,925	959		
5,800	1,819	4,500	1,624	3,200	1,367	1,900	951		

Source: *National Underwriter Social Security Manual, 2002 Edition.*

Plan Aid Table 6c: Inflation Factors

Years to Retirement	Inflation Rate				
	2.0%	2.5%	3.0%	3.5%	4.0%
1	1.02	1.03	1.03	1.04	1.04
2	1.04	1.05	1.06	1.07	1.08
3	1.06	1.08	1.09	1.11	1.12
4	1.08	1.10	1.13	1.15	1.17
5	1.10	1.13	1.16	1.19	1.22
6	1.13	1.16	1.19	1.23	1.27
7	1.15	1.19	1.23	1.27	1.32
8	1.17	1.22	1.27	1.32	1.37
9	1.20	1.25	1.30	1.36	1.42
10	1.22	1.28	1.34	1.41	1.48
11	1.24	1.31	1.38	1.46	1.54
12	1.27	1.34	1.43	1.51	1.60
13	1.29	1.38	1.47	1.56	1.67
14	1.32	1.41	1.51	1.62	1.73
15	1.35	1.45	1.56	1.68	1.80
16	1.37	1.48	1.60	1.73	1.87
17	1.40	1.52	1.65	1.79	1.95
18	1.43	1.56	1.70	1.86	2.03
19	1.46	1.60	1.75	1.92	2.11
20	1.49	1.64	1.81	1.99	2.19
21	1.52	1.68	1.86	2.06	2.28
22	1.55	1.72	1.92	2.13	2.37
23	1.58	1.76	1.97	2.21	2.46
24	1.61	1.81	2.03	2.28	2.56
25	1.64	1.85	2.09	2.36	2.67
26	1.67	1.90	2.16	2.45	2.77
27	1.71	1.95	2.22	2.53	2.88
28	1.74	2.00	2.29	2.62	3.00
29	1.78	2.05	2.36	2.71	3.12
30	1.81	2.10	2.43	2.81	3.24
31	1.85	2.15	2.50	2.91	3.37
32	1.88	2.20	2.58	3.01	3.51
33	1.92	2.26	2.65	3.11	3.65
34	1.96	2.32	2.73	3.22	3.79
35	2.00	2.37	2.81	3.33	3.95
36	2.04	2.43	2.90	3.45	4.10
37	2.08	2.49	2.99	3.57	4.27
38	2.12	2.56	3.07	3.70	4.44
39	2.16	2.62	3.17	3.83	4.62
40	2.21	2.69	3.26	3.96	4.80
41	2.25	2.75	3.36	4.10	4.99
42	2.30	2.82	3.46	4.24	5.19
43	2.34	2.89	3.56	4.39	5.40
44	2.39	2.96	3.67	4.54	5.62
45	2.44	3.04	3.78	4.70	5.84
46	2.49	3.11	3.90	4.87	6.07
47	2.54	3.19	4.01	5.04	6.32
48	2.59	3.27	4.13	5.21	6.57
49	2.64	3.35	4.26	5.40	6.83
50	2.69	3.44	4.38	5.58	7.11

inflation-adjusted dollars, which should be entered in box (i). This is the actual dollar amount you might plan to receive from Social Security in the first year of retirement, and it should increase with inflation for the rest of your life. If you are concerned about the Social Security system, and think that you may not get all of the benefits you are being promised, you can reduce this amount by any percentage you feel is appropriate. Just make a note of it by the input box so you don't forget what you did.

After reviewing the example, fill in Plan Aid 6b: Your Plan now, to determine your own hypothetical annual Social Security benefit. Make sure to use your own numbers when pulling information from previous worksheets.

ADJUSTING SOCIAL SECURITY IF YOU PLAN TO RETIRE EARLY

Some people may plan to retire before they expect to start collecting Social Security. For example, if you plan to retire at age fifty-seven, and don't expect to start collecting until you're sixty-five, you will go nine years in retirement without receiving any Social Security benefits. In cases like this, you need to make an adjustment to your retirement plan, since it will otherwise assume that you will start collecting benefits the year you retire—which obviously won't be the case.

ADJUSTING FOR DELAYED SOCIAL SECURITY BENEFITS

If you plan to retire before you start collecting Social Security, you have to make an adjustment to your plan—and we'll get to that in a little while. In order to make the correction, you simply have to calculate how many years you plan to be retired before you start getting benefits, and multiply that number of years by the annual Social Security benefit you calculated in box (i). Make a note of the resulting amount at the bottom of Plan Aid 6b: Your Plan. This is an estimate of the benefits that have automatically been built into your plan, but which you won't actually get. You'll be able to compensate for them in a little while.

Traditional Pension Plans

Although traditional pension plans seem to be going the way of the dinosaur, many people still participate in them. If you are lucky enough

**Plan Aid 6b: Your Plan
Social Security Benefits**

Current Annual Salary .... (a) $ _____
  (From item (d), Plan Aid 3b: Your Plan, on page 77)

Year You Were Born .... (b) _____

Social Security Average Earnings .... (c) $ _____
  Look Up on Plan Aid Table 6a, Using Items (a) and (b) above

Hypothetical <u>Monthly</u> Benefit (current dollars) .... (d) $ _____
  Look Up on Plan Aid Table 6b, Using Item (c) above

Hypothetical <u>Annual</u> Benefit (current dollars) .... (e) $ _____
  (d) x 12

Number of Years Until Retirement .... (f) _____
  (From item (c), Plan Aid 1b: Your Plan, on page 13)

Inflation Rate Assumption .... (g) _____ %
  (From item (j), Plan Aid 4b: Your Plan, on page 86)

Inflation Factor .... (h) _____
  Look Up on Plan Aid Table 6c, Using Items (f) and (g) above

Hypothetical <u>Annual</u> Social Security Benefit .... (i) $ _____
  Future Value Dollars in Year 1 of Retirement   (e) x (h)

For illustration purposes only. All assumptions and computational results are hypothetical in nature. There are no guarantees that you will achieve the results shown. You should consult with a financial professional.

to have one, you should consider how it will impact your retirement by following *Step #5: Account for Protected Pensions.*

Traditional pension plans provide benefits in a variety of ways. Some provide a fixed monthly amount of income during retirement, while others pay a lump-sum balance when you stop working—and require you to manage it for the rest of your life. If you have a traditional pension, you need to find out which kind of payout you will get, and then build it into your financial plans accordingly.

CONSIDERING ONLY INFLATION-ADJUSTED, MONTHLY-PAYOUT PLANS

In this chapter we only consider pension plans that provide *monthly* income, and then only those that provide income that is *adjusted for inflation* every year. In other words, we only deal with monthly payout pension plans that have built-in cost of living increases. Later on we will consider lump-sum payout plans and monthly payout plans that are *not* adjusted for inflation—but they need to be accounted for in a different way.

WHICH TYPE OF PENSION PLAN YOU HAVE

If you have a pension plan at work or with a former employer, the first thing you need to do is determine what kind of payout option it provides. If it is a monthly payout plan, you also have to find out if it will be adjusted for inflation. You should be able to get this information, as well as the amount of your projected benefit, from your human resource department.

MOST PENSION PLANS *DO NOT* COME WITH COST OF LIVING INCREASES

Most corporate pension plans *do not* come with inflation-adjustment features—although there are exceptions. Generally, it's more common for government and military pensions to provide annual cost of living increases. If you work for a federal, state or local government agency, or the military, the odds are pretty good that if you have a pension, it will be inflation-adjusted. If you have a private-sector pension plan, it probably won't be. But again, nothing is certain, so you have to check with your human resource department to be sure.

USE THE MOST CURRENT PENSION INFORMATION YOU CAN GET

Keep in mind that the amount of your projected pension benefit may change from year to year, based upon your income and number of years on the job—so be sure to use the most current projections. Generally, though not always, the amount of benefits projected by your human resource department will be the amount you are actually scheduled to get in the first year of retirement. So, unlike Social Security, you shouldn't have to adjust it for inflation. But double check just to be sure.

CREATE YOUR OWN PLAN: INFLATION-ADJUSTED PENSION BENEFITS

Use Plan Aid 7a: Example to see how easy it is to estimate your own pension benefits. Simply enter the *Hypothetical Monthly Benefit* you expect to get in box (j), and then multiply it by twelve to determine your *Hypothetical Annual Benefit*, which should be entered in box (k). That's it. You now have an idea of how much income you might expect to get from your pension plan in the first year of retirement—and of course it's expected to go up with inflation each year after that.

Plan Aid 7a: Example
Inflation-Adjusted Pensions

Hypothetical <u>Monthly</u> Benefit	(j) $ **500**
Hypothetical <u>Annual</u> Benefit	(k) $ **6,000**
Future Value Dollars in Year 1 of Retirement	*(j) x 12*

For illustration purposes only. All assumptions and computational results are hypothetical in nature. There are no guarantees that you will achieve the results shown. You should consult with a financial professional.

After reviewing the example, fill in Plan Aid 7b: Your Plan now, to determine your own hypothetical annual inflation-adjusted pension benefit. And again, make sure to use the most up-to-date pension estimates you can get. If you don't have this kind of pension plan you can leave this part blank.

Plan Aid 7b: Your Plan
Inflation-Adjusted Pensions

Hypothetical <u>Monthly</u> Benefit	(j) $
Hypothetical <u>Annual</u> Benefit	(k) $
Future Value Dollars in Year 1 of Retirement	*(j) x 12*

For illustration purposes only. All assumptions and computational results are hypothetical in nature. There are no guarantees that you will achieve the results shown. You should consult with a financial professional.

Other Inflation-Adjusted Income

Some people expect to have other sources of income in retirement too—and you want to take everything into account. That's why you have to follow *Step #6: Anticipate Other Income.*

An example might be the income you plan to earn on rental property. You might reasonably expect these amounts to be inflation-adjusted during retirement because in most circumstances you have the ability to raise rents to keep up with the cost of living. Other sources of income might include royalty payments or business proceeds that you expect to get from other endeavors. Again, they should only be included if you expect them to increase with inflation.

Like the inflation-adjusted pensions we just discussed, the amounts you include should be the projected monthly income you might expect as of the first year of retirement—so be sure to consider how much you will be getting then, rather than how much you might be getting today.

CREATE YOUR OWN PLAN: OTHER INFLATION-ADJUSTED INCOME

Use Plan Aid 8a: Example to estimate the inflation-adjusted income you plan to receive from other sources during retirement. Simply enter the *Hypothetical Monthly Income* you expect to get in box (l), and then multiply it by twelve to determine your *Hypothetical Annual Income*, which should be entered in box (m). This should give you an idea of how much income you are hoping to get from all other miscellaneous sources in the first year of retirement—and of course, it's expected to go up with inflation each year after that.

Plan Aid 8a: Example
Other Inflation-Adjusted Income

Hypothetical <u>Monthly</u> Income	(l) $ **250**
Hypothetical <u>Annual</u> Income	(m) $ **3,000**
Future Value Dollars in Year 1 of Retirement	*(l) x 12*

For illustration purposes only. All assumptions and computational results are hypothetical in nature. There are no guarantees that you will achieve the results shown. You should consult with a financial professional.

After reviewing the example, fill in Plan Aid 8b: Your Plan now, to determine your own hypothetical annual inflation-adjusted income from other sources. And again, make sure to use the amounts of income you think you will be earning as of the first year of retirement—not what you are getting from these sources today. If you don't have any other miscellaneous sources of retirement income you can leave this part blank.

Plan Aid 8b: Your Plan
Other Inflation-Adjusted Income

Hypothetical <u>Monthly</u> Income .... (l) $

Hypothetical <u>Annual</u> Income .... (m) $

    Future Value Dollars in Year 1 of Retirement   *(l) x 12*

For illustration purposes only. All assumptions and computational results are hypothetical in nature. There are no guarantees that you will achieve the results shown. You should consult with a financial professional.

TOTAL INFLATION-ADJUSTED INCOME FROM ALL SOURCES
It's time now to add up all the inflation-adjusted income you hope to get from these other sources. Then, you should be able to subtract them from your total retirement income need, in order to determine how much you may have to generate from your own retirement assets.

CREATE YOUR OWN PLAN: TOTAL OTHER INFLATION-ADJUSTED INCOME
In the first part of Plan Aid 9a: Example, you simply pull together all of the other sources of inflation-adjusted income we've been talking about. The *Hypothetical <u>Annual</u> Social Security Benefit* in box (a) comes from item (i), Plan Aid 6a: Example on page 96. *The Hypothetical <u>Annual</u> Inflation-Adjusted Pensions* amount in box (b) comes from item (k), Plan Aid 7a: Example on page 103. The *Hypothetical <u>Annual</u> Other Inflation-Adjusted Income* amount in box (c) comes from item (m), Plan Aid 8a: Example on page 104. Simply add them all up and put the total in box (d), *Hypothetical <u>Annual</u> Total Inflation-Adjusted Income.*

    This is the total amount of inflation-adjusted income, from all available sources, that you might plan to get during retirement. It represents

Plan Aid 9a: Example
Total Other Inflation-Adjusted Income

Hypothetical <u>Annual</u> Social Security Benefit .... (a) $ **42,094**
(From item (i), Plan Aid 6a: Example on page 96)

Hypothetical <u>Annual</u> Infl. Adj. Pensions .... (b) $ **6,000**
(From item (k), Plan Aid 7a: Example on page 103)

Hypothetical <u>Annual</u> Other Infl. Adj. Income .... (c) $ **3,000**
(From item (m), Plan Aid 8a: Example on page 104)

Hypothetical <u>Annual</u> Total Infl. Adj. Income .... (d) $ **51,094**
        Future Value Dollars in Year 1 of Retirement   *(a) + (b) + (c)*

Hypothetical Retirement Income Need — Year 1 ...... (e) $ **157,800**
(From item (q), Plan Aid 5a: Example on page 90)

Hypothetical Asset-Funded Retirement Income .... (f) $ **106,706**
        Future Value Dollars in Year 1 of Retirement   *(e) - (d)*

For illustration purposes only. All assumptions and computational results are hypothetical in nature. There are no guarantees that you will achieve the results shown. You should consult with a financial professional.

your income from all sources other than your own retirement assets—except for employer-sponsored pension plan amounts that you will get in a lump-sum or which will come in the form of monthly payments that are *not* adjusted for inflation, both of which we will consider in a little while.

HOW MUCH INCOME WILL HAVE TO COME FROM YOUR OWN RETIREMENT ASSETS? The final step is to subtract the amount of income you think you will be getting from these other sources from the total amount of income you may need for retirement. To do this, simply input your *Hypothetical Retirement Income Need—Year 1* into box (e)—which comes from item (q), Plan Aid 5a: Example on page 90, and then subtract the *Hypothetical Annual Total Inflation-Adjusted Income* in box (d) to determine your *Hypothetical Asset-Funded Retirement Income*, which you should input into box (f). This is the amount of income you may need to provide for yourself, out of your own retirement assets, in the first year of retirement—and of course, it will have to go up each year for inflation, as we have discussed many times.

After reviewing the example, fill in Plan Aid 9b: Your Plan now, to determine your own hypothetical asset-funded retirement income. This is the amount *you* may have to come up with, in addition to all of your other sources of income, to provide the lifestyle you may be looking for in the first year of retirement. You will then have to manage your assets throughout retirement to keep that amount increasing with inflation.

Plan Aid 9b: Your Plan
Total Other Inflation-Adjusted Income

Hypothetical <u>Annual</u> Social Security Benefit .... (a) $ _____
   (From item (i), Plan Aid 6b: Your Plan on page 101)

Hypothetical <u>Annual</u> Infl. Adj. Pensions .... (b) $ _____
   (From item (k), Plan Aid 7b: Your Plan on page 103)

Hypothetical <u>Annual</u> Other Infl. Adj. Income .... (c) $ _____
   (From item (m), Plan Aid 8b: Your Plan on page 105)

Hypothetical <u>Annual</u> Total Infl. Adj. Income .... (d) $ _____
   Future Value Dollars in Year 1 of Retirement   *(a) + (b) + (c)*

Hypothetical Retirement Income Need — Year 1 ...... (e) $ _____
   (From item (q), Plan Aid 5b: Your Plan on page 90)

Hypothetical Asset-Funded Retirement Income .... (f) $ _____
   Future Value Dollars in Year 1 of Retirement   *(e) - (d)*

For illustration purposes only. All assumptions and computational results are hypothetical in nature. There are no guarantees that you will achieve the results shown. You should consult with a financial professional.

SETTING YOUR ASSET ACCUMULATION TARGET

The reason you have to calculate your asset-funded retirement income is because you use it to help figure out how much you may need to accumulate in the rest of your retirement accounts. You can't possibly figure out how much you need to accumulate if you don't know how much income will be required to take care of yourself—and that's what you just determined.

Armed with this information, you should now be in a position to calculate how much you may need to accumulate in your retirement accounts to provide the amount of income *you* are responsible for. This total accumulation target will give you something to shoot for, and it's the foundation of the rest of your saving and investment decisions.

PART THREE

Managing Your Money During Retirement

In this section, we will cover:

Step #7: Plan to Invest Right in Retirement;

Step #8: Set a Good Accumulation Target; and

Step #9: Keep Taxes in Mind.

After completing this part of the book, you should have learned about managing money during retirement, considered the impact of taxes on your retirement plan, and set an overall asset accumulation target.

11

Invest Right During Retirement

You can't figure out how much you may need to accumulate *for* retirement unless you have a general understanding of how to manage it *during* retirement. After all, how can you set a target if you don't know what you're going to do with the money when you get there?

Unfortunately, in retirement, many people fall back on old rules of thumb. They either put all their money into conservative investments, live as frugally as they can, and hope they don't run out too soon, or they use some kind of one-size-fits-all asset allocation strategy to figure out how much they should put in the stock market—usually based upon their age and some fuzzy notion of their "risk tolerance." This isn't good enough anymore.

The Twelve Principles of Twenty-First-Century Retirement Investing

In my first book, *The Grangaard Strategy®: Invest Right During Retirement*, I used the Twelve Principles of Twenty-First-Century Retirement Investing to show older investors what they need to know about managing money during retirement. I use the same twelve principles here to outline what you need to know to do a better job planning *for* retirement.

Replacing Your Paycheck During Retirement

Essentially, at retirement, you need to put yourself back into the same position you were in before you retired. While you're working, you get your income, or liquidity, from your wages. As a result, because you have your income needs taken care of, you can be more comfortable investing some of your retirement savings in the stock market to go after potentially higher rates of return. You know you won't need to sell them anytime soon to get money to live on because you get a paycheck every couple weeks—so you can be a long-term investor on the stock market side of your portfolio.

However, once you retire, you have to get both your growth and your income from the same pot of retirement assets—which is a whole different ball game. Managing a rollover IRA to provide safe, steady, dependable income for longer and longer retirement periods is much more difficult than going to the bank to cash a paycheck—but that's exactly what you have to do. You have to manage your money to get the growth you need in the stock market while at the same time replacing the paychecks you no longer have.

Principle #1 Expect to Outlive the Averages

There has never been a time when so many people have retired so early, lived so long and been so completely on their own. The research is clear. The growing population of older Americans has to make their money last a lot longer. According to *65+ in the United States*, a study by the U.S. Bureau of the Census, the "old-old," those over the age of 85, are the fastest-growing segment of the population, and "recent improvements in the chances of survival at the end of the age spectrum have emerged as the most important factor in the growth of the oldest old."

Don't Plan to Run Out of Money Too Soon

Current life expectancy tables indicate that the average life expectancy of a 65-year-old today is about twenty years. But that's only an average, and averages can be very misleading. They don't relate to you, or to me, or to anyone else. The fact is, very few of us will actually live to an average age of 85. About half of us won't live that long, while the other half will live longer—and some of us a lot longer. The problem is, none of us know which half we're in. And because we don't, we all have to plan to live much longer than average.

Principle #2 Adjust for Changing Income Needs

Living longer is a good thing, but it can be a real financial challenge for retirees and their families, because the longer you live, the greater your exposure will be to inflation. So you need to make your money last a lot longer while at the same time overcoming the drag of inflation—which means that you will need to have more and more income each year in retirement.

Principle #3 Create Dependable Income for the Rest of Your Life

One of the first things you need to do in retirement is figure out where your inflation-adjusted income is going to come from. In essence, you need to replace your paycheck. You need to set yourself up with safe, steady, dependable income before you can make any other investment decisions—and you have to deal with this problem before you can put any of your money into the stock market.

Use Income Ladders to Create Dependable Income for the Rest of Your Life

To provide the income you need during retirement you can use an investment strategy called Income Ladders. They are a very important part of successful retirement investing. Not only can they give you the dependable income you need, but they also play an important role in helping you manage the rest of your portfolio, because they can help reduce much of the risk of owning stocks.

WHAT ARE INCOME LADDERS?

Income Ladders are investment portfolios designed to take care of your income needs in retirement. They are constructed with money you set aside in less risky fixed-income investments like bonds or annuities, which provide dependable income for a specific period of time.

Whether you invest in bonds or take advantage of easy-to-use products like annuities, it's important to understand how Income Ladders work. I use bonds in my example because they provide an easy way to illustrate the concept. If you use bonds in your portfolio you will have to build your own Income Ladders, or work with an advisor to help you do it—and you should be aware that there are transaction costs associated with the purchase of bonds and their principal value and yield will fluctuate with market conditions. If you use annuities, an insurance company will take care of most of it for you—and in some cases may even be able to provide a little extra income as well.

INCOME LADDERS: HOW THEY WORK WITH BONDS

My example assumes that you want to set aside ten years' worth of safe, steady, dependable income. You won't always use ten-year Income Ladders, but they're fairly common, because they give you plenty of time to ride out the ups and downs in the stock market.

The Income Ladder consists of a portfolio of $225,829 worth of individual bonds with a variety of maturity dates. Some mature in one year, some in two years, some in three years, and so on. You purchase bonds with different maturity dates because you want to be able to spend both interest and principal throughout the ten-year period. By combining the value of the bonds maturing at the end of each year with the interest earned on all the bonds that year you should be able to set yourself up with the income you need for the following year.

INCREASING INCOME IN RETIREMENT: COMPENSATING FOR INFLATION

It may seem at the bottom of the Income Ladder example in Illustration 19 that you're trying to provide an increasing standard of living—but you're not. To maintain the same lifestyle, your income has to go up with inflation, so your Income Ladders are built to produce more and more income each year.

BUILDING YOUR LADDER

After establishing your inflation-adjusted income needs you can start building the ladder. Since we are using bonds in the example, you will purchase an assortment of individual fixed-income securities with a variety of annual maturity dates—I call them "bond buckets." A "bucket" is simply a bunch of individual bonds that all mature at the same time. Since you plan to get income on an annual basis, you need to purchase bonds with nine different maturity dates. That way, you can spend some of the principal each year. It's important to review the credit quality of the issuer too, as lower credit ratings may indicate higher risks of default on principal and interest payments.

The total amount of bonds you put into each bucket depends on interest rates and when you plan to use the principal. At a 6 percent rate, the $30,773 worth of bonds in Bucket 9 should earn $1,846 of interest for nine years and would then be used for income in year ten. At a 4.5 percent rate, the $18,322 worth of bonds in Bucket 3 should earn $824 of interest for three years and would then be used for income in year four. The total amount of bonds in all the buckets—$225,829, plus all the interest on all the bonds, should take care of your income needs for the entire ten-year period.

HOLDING FIXED-INCOME INVESTMENTS UNTIL THEY MATURE

An important point to emphasize is that with Income Ladders you almost always hold your fixed-income investments until they mature. In fact, this is one of the essential features of an Income Ladder—you generally don't sell bonds ahead of schedule. The reason you don't is because your Income Ladders are built to rely on the interest *and principal* you are expecting to get back each year. The only way you can predict how much you are going to get is to hold your bonds until they mature—because at maturity, you should get back the face value you are expecting.

Illustration 19: Income Ladder of Bonds

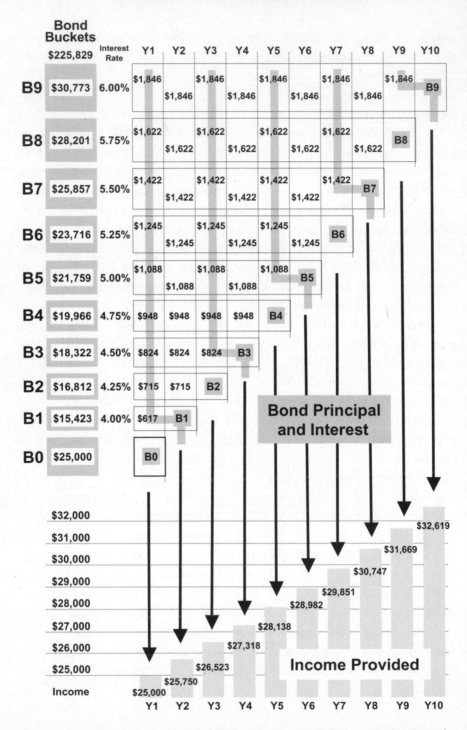

Rates of return are hypothetical. For illustration purposes only. Not representative of an actual investment. Bond principal and yields may fluctuate with market conditions. Higher interest rates and lower credit quality may increase the risk of default.

HOW OFTEN DO YOU WANT TO GET YOUR PAYCHECK DURING RETIREMENT?

You don't have to get your income at the beginning of each year. The example assumes that you want income on an annual basis, but in reality, many people prefer to get their "paychecks" at the beginning of each quarter or even at the beginning of each month.

You can accommodate many different income schedules by adding additional bond buckets to your Income Ladders. For example, if you want to get income on a quarterly basis, you can create thirty-nine quarterly bond buckets instead of nine annual bond buckets. This will provide principal payments at the beginning of each quarter, rather than at the beginning of each year.

Theoretically, you can do the same thing for monthly income too, by adding even more bond buckets. But it starts to get very complicated when you have to build Income Ladders requiring over a hundred different bond maturities. In fact, it isn't practical at all. That's why so many people use single-premium immediate annuities for their Income Ladder investments—because they provide income on a monthly basis and get you out from under the complexity of buying, owning and managing large bond portfolios. In essence, when you buy a single-premium immediate annuity, the insurance company is building and managing an Income Ladder for you and using their financial strength to invest appropriately and back up the payments they promise to make.

SINGLE-PREMIUM IMMEDIATE ANNUITIES (SPIAs)

Single-premium immediate annuities, also know as SPIAs, are contracts that you purchase from an insurance company that provide a specific amount of income every month for a specific period of time. The fact that they are "single-premium" annuities simply means that you only pay the insurance company one time, and one amount, for the stream of income they promise to provide. They are "immediate" annuities in the sense that they start paying out monthly income as soon as you buy them.

Single-premium immediate annuities are a much easier way to get monthly income compared to going out and buying a hundred or more bond maturities to create a monthly Income Ladder. Not only that, but many SPIAs today actually offer inflation protection too—so they can provide income each month going up with inflation every year.

SPIAs are not the only kind of annuity that can help you take care of your Income Ladder needs. More and more of the variable annuities offered today provide retirement income options that can also help you replace your paycheck without having to buy and manage complicated portfolios of individual bonds.

VARIABLE ANNUITIES

Variable annuities can be valuable during retirement despite the fact that they generally have additional fees such as mortality and expense risk charges and administrative fees, which are not typically found with other types of investments. Not only do they provide a way for you to protect your investment growth from current taxation, but many of them actually have built-in features that work very much like Income Ladders.

Variable annuities are contracts sold by insurance companies that allow you to invest your money without having to pay income taxes on your investment gains until you take them out during retirement. Your ability to delay paying taxes on your investment earnings can help you accumulate more money. Another nice thing about variable annuities is that they allow you to invest in a variety of accounts that are invested in the stock market and are often managed by a number of different investment managers—so you can go after higher rates of return in the stock market without being subjected to ongoing taxes.

MOVING YOUR MONEY AROUND TAX-FREE

An important aspect of variable annuities is that through the use of what's called a 1035 exchange, you may be able to move your money from a variable annuity into a SPIA without having to pay income taxes—so you can go after the growth you need in the stock market and be able to move it into future Income Ladders without paying taxes at the time of each conversion. This can help you generate more income during retirement. However, you must also keep in mind that while taxes or IRS penalties will not be incurred, there may still be surrender fees charged by the issuing insurance company for early withdrawal. So be sure to do your homework.

EXCITING NEW DEVELOPMENTS IN THE WORLD OF VARIABLE ANNUITIES

Some of the newer variable annuities even have features that make it possible to create your own Income Ladders right inside the contracts themselves. For example, they allow you to take some of your money out of the stock market accounts and turn it into a stream of income for a fixed period of time—just like a SPIA, except that you do it all inside the same contract. This is called "partial term-certain annuitization," and not all contracts allow it, so you have to shop around. Some variable annuities have guarantees backed by the issuer that protect you from fluctuating stock markets by providing minimum rates of return—even on the money you put into stocks. Some of them actually allow you to lock in and protect prior year stock market gains. The combination of these features and others can make variable annuities an important part of your retirement plans.

Of course, tax-qualified contracts such as IRAs, 401(k) plans, etc. are tax-deferred regardless of whether or not they are used in conjunction with an annuity. Nevertheless, annuities do provide other features and benefits, including guaranteed death benefits backed by the issuer and a variety of other options that can be very helpful, for which mortality and expense risk fees are charged.

THINGS TO REMEMBER ABOUT ANNUITIES

There are a few things you should always think about when considering annuities. An investment in a variable annuity does involve investment risk, including possible loss of principal. Annuities are designed for long-term retirement investing, and withdrawals of taxable amounts are subject to income tax and, if taken prior to age 59½, a 10 percent federal tax penalty may apply. Also, early withdrawals may be subject to withdrawal charges, and annuity contracts, when redeemed, may be worth more or less than the total amount you invested.

You should also know that the purchase of a variable annuity cannot be required for, and cannot be a term of, the provision of any banking service or activity, and an investment in the securities underlying a variable annuity is not guaranteed or endorsed by any bank, is not a deposit or obligation of any bank, and is not federally insured by the FDIC, the Federal Reserve Board or any other federal government agency. Any guarantees offered in an annuity contract are backed only by the claims-paying ability of the issuer. Obviously, you should always discuss the appropriateness of annuities with a financial professional—whether you are using them before or during retirement.

HOW TO KEEP YOUR KETTLE FULL

During retirement you replace your paycheck with Income Ladders—but you will probably continue to get your growth from the stock market. Compounding is the engine that drives that growth. It also gives your assets a chance to grow fast enough to keep your Income Ladders replenished throughout longer and longer retirement periods.

Principle #4 Count on Compounding During Retirement

Longer retirement periods mean longer compounding periods, and longer compounding periods may allow you to earn more interest on interest, or returns on returns, during retirement. In fact, most of the income you generate and spend throughout retirement will probably come from the compounded returns on your retirement assets—not from the assets themselves.

Compounding During Retirement

Illustration 20 shows what can happen in the stock market during retirement if you have your money invested in an IRA earning an 11 percent rate of return. It assumes that you already have money set aside in an Income Ladder and that you're comfortable with the risks associated with going after potentially higher returns. After only five years the compounded growth on the $100,000 investment is over $68,000. After ten years, the growth itself is almost $184,000. After twenty years, your initial investment will grow to over $800,000 and after thirty years it grows to almost $2.3 million—with all but the first $100,000 attributable to compounded earnings.

Of course, you periodically have to use some of the growth from your stock market investments to maintain your income—so you won't be able to leave it all invested for the whole thirty years. During a long retirement period you will probably sell stocks many times to create Income Ladders—sometimes after five years, sometimes after ten years, sometimes after fifteen years, and so on for the rest of your life. However, no matter when you decide to sell, the power of compounding will always be working to your advantage, because as the example shows, the balance in your account at the end of any holding period is likely to consist largely of compounded growth.

COMPOUNDING HIGHER RATES OF RETURN

In the example, you were able to achieve large increases in your account values because you invested in assets like stock market investments that can reasonably be expected to earn long-term average annual rates of return in the range of 11 percent per year. If you get lower rates of return you will have less compounded growth, which will obviously have a negative effect on your overall retirement lifestyle.

PUTTING YOUR MONEY INTO MORE CONSERVATIVE INVESTMENTS

If you decide to invest more conservatively, and put the entire $100,000 in a vehicle like intermediate-term government bonds, and realize a historical 5.3 percent long-run average annual rate of return, based upon data from the *Wall Street Journal* and the CRSP Government Bond File, you will accumulate far less compounded growth over each five-year period compared with stock market investments. For example, using historical returns, after only five years you would have 30 percent more in stocks than bonds. After ten years you would have 69 percent more in stocks. After twenty years you would have almost 200% more in stocks and after thirty years almost 400% more.

If you plan to live on growth during retirement, like many of us will have to, Illustration 21 shows that it may be difficult to make it work using fixed-income rates of return. Fixed-income investments are a fundamental part of your strategy for building Income Ladders, but they are generally not the way to go for the growth part of your portfolio. That's why it's so important to select your investments wisely during retirement.

Illustration 20: The Power of Compounding During Retirement

Comparison of Capital and Growth on
$100,000 at 11% Average Annual Return
for Various Length Investment Periods

5 Years
Total $168,506

Capital $100,000

Earnings $68,506

10 Years
Total $283,942

Capital $100,000

Earnings $183,942

15 Years
Total $478,459

Capital $100,000

Earnings $378,459

20 Years
Total $806,231

Capital $100,000

Earnings $706,231

25 Years
Total $1,358,546

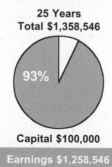

Capital $100,000

Earnings $1,258,546

30 Years
Total $2,289,230

Capital $100,000

Earnings 2,189,230

For illustration purposes only. Not representative of an actual investment. Past performance is not a guarantee of future results. Rates of return are hypothetical, and an investor's results may vary. Investments with the potential to earn higher rates of return are generally offset with a higher degree of risk.

Illustration 21: The Power of Compounding Different Rates of Investment Return During Retirement

Accumulated Value of $100,000 Invested in Stocks vs Bonds over Various Length Investment Periods
(Historical Rates of Return)

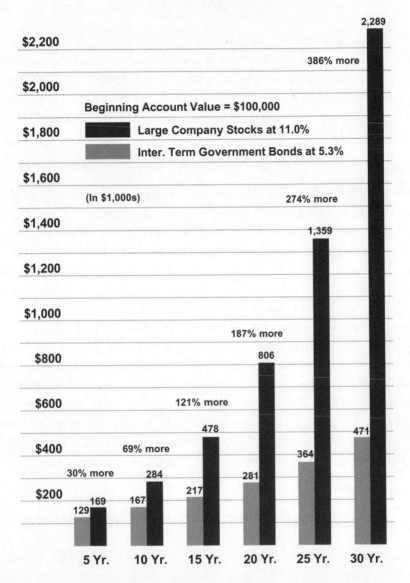

Beginning Account Value = $100,000

- Large Company Stocks at 11.0%
- Inter. Term Government Bonds at 5.3%

(In $1,000s)

Period	Bonds	Stocks	Difference
5 Yr.	129	169	30% more
10 Yr.	167	284	69% more
15 Yr.	217	478	121% more
20 Yr.	281	806	187% more
25 Yr.	364	1,359	274% more
30 Yr.	471	2,289	386% more

Source: Calculated by Paul Grangaard using data presented in *Stocks, Bonds, Bills and Inflation*®
2001 Yearbook, © 2001 Ibbotson Associates, Inc. Based on copyrighted works by Ibbotson and Sinquefield.
All rights reserved. Used with permission. Large Company Stocks are based on the S&P Composite Index which
includes 500 of the largest stocks in the United States from 1957 to the present and 90 of the largest stocks
prior to 1957. Intermediate-Term Government Bonds are based on data from The Wall Street Journal and the
CRSP Government Bond File. For illustration purposes only. Not representative of an actual investment. Past
performance is not a guarantee of future results. An investment cannot be made directly in an index. Prices of
Large Company Stocks will fluctuate and Government Bonds are guaranteed by the U.S. Government and, if
held to maturity, offer a fixed rate of return and fixed principal value. Rates of return are hypothetical, and an
investor's results may vary. Investments with the potential to earn higher rates of return are generally offset with
a higher degree of risk.

Principle #5 Invest in the Right Stuff

Your choice of investments will play a critical role in your financial well-being during retirement. Most people simply don't understand the difference between compounding a historical fixed-income rate of return of 6 percent and a historical stock market rate of return of 11 percent—but the impact on your retirement lifestyle can be quite dramatic.

Being Too Aggressive or Too Conservative Can Cost You Big Bucks

Many people need to invest some of their retirement assets in the stock market to have a shot at earning higher rates of return. It may be the only way they can ever hope to maintain a reasonable inflation-adjusted lifestyle throughout longer and longer retirement periods. But you probably don't want to have so much invested in the stock market that there's nothing left over for safer, income-producing investments.

You probably also don't want to put all of your money into safer, lower-return assets either. This is one of the most common mistakes people make. At retirement, most people are inclined to protect their financial assets—as they should! After all, they have to last a long time. Unfortunately, this sense of urgency to protect your assets may also cause you to invest too conservatively. Protecting your retirement assets is a good idea, but it has to be viewed within the broader context of protecting your overall retirement lifestyle—which may often require you to own some investments with the potential for higher rates of return.

Principle #6 Be a Long-term Investor During Retirement

You can address many of these challenges during retirement by maintaining a long-term investment perspective. Having the time you need to make better investment decisions can have a dramatic effect on your ability to achieve your objectives and can protect you from having to invest too conservatively. In other words, having a long-term investment perspective can help you gain more comfort as a stock market investor during retirement.

Using "Reasonable" Hypothetical Rates of Return

Two sides of the same coin in retirement planning are establishing "reasonable" hypothetical rates of return for your stock market investments and reducing the likelihood that you will earn anything other than those reasonable rates. You want to reduce the possibility of getting rates of return other than what you plan for because you eventually need to create Income Ladders with the growth you hope to earn on your stock market investments. One of the biggest challenges you face as a retirement investor is knowing when and how to harvest that growth.

Since you will be basing many of your current and future spending decisions on the long-term rates of return you might plan to earn in the stock market, getting less than the reasonable hypothetical rates you are anticipating may cause your plans to go seriously awry. Knowing when to sell stocks to lock in your investment gains is one of the best ways to increase the odds that you will get what you are expecting, and also one of the most important elements of a well-managed retirement portfolio.

Selling Stock Market Investments

During retirement most people sell more stock market investments—or equities—than they buy. During the accumulation phase of life, while you're working and saving for retirement, you generally buy more equities than you sell, and then stay invested to go after the higher rates of return they have historically provided. The higher rates of return in the stock market are what make it possible for many of us to accumulate enough money to retire in the first place. However, once we retire, most of us have to start selling those stocks to create the Income Ladders we may need to replace our paychecks.

Picking a Time to Sell Stocks During Retirement

Since you are probably going to be an overall seller of equities during retirement, you want to be very careful about when you sell and at what prices. You obviously want to sell when markets are up. You certainly don't want to get yourself into a position in which you are forced to sell equities in down markets simply because you are out of cash and need some more money to pay the bills. One of the most important things to understand about retirement investing is that you always want to be in a position to choose a good time to sell stocks, and never in a position in which you could be forced to sell at the wrong time. This is one of the best ways to protect yourself against the possibility of getting rates of return other than what you are reasonably expecting and building into your plan—because it's only when you sell stocks that you lock in your investment gains and losses.

Stock Market Holding Periods in Retirement

The big question in retirement is how to stay invested in the stock market for the growth you may need while reducing the possibility of getting rates of return other than what you're expecting—especially when you know that the stock market will be bouncing around all over the place from year to year.

One of the best answers is stock market holding periods. They are an important part of reducing the likelihood of getting anything other than the reasonable rates of return you are building into your plan. You have already seen how important holding periods are in reducing investment risks before retirement. They are even more important in managing your assets during retirement.

WHY MOST PEOPLE LIKE LONGER HOLDING PERIODS DURING RETIREMENT
The longer you can stay invested in the stock market, or in other words, the longer your stock market holding periods, the more likely you are to actually get the long-run historical rates of return that you are reasonably planning for. As a result, most people want to create the longest pos-

sible holding periods during retirement to get as much comfort as they can that they will be able to earn the rates of return they are expecting.

YOU GET LESS INCOME WITH LONGER HOLDING PERIODS

However, longer holding periods generally lead to less income during retirement. It works this way because longer holding periods force you to wait longer to sell stocks, and, as a result, you have to keep more money out of the stock market to begin with, because it has to last longer. In other words, you have to create larger Income Ladders to take care of your retirement paycheck for longer holding periods. With more money out of the stock market, you will probably get less overall growth. With less overall growth, you will most likely end up with less income. So while it's true that you want the longest possible holding periods during retirement, you also have to balance your need for comfort and predictability in the stock market with the equally important need for reasonable amounts of income.

REDUCING VARIABILITY WITH LONGER HOLDING PERIODS

Illustration 22 shows once again how longer holding periods tend to reduce the odds of getting rates of return other than what you are expecting. As holding periods increase, you achieve fairly dramatic reductions in the variability of historical returns around the long-run average. The reduction in variability is quite significant as you move from one-year to five-year holding periods and from five-year to ten-year holding periods. But even though you continue to reduce variability as you move beyond ten years, it doesn't really come down very much more until you get out beyond twenty years. This is due to the fact that you can only reduce variability around the long-run average up to a point. You can never get rid of market fluctuations altogether. But you are able to squeeze a lot of the variation and unpredictability out of the stock market by the time you get out to about ten-year holding periods.

In fact, you actually accomplish about 61 percent of the total historical reduction in variability just by going from one-year to five-year holding periods. By the time you get out to ten-year holding periods you have accounted for about 83 percent of the total reduction in variability that

Illustration 22: Large Company Stock Returns
Various Holding Periods (1926 through 2000)

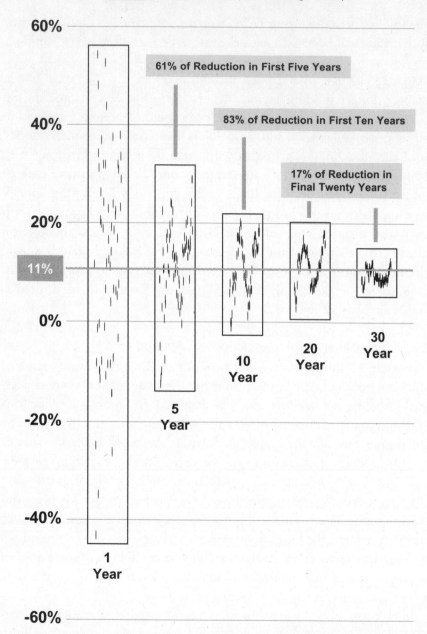

61% of Reduction in First Five Years

83% of Reduction in First Ten Years

17% of Reduction in Final Twenty Years

can be achieved over thirty-year investment periods. It takes twenty more years to pick up the final 17 percent. That's why you can eliminate so much of the variability in historical returns, and increase the predictive accuracy of your planning assumptions, by establishing and using retirement holding periods somewhere in the range of ten years—because you get most of the benefit by then anyway.

USING TEN-YEAR HOLDING PERIODS AS A PLANNING BENCHMARK

Because of their significance for planning during retirement, I like to focus on ten-year holding periods—not because you should always use them, but because they provide a good benchmark. Consequently, it's instructive to consider the average annual rates of return for all sixty-six ten-year holding periods between 1926 and 2000 to see what they can tell us about managing stock market investments during retirement.

Even though there is still some variability in ten-year average annual rates of return, most ten-year holding periods tend to fall fairly close to or in excess of the 11 percent long-run average.

For example, the upper half of Illustration 23 shows that only 4.6 percent of all sixty-six historical ten-year holding periods had negative ten-year average annual returns. So historically speaking, the chance of losing money in the stock market over ten-year holding periods is pretty small—although of course it is always a possibility.

Slightly over 9 percent of all historical ten-year holding periods delivered average annual rates of return between zero and 5 percent. Almost 32 percent achieved average annual rates between 5 and 10 percent. Over 22 percent delivered rates of return between 10 and 15 percent, and an incredible 31.8 percent, or almost a third of them, actually delivered average annual rates of return of 15 percent or more!

In fact, to get a better perspective on the degree to which rates of return tend to be skewed toward the higher end of the range, the lower half of Illustration 23 summarizes the same data on a cumulative basis. It shows that 31.8 percent of the time, large company stocks delivered average annual rates of return greater than 15 percent. It also shows that 54.5 percent of the time you would have earned 10 percent or more, and that over 86 percent of the time you would have earned at least 5 percent average annual rates of return!

Illustration 23: Average Annual Large Company Stock Returns
All 66 Ten-Year Holding Periods (1926 through 2000)

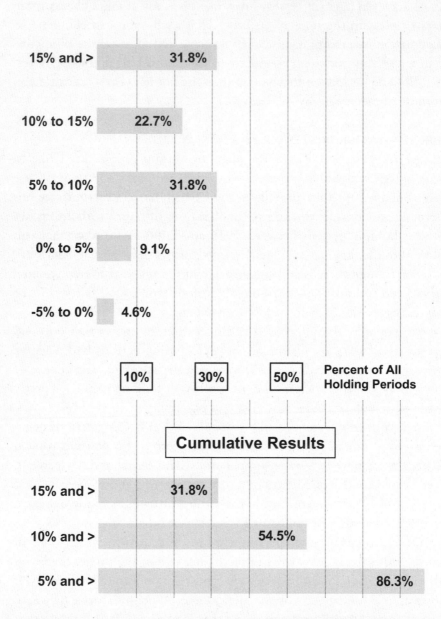

	Percent of All Holding Periods
15% and >	31.8%
10% to 15%	22.7%
5% to 10%	31.8%
0% to 5%	9.1%
-5% to 0%	4.6%

10%   30%   50%   Percent of All Holding Periods

Cumulative Results

15% and >	31.8%
10% and >	54.5%
5% and >	86.3%

These are important results—because 5 percent is very close to the seventy-five-year long-run average annual rate of return of 5.3 percent for fixed-income investments like intermediate-term government bonds. So in most instances, over ten-year holding periods, large company stocks delivered rates of return very close to or better than their long-run historical average of 11 percent, while almost always providing returns at least as good as or better than the seventy-five-year average for alternative fixed-income type investments.

SELLING STOCKS DURING RETIREMENT

Since you are probably going to be an overall seller of stock market investments during retirement, you have to be very careful about deciding when to sell, because you don't want to undo what the magic of compounding over longer holding periods might already have accomplished. Being forced to sell stocks at the wrong time is one of the biggest problems you face in retirement.

Principle #7 Know When to Sell

Throughout retirement you will need to determine when to sell stock market investments to get the money you need to live on. That's why knowing when to sell is so important. Even though you may create ten-year holding periods for your stock market investments, you won't necessarily hold on to them for the full ten years. In fact, in most instances, you will sell them before the end of a typical ten-year period. You do this because as a retirement investor you never want to get too close to the point at which you will be forced to sell stocks, because you never know what will be happening in the market at that time.

The problem for retirement investors is establishing criteria to use in deciding when to sell. We'll look at two strategies. One of them has to do with meeting your rate of return objectives and the other has to do with achieving your account value objectives.

Hitting Your Rate of Return Objectives

Ten-year holding periods can reduce the possibility of getting rates of return other than what you expect, and they often allow you to do that without having to stay invested for the full ten years—it's just that you can if you want to. In fact, ten-year holding periods just set the outside limit on how long you can survive financially without selling stocks, but they do not tell you when to sell—unless of course you wait until the very end of the holding period to do it.

Hitting Your Account Values

You can also ask yourself what you expect your stocks to be worth at the end of the ten-year period and then just plan to sell whenever you get to that amount. In other words, rather than evaluating whether you are achieving your expected rates of return along the way, you consider instead whether or not you are hitting your anticipated ending values.

What should you do, for example, if you have as much value in your stocks after five years as you were expecting to have after ten? You would be smart to consider selling—wouldn't you? Of course you would. After all, you would have gotten to your expected amount five years ahead of schedule!

Pulling the Options Together: A Real Ten-Year Period

Illustration 24 consists of two closely related graphs of an actual ten-year period from 1932 to 1941. It shows how these two strategies can help you decide when to sell stocks. The upper graph relates to the annual rates of return over this period of time. The lightly shaded bars show the expected annual rates of return—which in this example are a slightly conservative 10 percent. The darker bars represent the actual rates of return earned in each of the ten years. As you would expect, they bounced around all over the place between some very good years and some very bad years. This is why you would have used a ten-year holding period in the first place—to give yourself the time you needed to ride out the ups and downs in the market while waiting to achieve an expected long-run average annual rate of about 10 percent.

The black line shows the actual year-to-date average annual rates of return at the end of each year. By the end of the second year, the 54 percent actual return in 1933 averaged with the loss of 8.2 percent in 1932 resulted in a two-year average annual rate of return of 18.9 percent. So losing 8.2 percent in the first year followed by a gain of 54 percent in the second year is the same as earning 18.9 percent in each of the two years. As you can see, the year-to-date actual average annual rates of return fluctuate from year to year as the market delivers its random pattern of ups and downs.

The illustration shows that you would have been at or above the expected 10 percent average annual rate of return in every year through 1939. In many years you would have been far ahead of expectations. By 1936 you would have earned a cumulative 22.5 percent five-year average annual rate of return, which was far better than the 10 percent you were expecting. Obviously, this would have been a great time to consider selling some of your stocks, since you were way ahead of where you thought you would be. In fact, you would have had many opportunities to sell stocks prior to the end of the ten-year period.

Ultimately, however, because of a couple bad years in 1940 and 1941, the nine- and ten-year average annual rates of return dropped well below your 10 percent expectations. This is why you never want to wait too long to sell stocks—because you never know for sure what might happen next.

Portfolio Values

The lower graph in Illustration 24 relates to the account values over the same ten-year period. The lightly shaded bars show what your account values would have been if you had invested $1,000 at the beginning of 1932 and earned the 10 percent average annual rate of return you were expecting over the entire ten-year period. By 1941 you would have expected your account to have grown to about $2,595. Of course, you know it never really happens this way, but it does illustrate what you would have been expecting from an overall planning perspective.

Illustration 24: Deciding When to Sell
Historical Example of Large Company Stocks
for the Period from 1932 to 1941

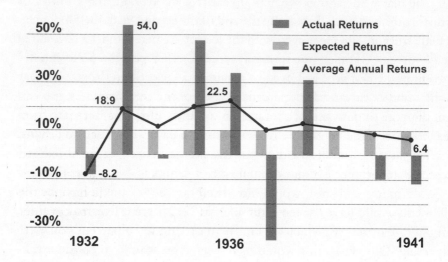

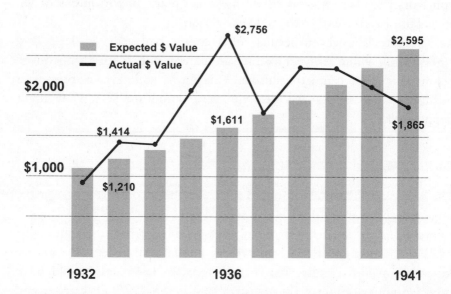

The black line in the lower graph shows the actual value of your investments at the end of each year as they rise and fall with the actual rates of return. By the end of the second year, the actual value of your investments was $1,414 compared to an expected value of $1,210. The actual two-year average annual rate of return of 18.9 percent was obviously much better than the average 10 percent rate that you were expecting—and your account value shows it.

By 1936, after having achieved a five-year average annual rate of return of 22.5 percent, your account value would have actually been $2,756, compared to the $1,611 that you would have been expecting after five years. Not only would you have had considerably more value in your account than you planned for, but you would have actually had quite a bit more than the $2,595 that you thought you would have by the end of the entire ten-year period! Would this be a good time to consider selling stocks? Of course it would. Any time you achieve the account values you expect from an entire holding period before the end of that period you need to consider selling—because you never know what will happen next.

In fact, because of the bad years in 1940 and 1941 your account values headed south fast, and you would have ended up with a final value of only $1,865—considerably less than the $2,595 that you were expecting. The problem is that you would almost certainly have been counting on that final value to provide the income you needed to support your lifestyle in future years.

Principle #8 Don't Let "Dollar Price Erosion" Catch You Off-Guard

By providing the time you need to make better decisions about when to sell, holding periods can also protect you against dollar cost averaging out of the stock market, or what I call "dollar price erosion." Dollar price erosion takes place when you sell more shares of stock when the market is down, and fewer shares when the market is up, to provide a consistent amount of income in retirement.

Investing Too Aggressively

It's important to understand dollar price erosion because some people are tempted to invest more aggressively then they should during retirement. By investing too aggressively, I mean owning too much stock. The reason this can be such a big problem is that if you put too much money into the stock market you won't have enough left to create the Income Ladders you need. If you can't create the Income Ladders you need you won't be able to establish the holding periods you need. If you don't have the holding periods you need you won't be able to choose appropriate times to sell stock market investments. If you are forced to sell stocks at the wrong time, you may not get the rates of return you are planning for. If you don't get the rates of return you are planning for, you probably won't have enough money to create future Income Ladders—and if you can't create future Income Ladders, you may not be able to maintain the lifestyle you need and want.

An Example of Dollar Price Erosion

Illustration 25 is made up of two separate but closely related examples. The first is shown in columns (3) through (6) and the second in columns (7) through (10). Together, they illustrate why selling stock market investments too frequently can be such a risky proposition. In both cases you start with $10,000 in the stock market, consisting of 1,000 shares of a large company stock mutual fund valued at $10 per share, and need to generate $739 of inflation-adjusted annual income for a thirty-year retirement period. Keep in mind that mutual funds are investments that fluctuate with market conditions, and do involve risk—because when they're redeemed, your shares may be worth more or less than original cost. Also, mutual funds are available by prospectus only, and you should always contact a financial professional or the mutual fund company for a copy of the prospectus. You should read it carefully before investing or sending money.

Illustration 25: Dollar - Price - Erosion

(1)	(2)	(3)	(4)	(5)	(6)	(7)	(8)	(9)	(10)
Year	Income Need	Rate of Return	Share Value	Shares Sold	Portfolio Value	Rate of Return	Share Value	Shares Sold	Portfolio Value
0			$10.00	(1,000)	$10,000		$10.00	(1,000)	$10,000
1	$739	10%	$11.00	73.90	$10,187	10%	$11.00	73.90	$10,187
2	$761	10%	$12.10	69.20	$10,369	10%	$12.10	69.20	$10,369
3	$784	10%	$13.31	64.79	$10,543	-10%	$10.89	64.79	$8,626
4	$808	10%	$14.64	60.67	$10,709	10%	$11.98	74.15	$8,600
5	$832	10%	$16.11	56.81	$10,865	10%	$13.18	69.43	$8,546
6	$857	10%	$17.72	53.19	$11,009	-10%	$11.86	65.02	$6,920
7	$882	10%	$19.49	49.81	$11,139	10%	$13.05	74.41	$6,641
8	$909	10%	$21.44	46.64	$11,254	10%	$14.35	69.67	$6,306
9	$936	10%	$23.58	43.67	$11,349	-10%	$12.91	65.24	$4,833
10	$964	10%	$25.94	40.89	$11,423	10%	$14.21	74.66	$4,255
11	$993	10%	$28.53	38.29	$11,473	10%	$15.63	69.91	$3,588
12	$1,023	10%	$31.38	35.85	$11,495	20%	$18.75	65.46	$3,078
13	$1,054	10%	$34.52	33.57	$11,486	10%	$20.63	56.19	$2,227
14	$1,085	10%	$37.97	31.44	$11,441	10%	$22.69	52.61	$1,256
15	$1,118	10%	$41.77	29.44	$11,355	20%	$27.23	49.26	$166
16	$1,151	10%	$45.95	27.56	$11,224	10%	$29.95	42.28	-$1,084
17	$1,186	10%	$50.54	25.81	$11,042	10%	$32.95	---	---
18	$1,221	10%	$55.60	24.17	$10,803	20%	$39.54	---	---
19	$1,258	10%	$61.16	22.63	$10,499	10%	$43.49	---	---
20	$1,296	10%	$67.27	21.19	$10,124	10%	$47.84	---	---
21	$1,335	10%	$74.00	19.84	$9,668	20%	$57.41	---	---
22	$1,375	10%	$81.40	18.58	$9,122	10%	$63.15	---	---
23	$1,416	10%	$89.54	17.39	$8,477	10%	$69.46	---	---
24	$1,458	10%	$98.50	16.29	$7,720	20%	$83.35	---	---
25	$1,502	10%	$108.35	15.25	$6,840	10%	$91.69	---	---
26	$1,547	10%	$119.18	14.28	$5,822	10%	$100.86	---	---
27	$1,594	10%	$131.10	13.37	$4,651	20%	$121.03	---	---
28	$1,642	10%	$144.21	12.52	$3,310	10%	$133.13	---	---
29	$1,691	10%	$158.63	11.72	$1,782	10%	$146.44	---	---
30	$1,742	10%	$174.49	10.98	$44	20%	$175.73	---	---
Totals		10%		1,000		10%		1,000	

Inflation-Adjusted Income

Since you want to inflation-protect your lifestyle you will notice in column (2) that you need more and more income each year. Starting at $739, the amount you need goes up by 3 percent inflation per year—to $761 in year two, to $784 in year three, and so on all the way up to $1,742 in year thirty.

Selling Shares That Are Growing at an Average Annual Rate of Return

In the first example you plan to earn a 10 percent rate of return each year. You know from previous discussions that it's probably reasonable to expect a 10 percent average annual rate of return over a thirty-year investment period, but you would certainly never expect to get 10 percent each and every year. You know that you will do better in some years and worse in others, and that only when you consider the entire period as a whole are you likely to average out to something close to the expected average of 10 percent.

However, to illustrate the point we are trying to make, we assume in this first example that you actually get 10 percent each and every year. As a result, the value of your shares in column (4) increases from $10.00 at the beginning of year one to $11.00 at the end of year one, to $12.10 at the end of year two, to $13.31 at the end of year three, and so on all the way up to $174.49 at the end of year thirty. Keep in mind that this illustration has been simplified and is not representative of an actual investment. Mutual funds include fees and expenses which have not been included here in order to simplify the example. If fees and expenses had been included, the results would be lower.

Selling Fewer and Fewer Shares Each Year

What happens next? Even though your need for income increases by 3 percent per year, the value of your stock market investments increases even faster—at 10 percent per year. As a result, you can maintain $739 per year of inflation-adjusted income while selling fewer and fewer shares each year. As shown in columns (4) and (5), as the value of your shares increases over time, you are able to sell fewer and fewer of them each year to get the money you need to live on.

By the end of the thirty-year period you will have sold all of your shares. So in the example, if you start with 1,000 shares valued at $10 each, and if those shares increase in value at 10 percent per year, for thirty years, with no fluctuations, your $10,000 should be able to provide $739 per year of inflation-adjusted purchasing power for thirty years. You will have achieved your objective. This is the way many software programs and financial planners calculate how you will spend your money during retirement. But it isn't that simple.

Selling Shares That Are Fluctuating in Value

To understand why dollar price erosion can be so detrimental, let's turn now to the second example in columns (7) through (10). The only difference in assumptions is that we get a little more realistic about the rates of return we expect to earn each year. You know that over thirty years the value, or price, of your stock market investments will jump around all over the place—and you also know that there is no way to predict the actual pattern of future returns. But to make things a little more realistic we'll change the rates of return in every third year, so that you lose 10 percent rather than earning 10 percent in years three, six, and nine, and earn 20 percent rather than 10 percent in every third year beyond that.

The values shown are simplified for the purposes of illustration, and the actual performance of the market would probably be quite different. But in the illustration, over the entire thirty-year period, you will still earn the same 10 percent average annual rate of return—it's just that you start out a little more slowly and then catch up in later years. You start with the same share price of $10.00 and end up with a price of $175.73. This is almost exactly the same as in the first example in which your shares started at $10.00 and grew to $174.49 by earning 10 percent each and every year. In both cases you achieve an average annual rate of return of almost exactly 10 percent.

Selling More Shares to Get the Same Amount of Income Each Year

In the second example, however, you end up selling more shares to get the same amount of income. Your shares are worth less because of the losses experienced in the early years, so you have to sell more of them to get the same amount of income. For example, at the beginning of year four you have to sell 74 shares at the previous year's ending price of $10.89 each, compared to the first example in which you only had to sell 61 shares at $13.31. Then, in year five, you have to sell 69 shares compared to only 57 in the first example—and so on all the way down to year thirty. In fact, in year twelve, you are actually forced to sell almost twice as many shares in the second example as in the first—65 shares instead of 36, to get the same $1,023 of income.

Running Out of Shares

Ultimately, because you are forced to sell so many more shares each year, by the time you get to year sixteen you actually run out. In fact, you will have sold almost all 1,000 shares by the end of year fifteen, and have only a fraction of the number you need to support yourself in year sixteen. And of course you won't have any shares left at all to take care of your income needs for the last fourteen years of your life!

And remember, this happens even though you ultimately would have earned a 10 percent average annual rate of return over the entire thirty-year period. But because you have three bad years in the first decade of retirement, you have to sell more shares at lower prices throughout the first sixteen years to get the income you need, and you end up selling far more shares each year than you can really afford to sell. By doing that, you don't even have a chance to make it up with the higher 20 percent rates of return you would have earned in later years because you don't have any shares left to earn those higher returns.

The problem is, if you sell shares out of a fluctuating account, and if you start out with a few bad years, you may end up selling so many shares to maintain your income in the early years that you run out before you have a chance to catch up later.

Diversification Is Important During Retirement Too

You need to make good decisions about when to sell stocks, but you also need to make good decisions about which stocks to sell. The next principle of twenty-first-century retirement investing addresses the importance of maintaining a well-diversified stock portfolio during retirement, which may increase the odds that you will have something in a good position to sell whenever you need to do so.

Principle #9 Diversify

The goal of stock market diversification during retirement is a little different than before retirement, because you have to stay focused on selling stocks. Essentially, you need to allocate your money to enough different stock market investments to increase the chances that there will always be something in a good position to sell whenever you need to get more income. Having a diversified portfolio of stock market investments with reasonable length holding periods can help you do that. Not only will you have more time to decide when to sell, but you will also have more options when it comes to deciding what to sell—and that's a powerful combination.

Principle #10 Keep It Tax Deferred

Reducing income taxes is an important part of any investment strategy, and it's particularly important in retirement. Since you will probably be selling stock market investments to get income during retirement, you want to be very careful about how you structure your portfolio to reduce the taxes you have to pay each time you sell stocks. There are many ways to protect yourself against what I call the "liquidity tax" and many types of investment products that can help.

Selling Stocks and Creating Income Ladders

Creating and spending Income Ladders over reasonably long holding periods should give your stock market investments a chance to grow at the higher rates of return you may need to create future Income Ladders and future holding periods. This process will probably repeat itself many times throughout a typical thirty-year retirement period, which means that in most cases you will be making a large number of stock sales during retirement. The issue you need to address from a tax perspective is the exposure you may have to paying income and/or capital gains taxes, or what I call "liquidity taxes," every time you sell stocks to purchase Income Ladder investments.

"Liquidity Taxes"

I call them "liquidity taxes" because you usually have to pay them when you sell stocks to get "more liquid" in your retirement portfolio—or in other words, when you sell stocks to get more income to live on. As you attempt to replace the income you had before you retired, you periodically move money out of the stock market and into Income Ladder investments that are structured to provide the income you want, when you want it. The good thing about using Income Ladders is that they make it possible for you to do this well in advance of when you actually need the money.

However, if you have to pay liquidity taxes every time you sell stock market investments to create Income Ladders, you might not be able to achieve the level of income you need, because you may not be able to afford to pay all of these taxes up front. You don't want to be forced to pay income and capital gains taxes too soon just because you want to move some money into "more liquid" investments. You almost always have to pay taxes when you take money out of your Income Ladders, but that's a very different matter than having to pay them all up front just because you want to convert some stocks into Income Ladders in anticipation of future income needs.

Investing in Tax-Deferred Accounts

If you already have your money in tax-deferred accounts like IRAs, retirement plans, and variable annuities, you don't have to worry about this liquidity tax issue. In each of these accounts you don't have to pay income taxes until you actually take the money out of your Income Ladders. In other words, you can buy and sell investments without paying taxes as long as you don't take the money out of the account. If you just move it around, like you do when you sell stock market investments to create Income Ladders, you don't have to pay any taxes at the time of the transaction because you only pay taxes when you take the money out and spend it. This can make a big difference in the amount of income you will be able to generate over longer retirement periods.

Investing in Taxable Accounts

However, if you have some of your money in taxable accounts, you will probably have to pay annual income taxes on some of the earnings, while also paying taxes on the rest of the earnings at the time you sell investments to create Income Ladders. In taxable accounts, if you haven't paid income taxes on all of your earnings by the time you sell stocks to purchase Income Ladder investments, you will most likely have to pay the rest of the taxes at that time. In other words, you incur a liquidity tax. You are forced to pay taxes simply because you want to restructure your portfolio to include more fixed-income investments.

As a result, you often end up paying taxes much sooner than you would if you were in a tax-deferred account, because in tax-deferred accounts you don't have to pay annual income taxes or liquidity taxes. In tax-deferred accounts you only pay taxes when you take money out of your Income Ladders. In essence, you are able to defer the payment of income taxes on all of your investment gains, allowing you to keep all that extra money invested in the stock market where it has a chance to grow and compound at potentially higher rates of return.

More Income from Tax-Deferred Accounts

In many cases you are able to generate more income from the same amount of assets if they are invested in tax-deferred accounts like IRAs, retirement plans, and annuities than if you leave them in taxable accounts. That's why as a retiree you need to talk with financial professionals about the merits of getting your taxable investments into tax-deferred vehicles.

Taxable Accounts in Retirement

Any investments you already have in retirement plans at work, in regular or Roth IRAs, or in annuities, are already in tax-deferred accounts. So you generally don't need to do anything special with them from a tax perspective.

However, most people tend to get to retirement with a lot of taxable investments too. They save and invest in taxable accounts over the years, perhaps sell a home or other investments, or maybe even sell a business. Many people also receive gifts and inheritances. So for lots of reasons you may get to retirement with substantial amounts of money in taxable investments. You need to take a very hard look at these assets to determine whether or not you should move them into tax-deferred accounts.

You may wonder about how to get potentially larger amounts of money into tax-deferred vehicles. Most people know that there are significant limitations on how much you can put into IRAs each year, and since you will be retired you won't be able to use your retirement plans at work either. This only leaves a couple options. You can use some of the annuity products we've talked about—including single-premium immediate annuities, fixed annuities and variable annuities, or you can use certain kinds of trusts. Most of them have few limitations on how much can be invested at any given time, so it's usually fairly easy to move money into them whenever you want to.

Rethinking Annuities

In fact, many people need to change the way they think about some of these financial products—if they ever thought about them in the first place. A lot of people have grown up with the idea that annuities are only good for accumulating assets *for* retirement. This is generally not the case. It's certainly true that they are one of the best and most useful accumulation tools you have as a preretirement investor. But you should also recognize the tremendous value of the tax-deferral characteristics of annuities *during* retirement too, because in the twenty-first century you will probably need tax deferral in retirement as much as you do before retirement.

Different Ways of Being Taxed in Retirement

Illustration 26 can give you a better feel for the consequences of paying income taxes too soon in retirement. It shows three different methods of taxing the growth in a retirement portfolio. In each case you start with $1,000, assume that it grows at 10 percent per year for thirty years, and that you pay a combined state and federal income tax rate of 30 percent. However, in each example, you pay the tax differently.

Keep in mind that these are very simple examples and don't take into account many of the complexities concerning the way investment earnings are actually taxed. They are only intended to show in a very general way the consequences of paying income taxes at different times during retirement.

TAX EXAMPLE ONE—GROWTH TAXED ANNUALLY
If you assume that you invest in a taxable account and pay taxes on all of your investment earnings each year, a $1,000 investment will grow to about $7,612 over thirty years. You earn 10 percent each year on the cumulative balance and pay 30 percent of those earnings in taxes every year. So in year one your $1,000 investment earns $100, you pay $30 in taxes, and you end the year with $1,070 in your account.

By the time you get to year ten, you start with $1,838 in your account, earn $181, pay $52 in taxes, and end the year with $1,967. The process continues the same way until by the end of the thirty-year investment period you have $7,612 in the account.

Illustration 26: Liquidity Tax Analysis

Year	Taxed Annually Ending Balance	Taxed Annually Annual Tax	Taxed at End of 10-Year Periods Ending Balance	Taxed at End of 10-Year Periods Annual Tax	Taxed at End of 10-Year Periods with Tax Paid Over Following 10 Years Ending Balance	Taxed at End of 10-Year Periods with Tax Paid Over Following 10 Years Annual Tax
0	$1,000		$1,000		$1,000	
1	$1,070	$30	$1,100	$0	$1,100	$0
2	$1,145	$32	$1,210	$0	$1,210	$0
3	$1,225	$34	$1,331	$0	$1,331	$0
4	$1,311	$37	$1,464	$0	$1,464	$0
5	$1,403	$39	$1,611	$0	$1,611	$0
6	$1,501	$42	$1,772	$0	$1,772	$0
7	$1,606	$45	$1,949	$0	$1,949	$0
8	$1,718	$48	$2,144	$0	$2,144	$0
9	$1,838	$52	$2,358	$0	$2,358	$0
10	$1,967	$55	$2,116	$478	$2,594	$0
11	$2,105	$59	$2,327	$0	$2,805	$48
12	$2,252	$63	$2,560	$0	$3,038	$48
13	$2,410	$68	$2,816	$0	$3,294	$48
14	$2,579	$72	$3,097	$0	$3,576	$48
15	$2,759	$77	$3,407	$0	$3,885	$48
16	$2,952	$83	$3,748	$0	$4,226	$48
17	$3,159	$89	$4,123	$0	$4,601	$48
18	$3,380	$95	$4,535	$0	$5,013	$48
19	$3,617	$101	$4,989	$0	$5,467	$48
20	$3,870	$108	$4,476	$1,012	$5,965	$48
21	$4,141	$116	$4,923	$0	$6,447	$115
22	$4,430	$124	$5,416	$0	$6,976	$115
23	$4,741	$133	$5,957	$0	$7,558	$115
24	$5,072	$142	$6,553	$0	$8,198	$115
25	$5,427	$152	$7,208	$0	$8,902	$115
26	$5,807	$163	$7,929	$0	$9,677	$115
27	$6,214	$174	$8,722	$0	$10,529	$115
28	$6,649	$186	$9,594	$0	$11,467	$115
29	$7,114	$199	$10,554	$0	$12,498	$115
30	$7,612	$213	$9,469	$2,140	$13,632	$115

For illustration purposes only. Not representative of an actual investment.

TAX EXAMPLE TWO—GROWTH TAXED AT THE END OF EACH TEN-YEAR PERIOD

If you assume that you invest in a taxable account, but that you don't have to pay taxes on your investment earnings until the end of each ten-year period, the outcome is very different. The second example shows what happens if you only have to pay taxes every ten years—much like when you sell stocks to create Income Ladders. In other words, it assumes that all of your taxes are paid like liquidity taxes would be paid.

In this case, by the end of the thirty-year period you have about $9,469 in your account—$1,857 more than in the first example. In other words, you accumulate about 24% more because you pay the taxes later and are therefore able to leave the money invested longer.

In this case, your $1,000 compounds at 10 percent each year with no taxes taken out until the end of each ten-year period. Instead of paying taxes every year, you only pay them three times over the entire thirty-year period—and each time, you pay all the taxes that are due on the previous ten years' earnings. Ultimately, even though you are paying a liquidity tax every ten years, you still accumulate substantially more money this way.

TAX EXAMPLE THREE—GROWTH TAXED AT THE END OF EACH TEN-YEAR PERIOD WITH THE TAX PAID OVER THE FOLLOWING TEN YEARS

Now, let's assume that you invest in a tax-deferred account so you don't have to pay the liquidity tax all at once at the end of each ten-year period. Instead, let's assume that you are able to spread it over the following ten years like you would if you only had to pay tax when you took money out of an Income Ladder. In other words, you compute the tax at the end of each ten-year period, but pay it in equal annual installments over the following ten years. Of course this means that all those taxes you're not paying will be able to stay invested even longer—and the results are significant.

Over the thirty-year period you will end up with $13,632 in the account. That's $4,163 more than the second example and $6,020 more than the first example. By paying the tax in equal annual installments over the ten years following each ten-year period, you end up with substantially more in the account at the end of thirty years.

These are the kinds of differences you have to consider when you decide how to invest your taxable assets. This is the potential value of deferring both the annual taxes and the liquidity tax payments. Illustration 27 shows graphically just how dramatic the differences can be.

Principle #11 Have a Plan

Many people simply assume that they can think of their life in two phases—the preretirement phase and the retirement phase. Unfortunately, it isn't quite that easy. Both the preretirement phase and the retirement phase have to be broken down into a number of different periods as shown in Illustration 28.

The Accumulation Phase

The preretirement, or Accumulation Phase, is separated into an Early Accumulation Period and a "Late" Accumulation Period. The Early Period relates to the majority of your working years when you are focused primarily on accumulating assets for retirement. The Late Period covers the years just prior to retirement when you have to start thinking about repositioning your investments to generate the safe, steady, dependable income you need for the rest of your life.

The Early Period of the Accumulation Phase starts the day you get your first job and ends about five to seven years before retirement. The Late Period is made up of those last five to seven years. During this time you decide when and how much money to set aside for income purposes and how to invest the rest of your assets to go after the growth you may need to support yourself for the rest of your life. It's a critical time because you are really deciding when to change your overall investment approach from a growth and accumulation strategy to a growth and income strategy—and this decision has very important consequences.

The Retirement Phase

The Retirement Phase is separated into three ten-year time frames or holding periods. A holding period, as you know, is simply the length of time you can stay invested in the stock market to go after the growth you

Illustration 27: Liquidity Tax Graph

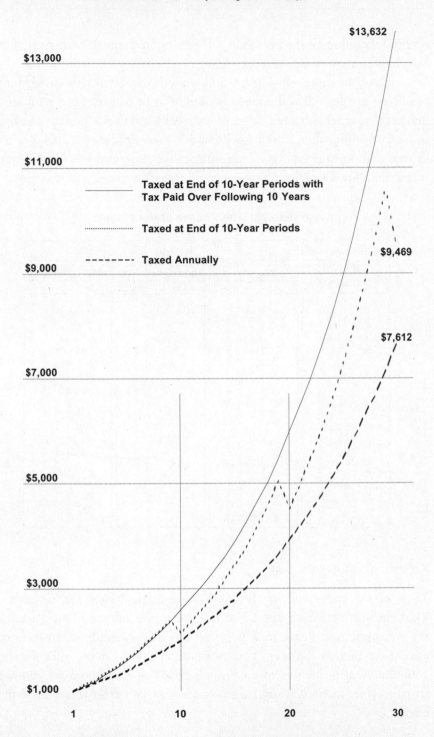

$13,632

$13,000

$11,000

——————— Taxed at End of 10-Year Periods with Tax Paid Over Following 10 Years

·················· Taxed at End of 10-Year Periods

- - - - - - Taxed Annually

$9,000

$9,469

$7,612

$7,000

$5,000

$3,000

$1,000

1   10   20   30

For illustration purposes only. Not representative of an actual investment.

need while reducing the possibility of getting investment returns that are less than you are reasonably expecting.

Each of the three ten-year holding periods can be further divided into two five-year periods. Often, you will plan to be able to hold your stock market investments for ten years, but actually sell them sooner than that. In fact, deciding when to sell stocks within your holding periods is one of the most important aspects of retirement investing, and you seldom hang on to them for a full ten years—even though you can if you want to.

Illustration 28: The Phases of Retirement

Accumulation		Retirement					
Early	Late	Holding Period 1		Holding Period 2		Holding Period 3	
		1a	1b	2a	2b	3a	3b
Age <58	Age 59 to 65	Age 65 to 75		Age 75 to 85		Age 85 to 95	

Accumulating Assets First

Throughout your working life you accumulate assets for retirement. Then, as you approach age 59 or 60, you move into the Late Period of the Accumulation Phase in which you ultimately decide when to create your first Income Ladder. You normally have to make this decision sometime within the five to six years before you retire because you need to have your income ready to go as soon as you stop receiving a paycheck.

Creating Your First Income Ladder

Income Ladders are the lower-risk, lower-return part of your portfolio that provides the safe, steady, dependable income you need during retirement, so you might wonder why you create the first one before you retire. You never know in advance when you will do it, but as you approach retirement, you do know that you will have to create an Income Ladder fairly soon. If you are still heavily invested in the stock market, like many people are at that time, this is just another way of saying that you know you are getting close to the point at which you will be forced to sell stock market investments. Since you never want to be forced to sell stocks when the market is down, and because you have no idea about what will be happening during the rest of the years prior to retirement, you always want to be on the lookout for a good time to sell—just like you will be for the rest of your life.

Making Your First Stock Sales

Ultimately, you have to decide when to create your first Income Ladder and sell some of your stock market investments. Or, if you have other assets that you want to use first—such as real estate, collectibles or other kinds of investments—you can sell them instead. You use the proceeds from the sale of stocks or other assets to purchase fixed-income securities to build your first Income Ladder. Then, the rest of your assets can stay invested, or be invested, in a diversified portfolio of stock market investments. If you prefer, you can always leave them invested in other assets as well—it's up to you. We focus on stocks because they tend to be more typical of the investments people bring with them into retirement. But everyone's life is different.

Spending Your Income Ladders

As your stock market or other investments are allowed to grow, you spend your Income Ladders to provide the lifestyle you need and want. By about age 75 you will probably exhaust your first Income Ladder and need to create a new one to provide the income you want for the next ten years. To do that, you will be able to sell some of your stock market investments and use the proceeds to purchase new Income Ladder investments. The rest of your assets can then remain invested in the stock market where you can plan for them to continue growing at the higher rates of return you are reasonably expecting.

You use the same process over and over again to generate both the income and growth you need to maintain your lifestyle throughout retirement. As shown in Illustration 29, you always have some of your money in Income Ladders for income, and some in the stock market for growth, and will probably have a fair amount left at the end.

Outdated Ideas About Retirement Financial Management

A number of issues come up because you are likely to have a reasonable amount of money left over at the end of your life. You've probably seen the bumper stickers that say something like "Ha, ha, we're out spending our kids' inheritance!" stuck on the back of camper rigs running up and down the freeways—or heard the old saying that the best retirement plan will have you "spending your last dollar on your last day." These are cute little sayings as long as you keep in mind that they're just for fun— because the reality is much different. This kind of thinking may have worked in the old days when you didn't live very long in retirement, but it won't work today.

The fact is, if you do a good job taking care of yourself during retirement, there will probably be a fair amount of money left over at the end of your life, and the question is—what do you want to do with it? Do you want to give it to charity? Do you want to give it to the church? Do you want to find a way to get as much as possible to your children and grandchildren? These are very important questions that may never even come up if you simply plan to manage your money the old-fashioned way—because there probably won't be much left to worry about anyway. But if you manage your money the way I suggest, there will probably be quite a bit left over, and you will certainly want to decide what to do with it.

Illustration 29: The Grangaard Strategy®
(A Conceptual Overview)

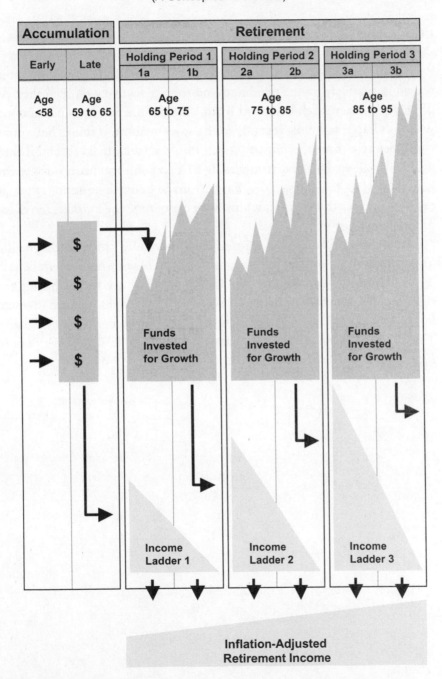

Principle #12 Take Action Now

Retirement investors often vacillate between the twin perils of investing too conservatively on the one hand and too aggressively on the other. As often as not they lurch back and forth between the extremes based upon what has happened most recently in the stock market. If things have gone well, they're tempted to put too much into the stock market, and if they haven't gone so well the tendency is to become too conservative. The goal is to stop vacillating. You have to make good, long-term, strategic decisions rather than getting whipsawed every time the markets move for or against you.

It's often said that the stock market is driven by "fear" and "greed." You absolutely cannot let these emotions control your investment behavior in retirement. You need to "thread the financial needle" by having the right amount invested in Income Ladders and the right amount invested in the stock market—and by managing the balance wisely over time. That's what I mean when I say that you have to follow *Step #7: Plan to Invest Right in Retirement*.

12

Setting Your Total Retirement Accumulation Target

Now that you know how to manage your money during retirement, and how much income you may have to get from your own assets, you can determine how much you might need to accumulate for yourself.

Making Assumptions About Retirement Asset Management

On the back of my business card I ask, "If you don't know how you're going to manage money during retirement, how can you possibly know how much to accumulate for retirement?" This is a very important question, and unfortunately, one that is seldom asked. But it points out that even if you're a younger investor, you still need to understand how to manage your money during retirement. It's really the only way you will be able to follow *Step #8: Set a Good Accumulation Target.*

Will You Need to Accumulate More or Less?

If you plan to manage your assets more efficiently and effectively during retirement, you can probably get by with less—and if you don't need to accumulate as much, you should also be able to spend more today and tomorrow.

Do It the Right Way in Retirement

The important thing for investors who still have some time before they stop working is to come up with a set of retirement planning assumptions that have a reasonable amount of historical integrity. You can then use these historical assumptions to develop a range of *retirement factors* that should allow you to estimate how much you may need to accumulate.

Getting a General Sense of the Future

You can be more or less aggressive with your assumptions about how you plan to manage your money during retirement. You have to choose from among a variety of different investment strategies—and while they're all generalizations, they should suffice pretty well for long-range planning purposes.

After all, you can't really know today what you will think about many of the investment decisions you'll be facing twenty-five, thirty, or even thirty-five years from now when you retire. But you can certainly use historically meaningful assumptions and a general sense of your overall investment behavior to make reasonable long-range projections. As you get closer to retirement, you will need to become more and more thoughtful about your assumptions—but until then, you should be able to use a much more general approach.

Aggressive, Conservative, or Moderate Retirement Portfolios

We will consider three different hypothetical retirement scenarios. The first represents a more **aggressive** retirement portfolio, the second a more **moderate** portfolio, and the third a more **conservative** strategy. In all of the scenarios please keep in mind that rates of return are hypothetical in nature and are not meant to predict or represent the future performance of any investment, and that actual rates of return will vary along with your actual results. You should also remember that higher return potentials come with a higher degree of investment risk and volatility. Although we can't address all of the details and variables discussed in Chapter 11, following are some of the key assumptions used to determine the retirement factors associated with each of the portfolios:

More Aggressive Retirement Portfolio
(Retirement Factor of 16.53):

Inflation Rate	3.0%
Income Ladder Rate of Return	5.0%
Large Company Stock Average Annual Rate of Return	10.0%
Large Company Stock Holding Period	10 years
Small Company Stock Average Annual Rate of Return	12.0%
Small Company Stock Holding Period	12 years

Portfolio Allocation: 50% Income Ladder Investments
　　25% Large Company Stock Investments
　　25% Small Company Stock Investments

As you can see, the above scenario uses assumptions that are very much in line with what we have been talking about throughout the book. It's probably the best guess about how you might manage your own money during retirement, based upon historical experience over the past seventy-five years. However, some people may be more comfortable with a more conservative portfolio. Of course, if you plan to invest more conservatively *in* retirement, you may also have to accumulate more money *for* retirement, so the following two hypothetical scenarios would generally lead to larger accumulation targets.

Moderate Retirement Portfolio
(Retirement Factor of 19.75):

Inflation Rate	3.5%
Income Ladder Rate of Return	4.5%
Large Company Stock Average Annual Rate of Return	9.0%

Large Company Stock Holding Period   11 years
Small Company Stock Average Annual Rate of Return   11.0%
Small Company Stock Holding Period   13 years
Portfolio Allocation: 50% Income Ladder Investments
    25% Large Company Stock Investments
    25% Small Company Stock Investments

Although there are many ways to make a portfolio more conservative, you will notice that in this case we increased the inflation rate, reduced hypothetical rates of return, and increased the holding periods for both large and small company stocks.

Some investors may want to be even more conservative than this, so the next hypothetical portfolio includes a set of assumptions that are even less aggressive.

More Conservative Retirement Portfolio
(Retirement Factor of 25.54):

Inflation Rate   4.0%
Income Ladder Rate of Return   4.0%
Large Company Stock Average Annual Rate of Return   8.0%
Large Company Stock Holding Period   12 years
Small Company Stock Average Annual Rate of Return   10.0%
Small Company Stock Holding Period   14 years
Portfolio Allocation: 50% Income Ladder Investments
    25% Large Company Stock Investments
    25% Small Company Stock Investments

To make this portfolio more conservative, we continued to increase inflation, further reduced the hypothetical rates of return, and made the stock market holding periods even longer.

Other Variables to Consider

You should keep in mind that the above scenarios are only three of a virtually unlimited number of retirement planning strategies you could explore. Other variables can be adjusted to affect the aggressiveness and/or conservativeness of your portfolio, and different combinations of assumptions can be used.

For example, you could change the allocation of assets between higher-risk small company stocks and lower-risk large company stocks. Alternatively, you could allocate more money to Income Ladders and less to the stock market. There are an infinite number of ways to change the characteristics of the portfolio—but many of them would lead to retirement factors somewhere in the range we just established anyway.

Good Enough for Long-Range Planning Purposes

For long-range planning purposes, especially for people who still have a fair amount of time before retirement, these factors should help you develop a long-term financial plan. Each of the portfolios is constructed to help provide inflation-adjusted income throughout retirement, and seek the growth potential of stock market investments to help reduce the risk that you will run out of money too soon.

Create Your Own Plan

Let's take a look at how you can use these retirement factors to establish your own retirement accumulation target. In Plan Aid 10a: Example, start by entering your *Hypothetical Asset-Funding Retirement Income* in box (c). This amount comes from item (f), Plan Aid 9a: Example on page 106.

Next, decide how conservative you want to be with your retirement portfolio, and select a *Retirement Factor* from the table at the bottom of the page, and enter it in box (d). Then, simply multiply the *Retirement Factor* in box (d) by the *Hypothetical Asset-Funded Retirement Income* in box (c), to determine your *Hypothetical Total Accumulation Target*, which should be entered in box (e).

Plan Aid 10a: Example
Setting the Total Accumulation Target

Hypothetical Asset-Funded Retirement Income .... (c) $ **106,706**
   (From item (f), Plan Aid 9a: Example on page 106)

Retirement Factor .... (d)   **16.53**
   (from box # 1 in the table below)

Hypothetical Total Accumulation Target .... (e) $ **1,763,850**
   Future Value Dollars in Year 1 of Retirement   *(c) x (d)*

RETIREMENT FACTORS		
More Aggressive Retirement Portfolio	(1)	**16.53**
Moderate Retirement Portfolio	(2)	**19.75**
More Conservative Retirement Portfolio	(3)	**25.54**

For illustration purposes only. Not representative of an actual investment. An individual investor's results may vary. All assumptions and computational results are hypothetical in nature. There are no guarantees that you will achieve the results shown. You should consult with a financial professional.

This is the total amount of assets that you may need to have available at retirement to provide the part of your retirement lifestyle that you think *you* will be responsible for. It is stated in terms of inflation-adjusted or "future value" dollars as of the first year of retirement. It's an estimate of the total amount of money you may need to accumulate given the income expectations you established.

After reviewing the example, fill in Plan Aid 10b: Your Plan now, to determine how much *you* may need to accumulate for retirement.

Plan Aid 10b: Your Plan
Setting the Total Accumulation Target

Hypothetical Asset-Funded Retirement Income .... (c) $
   (From item (f), Plan Aid 9b: Your Plan on page 107)

Retirement Factor .... (d)
   (from box #   in the table below)

Hypothetical Total Accumulation Target .... (e) $
   Future Value Dollars in Year 1 of Retirement   (c) x (d)

RETIREMENT FACTORS		
More Aggressive Retirement Portfolio .... (1)		**16.53**
Moderate Retirement Portfolio .... (2)		**19.75**
More Conservative Retirement Portfolio .... (3)		**25.54**

For illustration purposes only. Not representative of an actual investment. An individual investor's results may vary. All assumptions and computational results are hypothetical in nature. There are no guarantees that you will achieve the results shown. You should consult with a financial professional.

Adjusting for Social Security If You Plan to Retire Early

As we discussed in Chapter 10, some people may plan to retire before they start collecting Social Security, and as a result, they may need to make an adjustment to their retirement plan.

Adjusting for Delayed Social Security Benefits

If you plan to retire before you start collecting Social Security, and if you decided to adjust your plan because of it, you need to go back to Plan Aid 6b: Your Plan on page 101, and get the Social Security adjustment you calculated at the bottom of the page. Make a note of that amount on the bottom of Plan Aid 10b: Your Plan, and add it to your hypothetical total accumulation target in box (e). This amount has to be added back to account for the fact that because of the way we accounted for Social Security, you would have included too many years' worth of benefits in your plan. This adjustment corrects for that overstatement.

All of the Money Is Assumed to Be in Tax-Deferred Accounts

It's important to understand that the total hypothetical accumulation target you just calculated assumes that **all of the money you accumulate will be invested in tax-deferred accounts** like IRAs or 401(k) plans during retirement. The asset management strategy discussed in Chapter 11 assumes that your money will be managed in tax-deferred accounts—and of course that's the strategy we used to come up with the retirement factors you just used to set your target.

Your Assets Are Also Assumed to Be Generating Taxable Income

As I've already said many times, we are planning for the amount of "pre-tax" income you may need in retirement, so you have to assume that your assets will be invested in accounts that generate 100 percent taxable income—whether they actually do or not. As you will see, you start with this assumption in order to establish a baseline for making apples-to-apples comparisons between the hypothetical values of your various retirement accounts.

Creating a Benchmark for Comparison Purposes

By setting your targets this way—assuming that your money is invested in **tax-deferred accounts generating 100 percent taxable income**, you create a benchmark against which you can adjust the hypothetical value of assets that provide either partially or totally tax-free income—such as annuities and Roth IRAs, as well as the value of assets that are not invested in tax-deferred accounts at all—like taxable mutual funds.

As you will see, **the hypothetical value of many of your retirement assets will have to be adjusted to reflect their value as if they were gener-**

ating 100 percent taxable income from within tax-deferred investment accounts—because that's how you set your targets in the first place. If you don't do it this way, you will never be able to combine the value of various accounts, because you won't have a common denominator that allows you to tie everything together. This will all become much more obvious as you work through the rest of your plan and consider the value of each of your retirement accounts.

13

Think About Taxes

Because you are planning for *pretax income* and assuming that your retirement portfolios will be managed inside *tax-deferred accounts*, you need to adjust the hypothetical value of some of your assets. For example, Roth IRAs are tax-deferred investment vehicles, but they generate *tax-free* income, because you generally don't have to pay taxes on money coming out of a Roth. On the other hand, taxable accounts are obviously *not* tax-deferred, but they *do* generate taxable income. So for many different reasons, if you want to value all these assets properly for planning purposes, you have to restate them as if they were generating *taxable income* from within *tax-deferred* accounts.

Most Assets *Do* Need to Be Adjusted

The only accounts that you will not have to adjust are your regular IRAs and your retirement accounts at work—like your 401(k) and 403(b) plans—because they're the only ones that generate 100 percent taxable income from within tax-deferred accounts. The rest of your assets will need to be adjusted up or down before they can be included in your plan.

An Example of Roth IRAs

The reason you need to adjust the value of Roth IRAs is because they generate tax-free income during retirement. Therefore, a given amount of income from a Roth IRA is actually worth more—in terms of how much you have available to spend after taxes—than if it was coming out of an account that generated taxable income.

Roth IRA Balances Are Actually Worth More

This also means that a given amount of money in a Roth IRA is actually worth more than the same amount of money in an account generating taxable income. In other words, because Roth IRAs provide the same amount of income, but don't require you to pay taxes on it, they're actually worth more in terms of their ability to support your lifestyle. Therefore, to account for them properly in your plan, you have to increase the hypothetical projected value of your Roth IRAs to reflect their value as if they were generating taxable income.

USING THE ENHANCED VALUE FOR PLANNING PURPOSES

It's this enhanced "as if" value that you include in your financial plan. Remember, you set your *Hypothetical Total Accumulation Target* based upon how much you need to accumulate to provide a certain amount of *taxable* income during retirement. If you want to know how much of that accumulation might be taken care of by your Roth IRAs, you have to revalue them. If you don't, you will understate their value and end up with a larger accumulation target than you actually need.

TAKE A LOOK AT THE NUMBERS

Let's say you have a total accumulation target of $500,000 after considering Social Security, pensions and all other sources of income. Further, assume that you are planning to accumulate about $100,000 in your Roth IRAs by the time you retire.

It would be incorrect to subtract the anticipated $100,000 Roth IRA balance from your $500,000 target to determine how much you need to accumulate in your other accounts—because the Roth IRA will be kicking out tax-free income. Since the $500,000 target was set initially assuming that all of your assets would be generating taxable income, the Roth IRAs will actually take care of a bigger share of the total, because every dollar coming out of the Roth IRA is actually worth more than a dollar coming out of another account as taxable income.

For example, if you are in a combined state and federal income tax bracket of 40 percent, the tax-free income you get from a Roth IRA is actually worth about 67 percent more than the same amount coming out of a taxable account. So $1,000 of Roth IRA income is as good as getting $1,667 of taxable income—and it's that $1,667 that you should use for planning purposes. You will only be getting $1,000 of income, but it's essentially the same as getting $1,667 and then paying 40 percent tax on it.

VALUING YOUR ROTH IRA ASSETS

The important thing to understand is that this means that the $100,000 you hope to have in your Roth IRA will actually be worth about 67 percent more than if it was in an account generating taxable income. So, instead of $100,000, you should subtract more like $167,000 from your target amount of $500,000 to come up with an accurate estimate of how much more you need to accumulate in the rest of your accounts. Rather than $400,000, you would really be able to get by with about another $333,000.

Making Adjustments for Other Kinds of Assets Too

Some of your other assets may also be invested in taxable accounts or annuities during retirement. Each of these investments has different tax consequences and each of them will need to be adjusted accordingly. Some will be adjusted up and some will be adjusted down, and you will consider each of them as you work through your plan.

Coming Up with Your Own Tax Rate Assumptions

To make the asset value adjustments we have been talking about, you have to come up with an estimate of your own combined state and federal income tax rate for planning purposes. Although it will necessarily be a rough estimate, and will probably fluctuate throughout your life, you have to make your best guess and then adjust it along the way as circumstances change—there's really no other way to do it.

MARGINAL VERSUS EFFECTIVE TAX RATES

There are two kinds of tax rates to which people commonly refer. Your *marginal tax rate* is the rate applied to your next dollar of income. It's important to know in a system like ours because tax rates tend to increase with the amount of income you report.

The other rate to which people often refer is your *effective tax rate*. This is the percentage you get when you divide the total tax you paid by your total income for any given year. It provides a much better sense of your overall tax rate and it's the amount you need to estimate for use in this book. Your last year's tax returns will be helpful in estimating this amount.

COMPUTING YOUR COMBINED EFFECTIVE TAX RATE

The easiest way to compute your combined effective state and federal tax rate is to use last year's tax returns. To get the total tax you paid, add the amount of tax from line 58 of your Federal Tax Return—Form 1040 to your total state income tax from your state tax return. Then, divide this total tax by your Adjusted Gross Income on line 33 of your Federal Form 1040. This will give you a reasonably good estimate of your combined state and federal tax rate. It won't be perfect, and you'll need to round it up or down to the nearest 10 percent anyway—but it should suffice for making the asset valuation adjustments we've been talking about.

BE SURE TO USE TAX RETURNS FROM A "REPRESENTATIVE" YEAR

If you had exceptionally high or low income last year you might want to calculate your combined tax rate using returns from a prior year. Just like when you projected your preretirement lifestyle using a "normal" amount for current earnings, you also want to use a "normal" year for tax purposes too. If you calculate a tax rate based upon an unusual year, you will project that year's abnormalities into your financial plan—which you don't want to do. Be sure to estimate a combined tax rate assumption that makes sense given your overall expectations about future income.

CREATE YOUR OWN PLAN

It will take just a few minutes to gather the information you need to compute the tax adjustment factors you'll use throughout the rest of the book. Using Plan Aid 11a: Example, start by estimating your *Combined Tax Rate Assumption* and enter it in box (a). Follow the steps outlined above to determine this amount, and then round it up or down to the nearest 10 percent—depending upon whether you want to be a little more conservative or a little more aggressive with your tax rate assumptions. Then, subtract your *Combined Tax Rate Assumption* from one, and note the answer as your *Tax Adjustment Percentage* in box (b). This percentage will be used to make valuation adjustments similar to the one we made in the Roth IRA example earlier in this chapter.

Plan Aid 11a: Example
Income Tax Rates and Assumptions

Combined Tax Rate Assumption .... (a)   **30.0** %
   (Select 0%, 10%, 20%, 30%, 40%, or 50%)

Tax Adjustment Percentage .... (b)   **70.0** %
   1 - (a)

Taxable Account Adjustment Factor .... (c)   **.97**
   Look Up on Plan Aid Table 11a, Using Item (a) above

Tax-Deferred Account Adjustment Factor .... (d)   **1.21**
   Look Up on Plan Aid Table 11b, Using Item (a) above

For illustration purposes only. All assumptions and computational results are hypothetical in nature. There are no guarantees that you will achieve the results shown. You should consult with a financial professional.

Next, go to Plan Aid Tables 11a and 11b. Use Table 11a to determine the *Taxable Account Adjustment Factor* for box (c) and Table 11b to determine the *Tax-Deferred Account Adjustment Factor* for box (d). These factors can be determined by finding your combined tax rate assumption across the top of each table, and dropping down to the related factor. You will use these amounts to adjust the value of your taxable or partially taxable accounts before including them in your plan.

Plan Aid Table 11a: Adjustment Factors If Assets Remain in Taxable Accounts During Retirement

Combined Tax Rate Assumption					
0%	10%	20%	30%	40%	50%
1.00	1.00	0.98	0.97	0.94	0.91

Plan Aid Table 11b: Adjustment Factors If Assets Are Moved into Tax-Deferred Accounts During Retirement

Combined Tax Rate Assumption					
0%	10%	20%	30%	40%	50%
1.00	1.06	1.13	1.21	1.33	1.50

After following the example, fill in Plan Aid 11b: Your Plan now, to establish the tax-adjustment factors that *you* will use in your own financial plan.

You Determine How You Will Be Taxed

These factors and lookup tables should help you evaluate the potential consequences of investing in different kinds of assets during retirement. They can't possibly take into account all of the unique tax issues you might encounter in your own life and they don't include all of the com-

Plan Aid 11b: Your Plan
Income Tax Rates and Assumptions

Combined Tax Rate Assumption .... (a)   %

    (Select 0%, 10%, 20%, 30%, 40%, or 50%)

Tax Adjustment Percentage .... (b)   %

                                                       1 - (a)

Taxable Account Adjustment Factor .... (c)

      Look Up on Plan Aid Table 11a, Using Item (a) above

Tax-Deferred Account Adjustment Factor .... (d)

      Look Up on Plan Aid Table 11b, Using Item (a) above

For illustration purposes only. All assumptions and computational results are hypothetical in nature. There are no guarantees that you will achieve the results shown. You should consult with a financial professional.

plexities of managing an entire portfolio during retirement. But they can help you do a better job in estimating the relative value of your various retirement accounts.

To a large extent you determine how your investments are going to be taxed, based upon the kinds of accounts you put them in—so you should consult with your advisors to determine the best approach in your own circumstances. But no matter what, you have to follow *Step #9: Keep Taxes in Mind*, to develop a good financial plan for the rest of your life.

PART FOUR

Taking Stock of What You Already Have

In this section, we cover:

Step #10: Put a Value on Pensions;

Step #11: Project Retirement Plan Balances;

Step #12: Project IRA Balances;

Step #13: Project Roth IRA Balances;

Step #14: Project Annuity Balances;

Step #15: Project Taxable Account Balances; and

Step #16: Measure the "Missing Money."

After completing this part of the book, you should have determined the future value of your *existing* assets and figured out how much more you may still need to accumulate for retirement.

14

Pensions

It's time to consider monthly pensions that are *not* adjusted for inflation, as well as the kind of pensions that pay a single lump-sum amount when you retire. You have to do this to follow *Step #10: Put a Value on Pensions.*

A Quick Review

Because some of your income is likely to come from sources other than your own investments, the hypothetical asset accumulation target you set earlier was limited to the amount you may need to accumulate to generate the retirement income that you think *you* might be responsible for. To determine that amount, you started by reducing your total retirement income need by the other sources of income you might plan to have—like Social Security, rents and royalties, and inflation-adjusted pensions. Then, you multiplied that reduced amount by your retirement factor to determine how much you may need to accumulate to provide *your* share of the lifestyle you want in retirement.

You Did Not Include Pensions That Are Not *Adjusted for Inflation*

However, you did *not* subtract from your retirement income any pensions you have which are *not* adjusted for inflation—because it would have overstated their value to do it that way. To account for their smaller value, you have to convert them into what I call an "equivalent lump-sum asset value," rather than treating them as an annual stream of income.

In other words, you have to figure out how much they would be worth as a single lump-sum payment, and then subtract that amount from the total you think you need to accumulate, rather than subtracting the annual payment from your income prior to setting your target. This is one of the easiest ways to compensate for the lower value of income amounts that are *not* adjusted for inflation, because if you make the same computation for inflation-adjusted income streams, you'll find that they have considerably larger equivalent lump-sum asset values.

AN EXAMPLE OF EQUIVALENT LUMP-SUM ASSET VALUES

Let's say you have a pension that provides $20,000 per year for a thirty-year retirement period, and it's *not* inflation-adjusted. Over the thirty-year period, you will get a total of $600,000 of annual pension payments. If instead you went out and purchased a single-premium immediate annuity (SPIA) to provide the same amount of annual income, you would have to pay about $323,000 if you could get an interest rate of about 5 percent. In other words, a non-inflation-adjusted pension of $20,000 per year for thirty years is worth about $323,000.

However, it would be worth a lot more if it was adjusted for inflation. At a conservative 4 percent inflation rate, a $20,000 annual pension today would increase to over $62,000 by the thirtieth year of retirement. In fact, over the entire thirty-year period, you would get a total of $1,122,000 of annual pension payments—or almost twice as much. If you had to go out and buy a thirty-year SPIA to provide $20,000 per year of *inflation-adjusted* income, it would cost you about $524,000, or in excess of $200,000 more at the same 5 percent rate of return. In other words, the inflation-adjusted pension in the example is worth about 62 percent more than the one that isn't adjusted for inflation.

BUILDING THE NON-INFLATION-ADJUSTED PENSION INTO YOUR PLAN

You can see that the inflation-adjusted pension is far more valuable. That extra value is reflected in the fact that you can build it into your plan by simply subtracting it from the amount of inflation-adjusted income you need prior to setting your accumulation target. In other words, you can treat it as a dollar-for-dollar reduction in your need for retirement income.

But you can't do that for pensions that are *not* adjusted for inflation. Instead, you have to compute a "lump-sum equivalent asset value," which will be less than it would be if the pension was adjusted for inflation. Then, you subtract that amount from your overall retirement accumulation target. In other words, you treat the non-inflation-adjusted pension as an "asset value" rather than an income stream. And because the "asset value" is less than it would be if the pension was inflation-adjusted, you automatically compensate for its lower value.

Create Your Own Plan: Pensions That Are Not Adjusted for Inflation

If you have a pension that is *not* inflation-adjusted, Plan Aid 12a: Example will help you figure out how much it may be worth. Start with your *Hypothetical Monthly Benefit*, and input it into box (a). You should be able to get this information from your human resource department—and it's usually given as the amount you will get in the first year of retirement. Double-check to be sure this is the case. Also, keep in mind that the amount of your projected benefit may change from year to year based upon your income and longevity, so be sure to use the most current available projections. Then, multiply the monthly benefit in box (a) by twelve to determine your *Hypothetical Annual Benefit*, and enter it in box (b).

In order to calculate the asset-value of your non-inflation-adjusted pension, you need to use a lookup table and make some calculations that are based on some fairly complicated math, which we don't want to get into. Suffice it to say that to do the calculations, you need to figure out what percentage of your income may be taken care of by your non-adjusted pension in the first year of retirement, and then use that percentage to find a factor that will allow you to compute the asset value of the pension.

So, the next step is to input your *Hypothetical Asset-Funded Retirement Income* into box (c). This is the same amount you used in item (f), Plan Aid 9a: Example on page 106. Then, by dividing your *Hypothetical*

Plan Aid 12a: Example
Putting a Value on Non-Inflation-Adjusted Pension Plans

Hypothetical <u>Monthly</u> Benefit .... (a) $ **500**

Hypothetical <u>Annual</u> Benefit .... (b) $ **6,000**
     Future Value Dollars in Year 1 of Retirement   *(a) x 12*

Hypothetical Asset-Funded Retirement Income .... (c) $ **106,706**
   (From item (f), Plan Aid 9a: Example on page 106)

Pension as a Percent of Asset-Funded Income .... (d) **5.6** %
                                     (b) ÷ (c)

Pension Value Factor .... (e) **.053**
         Look Up on Plan Aid Table 12, Using Item (d) above

Hypothetical Total Accumulation Target .... (f) $ **1,763,850**
   (From item (e), Plan Aid 10a: Example on page 160)

Hypothetical Value of Annual Pension .... (g) $ **93,484**
     Future Value Dollars in Year 1 of Retirement   *(e) x (f)*

For illustration purposes only. All assumptions and computational results are hypothetical in nature. There are no guarantees that you will achieve the results shown. You should consult with a financial professional.

Annual Benefit in box (b) by that amount, you can determine your *Pension as a Percent of Asset-Funded Income,* which should be entered in box (d). Starting with this amount, and rounding it up or down to the nearest whole percentage, you can turn to Plan Aid Table 12 to find the *Pension Value Factor* associated with your pension percent. Enter that factor in box (e).

The final step is to enter your *Hypothetical Total Accumulation Target* in box (f), which is the same amount used in item (e), Plan Aid 10a: Example on page 160, and then multiply it by the *Pension Value Factor* in box (e) to determine the *Hypothetical Value of Annual Pension* in box (g). This is the "equivalent lump-sum asset value" of your non-inflation-adjusted annual pension. It's the amount of your *Hypothetical Total Accumulation Target* that should be taken care of by the hypothetical value of your non-inflation-adjusted pension.

After reviewing the example, fill in Plan Aid 12b: Your Plan now, to

Plan Aid Table 12: Pension Value Factor Table

Pension Percent	Pension Value Factor	Pension Percent	Pension Value Factor
1.0%	0.009	51.0%	0.361
2.0%	0.018	52.0%	0.366
3.0%	0.026	53.0%	0.372
4.0%	0.035	54.0%	0.378
5.0%	0.044	55.0%	0.383
6.0%	0.053	56.0%	0.389
7.0%	0.062	57.0%	0.394
8.0%	0.071	58.0%	0.400
9.0%	0.079	59.0%	0.405
10.0%	0.088	60.0%	0.411
11.0%	0.097	61.0%	0.417
12.0%	0.106	62.0%	0.422
13.0%	0.115	63.0%	0.428
14.0%	0.124	64.0%	0.433
15.0%	0.132	65.0%	0.439
16.0%	0.141	66.0%	0.444
17.0%	0.150	67.0%	0.450
18.0%	0.159	68.0%	0.456
19.0%	0.168	69.0%	0.461
20.0%	0.177	70.0%	0.467
21.0%	0.184	71.0%	0.472
22.0%	0.191	72.0%	0.478
23.0%	0.198	73.0%	0.483
24.0%	0.206	74.0%	0.489
25.0%	0.213	75.0%	0.495
26.0%	0.220	76.0%	0.500
27.0%	0.227	77.0%	0.506
28.0%	0.233	78.0%	0.511
29.0%	0.238	79.0%	0.517
30.0%	0.244	80.0%	0.522
31.0%	0.249	81.0%	0.528
32.0%	0.255	82.0%	0.534
33.0%	0.261	83.0%	0.539
34.0%	0.266	84.0%	0.545
35.0%	0.272	85.0%	0.550
36.0%	0.277	86.0%	0.556
37.0%	0.283	87.0%	0.561
38.0%	0.288	88.0%	0.567
39.0%	0.294	89.0%	0.573
40.0%	0.300	90.0%	0.582
41.0%	0.305	91.0%	0.593
42.0%	0.311	92.0%	0.604
43.0%	0.316	93.0%	0.615
44.0%	0.322	94.0%	0.626
45.0%	0.327	95.0%	0.636
46.0%	0.333	96.0%	0.639
47.0%	0.339	97.0%	0.642
48.0%	0.344	98.0%	0.645
49.0%	0.350	99.0%	0.648
50.0%	0.355	100.0%	0.651

determine the value of *your* non-inflation-adjusted pension plan. If you don't have this kind of pension you can leave this part blank.

Plan Aid 12b: Your Plan
Putting a Value on Non-Inflation-Adjusted Pension Plans

Hypothetical <u>Monthly</u> Benefit .... (a) $

Hypothetical <u>Annual</u> Benefit .... (b) $
      Future Value Dollars in Year 1 of Retirement   *(a) x 12*

Hypothetical Asset-Funded Retirement Income .... (c) $
      (From item (f), Plan Aid 9b: Your Plan on page 107)

Pension as a Percent of Asset-Funded Income .... (d)   %
      (b) ÷ (c)

Pension Value Factor .... (e)
      Look Up on Plan Aid Table 12, Using Item (d) above

Hypothetical Total Accumulation Target .... (f) $
      (From item (e), Plan Aid 10b: Your Plan on page 161)

Hypothetical Value of Annual Pension .... (g) $
      Future Value Dollars in Year 1 of Retirement   *(e) x (f)*

For illustration purposes only. All assumptions and computational results are hypothetical in nature. There are no guarantees that you will achieve the results shown. You should consult with a financial professional.

Lump-Sum Pension Benefits

To wrap up our discussion of pension plans, you need to consider the kind of plans that pay a single lump-sum amount when you retire. A growing number of plans actually work this way, and many more provide lump-sum benefit as one among a number of different withdrawal options—so you have to at least consider the possibility of getting a lump-sum amount if you have a pension plan.

As always, you can get the information you need from your human resource department, and you should be careful to work with the most current available data.

Create Your Own Plan: Lump-Sum Pension Payments

To learn how to account for lump-sum pension payments, simply turn to Plan Aid 13a: Example and enter the amount you expect to get in box (h), *Hypothetical Lump-Sum Pension Benefit*. This is the amount of lump-sum pension benefits you may receive when you retire. It will be up to you to manage it for the rest of your life.

Plan Aid 13a: Example
Putting a Value on Lump-Sum Pension Benefits

Hypothetical Lump-Sum Pension Benefit .... (h) $ **50,000**
Future Value Dollars in Year 1 of Retirement

For illustration purposes only. All assumptions and computational results are hypothetical in nature. There are no guarantees that you will achieve the results shown. You should consult with a financial professional.

After reviewing the example, use Plan Aid 13b: Your Plan to account for your own expected lump-sum pension benefits. If you don't have this kind of pension plan you can leave this part blank.

Plan Aid 13b: Your Plan
Putting a Value on Lump-Sum Pension Benefits

Hypothetical Lump-Sum Pension Benefit .... (h) $
Future Value Dollars in Year 1 of Retirement

For illustration purposes only. All assumptions and computational results are hypothetical in nature. There are no guarantees that you will achieve the results shown. You should consult with a financial professional.

We Will Add It All Up Later

Later in the book we will summarize the hypothetical value of your pension plans together with the hypothetical value of other assets you may already have accumulated, to determine how much of your overall target might already have been taken care of.

15

Retirement Plans

Your retirement plans at work will probably be the backbone of your overall financial plan. That's why it's so important to follow *Step #11: Project Retirement Plan Balances.*

You have to consider your retirement plans in two ways. First, you need to estimate how much your current balances may be worth when you get to retirement, and then you have to project the hypothetical value of any future contributions that you and your employer intend to make.

Current Retirement Account Balances

There are many kinds of retirement plans—401(k) plans, 403(b) plans, Profit-Sharing Plans, SEP plans, SIMPLE Plans, Keogh Plans, and others. Whatever kind you have, the first step in building them into your financial plan is to determine your current account values.

To do this, add up the current balances in all your self-directed retirement plans at work, and/or any amounts you have remaining in plans at former employers. Armed with this information, you can estimate how much your current balances are likely to be worth when you get to retirement.

Create Your Own Plan

Follow the steps outlined in Plan Aid 14a: Example to learn how to estimate the hypothetical future value of your existing retirement plan assets. Start with the total value of all retirement plan balances in current and/or former employer plans, and enter that amount as your *Current Retirement Plan Balances* in box (i). Don't include assets from previous employer plans that you may have already rolled over into IRAs—we'll deal with them later. Only include amounts that are currently in employer-sponsored retirement accounts.

Next, enter the *Number of Years Until Retirement* in box (j). This is the same amount you calculated in item (c), Plan Aid 1a: Example on page 13.

Plan Aid 14a: Example
Current Retirement Plan Balances

Current Retirement Plan Balances .... (i) $ **50,000**

Number of Years Until Retirement .... (j) **22**
  (From item (c), Plan Aid 1a: Example on page 13)

Asset Growth Rate Assumption .... (k) **8.0** %
  (Use Plan Aid 15a: Example on page 183 to estimate rate of return)
  (Select 5%, 6%, 7%, 8%, 9%, 10%, 11%, or 12%)

Asset Growth Factor .... (l) **5.44**
  Look Up on Plan Aid Table 15, Using Items (j) and (k) above

Hypothetical Value of Retirement Plan Balances ..... (m) $ **272,000**
  Future Value Dollars in Year 1 of Retirement   *(i) x (l)*

For illustration purposes only. Not representative of an actual investment. An individual investors results may vary. All assumptions and computational results are hypothetical in nature. There are no guarantees that you will achieve the results shown. Higher volatility has historically been associated with higher rates of return, and average returns have had a tendency to fluctuate from year to year. You should consult with a financial professional.

Computing Your Weighted Average Rate of Return

Then, use Plan Aid 15a: Example to calculate your hypothetical weighted average asset growth rate assumption for the assets in your retirement plans. This is the hypothetical average annual rate of return you might expect to earn on your accounts until the day you retire. Since your assets are probably invested in a variety of different accounts and mutual funds, you need to compute a weighted average rate of return for the entire balance.

Calculating a hypothetical average annual rate of return for your retirement accounts is very easy. We've already worked through an example in Chapter 6, and we will do it the same way again.

Start by listing each type of asset in your accounts, and then determine the percentage of the total invested in each. You do this by listing the current value for each category, totaling them up, and calculating how much each one represents as a percent of the total. Do this for each kind of asset in your plans and double-check to make sure they add up to 100 percent.

After determining the percentage invested in each asset class, estimate the hypothetical rate of return you might expect to earn on each of them. Think back to our discussions in Chapters 3 and 4 about historical rates of return to get an idea of what you might reasonably expect.

Then, compute the hypothetical weighted average rate of return for the entire balance by multiplying the percentage of assets in each category by the hypothetical rate of return for that category, and adding them all up.

After estimating your weighted average rate of return, you can use it to project the hypothetical future value of your current retirement plan balances. Start by rounding the hypothetical weighted average rate of return either up or down to the nearest whole percentage, and then enter it as your *Asset Growth Rate Assumption* in box (k) on Plan Aid 14a: Example. If you want to be on the conservative side, you should round it down, and if you want to be a little more aggressive, you can round it up.

Then, turn to Plan Aid Table 15, and find the column related to your asset growth rate assumption and the row related to the number of years until retirement. Where they intersect in the table, you will find your *Asset Growth Factor*, which should be entered in box (l).

The final step is to multiply your *Asset Growth Factor* in box (l) by your *Current Retirement Plan Balances* in box (i) to compute the *Hypothetical Value of Retirement Plan Balances* in box (m). This is the amount your current retirement account balances might be worth when

Plan Aid 15a: Example
Weighted Average Rate of Return
Current Retirement Plan Balances

Type of Asset	Asset Value	% of Assets	Expect. Ret.	Wtd. Ret.
Treasury Bonds	$17,500	35.0%	5.5%	1.9%
Large Company Value Stocks	$12,500	25.0%	10.0%	2.5%
International Stocks	$12,500	25.0%	9.0%	2.3%
Small Company Growth Stocks	$2,500	5.0%	12.0%	0.6%
Mid-Cap Stocks	$5,000	10.0%	10.5%	1.1%
Tot. Assets & Wtd. Ave. Return	$50,000	100.0%		8.3%

For illustration purposes only. Not representative of an actual investment. An individual investor's results may vary. All assumptions and computational results are hypothetical in nature. There are no guarantees that you will achieve the results shown. Higher volatility has historically been associated with higher rates of return, and average returns have had a tendency to fluctuate from year to year. The prices of large company, small company, international, and mid-cap stocks will fluctuate. Investing in international stocks may carry additional risks such as differing securities regulations and more volatile political and economic environments. Treasury Bonds are guaranteed by the U.S. government and, if held to maturity, offer a fixed rate of return and principal value. You should consult with a financial professional.

Plan Aid Table 15:
Tax-Deferred Account Asset Growth Factor Table

Years to Retire	Asset Growth Rate Assumption							
	5.0%	6.0%	7.0%	8.0%	9.0%	10.0%	11.0%	12.0%
1	1.05	1.06	1.07	1.08	1.09	1.10	1.11	1.12
2	1.10	1.12	1.14	1.17	1.19	1.21	1.23	1.25
3	1.16	1.19	1.23	1.26	1.30	1.33	1.37	1.40
4	1.22	1.26	1.31	1.36	1.41	1.46	1.52	1.57
5	1.28	1.34	1.40	1.47	1.54	1.61	1.69	1.76
6	1.34	1.42	1.50	1.59	1.68	1.77	1.87	1.97
7	1.41	1.50	1.61	1.71	1.83	1.95	2.08	2.21
8	1.48	1.59	1.72	1.85	1.99	2.14	2.30	2.48
9	1.55	1.69	1.84	2.00	2.17	2.36	2.56	2.77
10	1.63	1.79	1.97	2.16	2.37	2.59	2.84	3.11
11	1.71	1.90	2.10	2.33	2.58	2.85	3.15	3.48
12	1.80	2.01	2.25	2.52	2.81	3.14	3.50	3.90
13	1.89	2.13	2.41	2.72	3.07	3.45	3.88	4.36
14	1.98	2.26	2.58	2.94	3.34	3.80	4.31	4.89
15	2.08	2.40	2.76	3.17	3.64	4.18	4.78	5.47
16	2.18	2.54	2.95	3.43	3.97	4.59	5.31	6.13
17	2.29	2.69	3.16	3.70	4.33	5.05	5.90	6.87
18	2.41	2.85	3.38	4.00	4.72	5.56	6.54	7.69
19	2.53	3.03	3.62	4.32	5.14	6.12	7.26	8.61
20	2.65	3.21	3.87	4.66	5.60	6.73	8.06	9.65
21	2.79	3.40	4.14	5.03	6.11	7.40	8.95	10.80
22	2.93	3.60	4.43	5.44	6.66	8.14	9.93	12.10
23	3.07	3.82	4.74	5.87	7.26	8.95	11.03	13.55
24	3.23	4.05	5.07	6.34	7.91	9.85	12.24	15.18
25	3.39	4.29	5.43	6.85	8.62	10.83	13.59	17.00
26	3.56	4.55	5.81	7.40	9.40	11.92	15.08	19.04
27	3.73	4.82	6.21	7.99	10.25	13.11	16.74	21.32
28	3.92	5.11	6.65	8.63	11.17	14.42	18.58	23.88
29	4.12	5.42	7.11	9.32	12.17	15.86	20.62	26.75
30	4.32	5.74	7.61	10.06	13.27	17.45	22.89	29.96
31	4.54	6.09	8.15	10.87	14.46	19.19	25.41	33.56
32	4.76	6.45	8.72	11.74	15.76	21.11	28.21	37.58
33	5.00	6.84	9.33	12.68	17.18	23.23	31.31	42.09
34	5.25	7.25	9.98	13.69	18.73	25.55	34.75	47.14
35	5.52	7.69	10.68	14.79	20.41	28.10	38.57	52.80
36	5.79	8.15	11.42	15.97	22.25	30.91	42.82	59.14
37	6.08	8.64	12.22	17.25	24.25	34.00	47.53	66.23
38	6.39	9.15	13.08	18.63	26.44	37.40	52.76	74.18
39	6.70	9.70	13.99	20.12	28.82	41.14	58.56	83.08
40	7.04	10.29	14.97	21.72	31.41	45.26	65.00	93.05
41	7.39	10.90	16.02	23.46	34.24	49.79	72.15	104.22
42	7.76	11.56	17.14	25.34	37.32	54.76	80.09	116.72
43	8.15	12.25	18.34	27.37	40.68	60.24	88.90	130.73
44	8.56	12.99	19.63	29.56	44.34	66.26	98.68	146.42
45	8.99	13.76	21.00	31.92	48.33	72.89	109.53	163.99
46	9.43	14.59	22.47	34.47	52.68	80.18	121.58	183.67
47	9.91	15.47	24.05	37.23	57.42	88.20	134.95	205.71
48	10.40	16.39	25.73	40.21	62.59	97.02	149.80	230.39
49	10.92	17.38	27.53	43.43	68.22	106.72	166.27	258.04
50	11.47	18.42	29.46	46.90	74.36	117.39	184.56	289.00

For illustration purposes only. Not representative of an actual investment. All assumptions and computational results are hypothetical in nature. Higher volatility has historically been associated with higher rates of return, and average returns have had a tendency to fluctuate from year to year.

you retire. In a very real sense, it's the part of your final accumulation target that may have already been taken care of by your previous retirement plan contributions. You obviously don't have this much in your account today, but if you expect your assets to keep growing until retirement you are calculating what your assets in these plans might be worth in the future.

After reviewing the example, use Plan Aid 14b: Your Plan to calculate how much you think *your* retirement account balances might be worth when you decide to stop working. Use Plan Aid 15b: Your Plan to estimate your own hypothetical weighted average rate of return. If you don't have any retirement plan accounts you can leave this part blank.

Plan Aid 14b: Your Plan
Current Retirement Plan Balances

Current Retirement Plan Balances .... (i) $

Number of Years Until Retirement .... (j)
(From item (c), Plan Aid 1b: Your Plan on page 13)

Asset Growth Rate Assumption .... (k)   %
(Use Plan Aid 15b: Your Plan on page 186 to estimate rate of return)
(Select 5%, 6%, 7%, 8%, 9%, 10%, 11%, or 12%)

Asset Growth Factor .... (l)
Look Up on Plan Aid Table 15, Using Items (j) and (k) above

Hypothetical Value of Retirement Plan Balances ..... (m) $
Future Value Dollars in Year 1 of Retirement   (i) x (l)

For illustration purposes only. Not representative of an actual investment. An individual investors results may vary. All assumptions and computational results are hypothetical in nature. There are no guarantees that you will achieve the results shown. Higher volatility has historically been associated with higher rates of return, and average returns have had a tendency to fluctuate from year to year. You should consult with a financial professional.

Plan Aid 15b: Your Plan
Weighted Average Rate of Return
Current Retirement Plan Balances

Type of Asset	Asset Value	% of Assets	Expect. Ret.	Wtd. Ret.
	$	%	%	%
	$	%	%	%
	$	%	%	%
	$	%	%	%
	$	%	%	%
	$	%	%	%
	$	%	%	%
	$	%	%	%
	$	%	%	%
	$	%	%	%
Tot. Assets & Wtd. Ave. Return	$	%		%

For illustration purposes only. Not representative of an actual investment. An individual investor's results may vary. All assumptions and computational results are hypothetical in nature. There are no guarantees that you will achieve the results shown. Higher volatility has historically been associated with higher rates of return, and average returns have had a tendency to fluctuate from year to year. You should consult with a financial professional.

16

Individual Retirement Accounts (IRAs)

One of the most important retirement vehicles is the Individual Retirement Account, or IRA. Not only can most people make contributions into their IRA accounts each year—subject to certain income and contribution limits that you should discuss with your financial advisors—but they're also very important as the vehicle into which you will probably transfer your retirement plan assets when you change jobs or retire. When used in this capacity they're often referred to as Rollover IRAs, and the important thing to remember is that they may allow you to maintain the tax-deferred status of your assets after you transfer them out of your employer-sponsored retirement plans.

The IRA Rules Can Get Complicated

The rules surrounding the use of IRAs can get rather complicated, and they also tend to change from year to year. It's not the purpose of this book to investigate all the details and issues concerning the use of IRAs—there are plenty of other books and resources for that. Just keep in mind that before you do anything with your retirement plans at work or with your IRAs, you should seek the advice of a competent financial advisor. You just don't want to run afoul of the rules.

What Is an IRA?

Simply put, an Individual Retirement Account is an investment vehicle that lets your money grow tax-free until you take it out during retirement. In other words, you don't have to pay taxes on the growth in your account until it's used to support your lifestyle after you stop working—just like your retirement plans at work. Normally, the opportunity to earn tax-deferred growth can lead to larger account balances.

One of the other great things about IRAs is that your annual contributions might also be tax-deductible, so you can often save more up front because of the tax deductions you may receive on the money you put in. Again, this is very similar to your retirement plans at work. So not only can you go after tax-free growth rates, but you should also be able to sock away more money in the first place. It's important to note that early withdrawals prior to age 59½ may be subject to a 10 percent federal penalty and ordinary income tax, so you want to be sure you know what you are doing.

And finally, IRAs can be extremely useful when you change jobs or stop working, because you can transfer money out of your retirement plans and into Rollover IRAs to maintain the tax-deferred status of your accounts. This is one of the most important features of IRAs, and most people use them this way many times throughout their lives. In fact, many retirees have substantial IRA balances after rolling money out of their retirement plans when they stop working.

IRAs and Financial Planning

IRAs may well be one of your biggest assets in retirement. That's why it's so important to follow *Step #12: Project IRA Balances*, because they will probably be an important part of your financial plan.

Just like retirement plans at work, you need to consider IRAs in two different ways. You start by estimating how much your current balances may be worth when you stop working, and then you project the hypothetical value of any future contributions you intend to make. At this point, we will only consider your current balances. We deal with future contributions later on.

Create Your Own Plan

Follow the steps outlined in Plan Aid 16a: Example to see how to estimate the hypothetical future value of your accounts. Start with the total current value of all your IRAs, and enter that amount as your *Current IRA Balances* in box (a). Since there are no limits on the number of IRAs you can have, be sure to include all of them in this calculation. Next, enter the *Number of Years Until Retirement* in box (b), which is the same amount you calculated in item (c), Plan Aid 1a: Example on page 13.

Plan Aid 16a: Example
Current IRA Balances

Current IRA Balances .... (a) $ **5,000**

Number of Years Until Retirement .... (b)   **22**
   (From item (c), Plan Aid 1a: Example, on page 13)

Asset Growth Rate Assumption .... (c)   **8.0** %
   (Use Plan Aid 17a: Example, on page 191 to estimate rate of return)
   (Select 5%, 6%, 7%, 8%, 9%, 10%, 11%, or 12%)

Asset Growth Factor .... (d)   **5.44**
   Look Up on Plan Aid Table 17, Using Items (b) and (c) above

Hypothetical Value of IRA Balances .... (e) $ **27,200**
   Future Value Dollars in Year 1 of Retirement   *(a) x (d)*

For illustration purposes only. Not representative of an actual investment. An individual investors results may vary. All assumptions and computational results are hypothetical in nature. There are no guarantees that you will achieve the results shown. Higher volatility has historically been associated with higher rates of return, and average returns have had a tendency to fluctuate from year to year. You should consult with a financial professional.

Computing Your Weighted Average Rate of Return

Then, use Plan Aid 17a: Example to calculate your hypothetical weighted average *Asset Growth Rate Assumption* for the assets in your IRAs. This is the average annual rate of return you might plan to earn on your IRAs until the day you retire. Since your accounts are probably invested in a variety of different assets and mutual funds, you need to compute a hypothetical weighted average rate of return for the entire amount.

As you can see, calculating a hypothetical average annual rate of return for your IRA accounts is exactly the same as calculating an average annual rate of return for your retirement plans at work. We've gone through the process a couple times already, so we're not going to do it again. Just review the example to get a feel for where the hypothetical rate of return is coming from.

After estimating your weighted average rate of return, you can use it to project the hypothetical future value of your IRA balances. Start by rounding it either up or down to the nearest whole percentage, and then enter it as your *Asset Growth Rate Assumption* in box (c) on Plan Aid 16a: Example. If you want to be on the conservative side you can round it down, and if you want to be a little more aggressive you can round it up.

Then, turn to Plan Aid Table 17 and find the column related to your asset growth rate assumption and the row related to the number of years until retirement. Where they intersect in the table, you will find your *Asset Growth Factor*, which should be entered in box (d).

The final step is to multiply your *Asset Growth Factor* in box (d) by your *Current IRA Balances* in box (a) to compute the *Hypothetical Value of IRA Balances* in box (e). This is the amount you might expect your current IRAs to be worth when you retire. In a very real sense, it's the part of your accumulation target that may have already been taken care of by your previous IRA contributions and retirement plan rollovers. You obviously don't have this much in your account today, but if you expect your IRAs to keep growing until retirement you are calculating what your assets in these accounts might be worth in the future.

After reviewing the example, use Plan Aid 16b: Your Plan to calculate how much you think *your* IRAs might be worth when you decide to stop working. Use Plan Aid 17b: Your Plan to estimate your own hypothetical weighted average rate of return. If you don't have any IRA accounts you can leave this part blank.

Plan Aid 17a: Example
Weighted Average Rate of Return
Current IRA Balances

Type of Asset	Asset Value	% of Assets	Expect. Ret.	Wtd. Ret.
Treasury Bonds	$1,750	35.0%	5.0%	1.8%
Large Company Value Stocks	$1,250	25.0%	9.5%	2.4%
International Stocks	$1,250	25.0%	8.5%	2.1%
Small Company Growth Stocks	$250	5.0%	11.0%	0.6%
Mid-Cap Stocks	$500	10.0%	10.0%	1.0%
Tot. Assets & Wtd. Ave. Return	$5,000	100.0%		7.8%

For illustration purposes only. Not representative of an actual investment. An individual investor's results may vary. All assumptions and computational results are hypothetical in nature. There are no guarantees that you will achieve the results shown. Higher volatility has historically been associated with higher rates of return, and average returns have had a tendency to fluctuate from year to year. The prices of large company, small company, international, and mid-cap stocks will fluctuate. Investing in international stocks may carry additional risks such as differing securities regulations and more volatile political and economic environments. Treasury Bonds are guaranteed by the U.S. government and, if held to maturity, offer a fixed rate of return and principal value. You should consult with a financial professional.

Plan Aid Table 17:
Tax-Deferred Account Asset Growth Factor Table

Years to Retire	Asset Growth Rate Assumption							
	5.0%	6.0%	7.0%	8.0%	9.0%	10.0%	11.0%	12.0%
1	1.05	1.06	1.07	1.08	1.09	1.10	1.11	1.12
2	1.10	1.12	1.14	1.17	1.19	1.21	1.23	1.25
3	1.16	1.19	1.23	1.26	1.30	1.33	1.37	1.40
4	1.22	1.26	1.31	1.36	1.41	1.46	1.52	1.57
5	1.28	1.34	1.40	1.47	1.54	1.61	1.69	1.76
6	1.34	1.42	1.50	1.59	1.68	1.77	1.87	1.97
7	1.41	1.50	1.61	1.71	1.83	1.95	2.08	2.21
8	1.48	1.59	1.72	1.85	1.99	2.14	2.30	2.48
9	1.55	1.69	1.84	2.00	2.17	2.36	2.56	2.77
10	1.63	1.79	1.97	2.16	2.37	2.59	2.84	3.11
11	1.71	1.90	2.10	2.33	2.58	2.85	3.15	3.48
12	1.80	2.01	2.25	2.52	2.81	3.14	3.50	3.90
13	1.89	2.13	2.41	2.72	3.07	3.45	3.88	4.36
14	1.98	2.26	2.58	2.94	3.34	3.80	4.31	4.89
15	2.08	2.40	2.76	3.17	3.64	4.18	4.78	5.47
16	2.18	2.54	2.95	3.43	3.97	4.59	5.31	6.13
17	2.29	2.69	3.16	3.70	4.33	5.05	5.90	6.87
18	2.41	2.85	3.38	4.00	4.72	5.56	6.54	7.69
19	2.53	3.03	3.62	4.32	5.14	6.12	7.26	8.61
20	2.65	3.21	3.87	4.66	5.60	6.73	8.06	9.65
21	2.79	3.40	4.14	5.03	6.11	7.40	8.95	10.80
22	2.93	3.60	4.43	**5.44**	6.66	8.14	9.93	12.10
23	3.07	3.82	4.74	5.87	7.26	8.95	11.03	13.55
24	3.23	4.05	5.07	6.34	7.91	9.85	12.24	15.18
25	3.39	4.29	5.43	6.85	8.62	10.83	13.59	17.00
26	3.56	4.55	5.81	7.40	9.40	11.92	15.08	19.04
27	3.73	4.82	6.21	7.99	10.25	13.11	16.74	21.32
28	3.92	5.11	6.65	8.63	11.17	14.42	18.58	23.88
29	4.12	5.42	7.11	9.32	12.17	15.86	20.62	26.75
30	4.32	5.74	7.61	10.06	13.27	17.45	22.89	29.96
31	4.54	6.09	8.15	10.87	14.46	19.19	25.41	33.56
32	4.76	6.45	8.72	11.74	15.76	21.11	28.21	37.58
33	5.00	6.84	9.33	12.68	17.18	23.23	31.31	42.09
34	5.25	7.25	9.98	13.69	18.73	25.55	34.75	47.14
35	5.52	7.69	10.68	14.79	20.41	28.10	38.57	52.80
36	5.79	8.15	11.42	15.97	22.25	30.91	42.82	59.14
37	6.08	8.64	12.22	17.25	24.25	34.00	47.53	66.23
38	6.39	9.15	13.08	18.63	26.44	37.40	52.76	74.18
39	6.70	9.70	13.99	20.12	28.82	41.14	58.56	83.08
40	7.04	10.29	14.97	21.72	31.41	45.26	65.00	93.05
41	7.39	10.90	16.02	23.46	34.24	49.79	72.15	104.22
42	7.76	11.56	17.14	25.34	37.32	54.76	80.09	116.72
43	8.15	12.25	18.34	27.37	40.68	60.24	88.90	130.73
44	8.56	12.99	19.63	29.56	44.34	66.26	98.68	146.42
45	8.99	13.76	21.00	31.92	48.33	72.89	109.53	163.99
46	9.43	14.59	22.47	34.47	52.68	80.18	121.58	183.67
47	9.91	15.47	24.05	37.23	57.42	88.20	134.95	205.71
48	10.40	16.39	25.73	40.21	62.59	97.02	149.80	230.39
49	10.92	17.38	27.53	43.43	68.22	106.72	166.27	258.04
50	11.47	18.42	29.46	46.90	74.36	117.39	184.56	289.00

For illustration purposes only. Not representative of an actual investment. All assumptions and computational results are hypothetical in nature. Higher volatility has historically been associated with higher rates of return, and average returns have had a tendency to fluctuate from year to year.

Plan Aid 16b: Your Plan
Current IRA Balances

Current IRA Balances .... (a) $

Number of Years until Retirement .... (b)
(From item (c), Plan Aid 1b: Your Plan, on page 13)

Asset Growth Rate Assumption .... (c)   %
(Use Plan Aid 17b: Your Plan, on page 194 to estimate rate of return)
(Select 5%, 6%, 7%, 8%, 9%, 10%, 11%, or 12%)

Asset Growth Factor .... (d)
Look Up on Plan Aid Table 17, Using Items (b) and (c) above

Hypothetical Value of IRA Balances .... (e) $
Future Value Dollars in Year 1 of Retirement   *(a) x (d)*

For illustration purposes only. Not representative of an actual investment. An individual investors results may vary. All assumptions and computational results are hypothetical in nature. There are no guarantees that you will achieve the results shown. Higher volatility has historically been associated with higher rates of return, and average returns have had a tendency to fluctuate from year to year. You should consult with a financial professional.

Plan Aid 17b: Your Plan
Weighted Average Rate of Return
Current IRA Balances

Type of Asset	Asset Value	% of Assets	Expect. Ret.	Wtd. Ret.
	$	%	%	%
	$	%	%	%
	$	%	%	%
	$	%	%	%
	$	%	%	%
	$	%	%	%
	$	%	%	%
	$	%	%	%
	$	%	%	%
	$	%	%	%
Tot. Assets & Wtd. Ave. Return	$	%		%

For illustration purposes only. Not representative of an actual investment. An individual investors results may vary. All assumptions and computational results are hypothetical in nature. There are no guarantees that you will achieve the results shown. Higher volatility has historically been associated with higher rates of return, and average returns have had a tendency to fluctuate from year to year. You should consult with a financial professional.

17

Roth IRAs

In some ways Roth IRAs are very much like regular IRAs and in some ways they're quite different. We're not going to investigate all the similarities and differences or get into all the details surrounding their use—because the rules can get complicated and often change from year to year anyway. As with all other investments, you need to get the advice of a competent financial advisor before making any moves with your Roth IRAs—because you don't want to go astray in this area.

What Is a Roth IRA?

Just like a regular IRA, you can put money into a Roth IRA each year subject to income and contribution limits that need to be discussed with your own financial advisors. However, unlike regular IRAs, your contributions into Roth IRAs are not tax deductible—so you have to fund them with after-tax dollars.

However, you get a significant benefit in return, because with Roth IRAs you don't have to pay income taxes on withdrawals you make during retirement. So not only does your money grow tax-free, but you also get to take it out tax-free. This is a significant advantage. As a reminder, please keep in mind that with Roth IRAs any withdrawals of earnings prior to age 59½ will be subject to a 10 percent penalty and ordinary income tax.

But it gets even better, because unlike regular IRAs, which require you to begin making taxable withdrawals at age 70½, you are never forced to take money out of your Roth IRAs—so you can let it grow tax-free as long as you like. Obviously, the opportunity to earn tax-free growth for longer investment periods can lead to higher account balances, and the ability to make tax-free withdrawals during retirement can lead to enhanced lifestyles as well.

Roth IRAs and Financial Planning

Like regular IRAs, you need to consider Roth IRAs in two different ways. We start by estimating how much your current balances may be worth when you stop working, and then project the hypothetical value of future contributions you intend to make. At this point, to follow *Step #13: Project Roth IRA Balances,* we will consider only current account balances, and deal with future contributions later on.

Create Your Own Plan

Follow the steps outlined in Plan Aid 18a: Example to learn how to estimate the hypothetical future value of your accounts. Start with the total current value of all of your Roth IRAs, and enter that amount as your *Current Roth IRA Balances* in box (f). Since there is no limit on the number of Roth IRAs you can have, be sure to include all of them in this calculation. Next, enter the *Number of Years Until Retirement* in box (g), which is the same amount you calculated in item (c), Plan Aid 1a: Example on page 13.

Computing Your Weighted Average Rate of Return

Then, use Plan Aid 19a: Example to calculate your hypothetical weighted average asset growth rate assumption for the assets in your existing Roth IRAs. This is the average annual rate of return you might expect to earn on your Roth IRAs until the day you retire.

Plan Aid 18a: Example
Current Roth IRA Balances

Current Roth IRA Balances .... (f) $ **5,000**

Number of Years Until Retirement .... (g) **22**
    (From item (c), Plan Aid 1a: Example on page 13)

Asset Growth Rate Assumption .... (h) **8.0** %
    (Use Plan Aid 19a: Example on page 198 to estimate rate of return)
    (Select 5%, 6%, 7%, 8%, 9%, 10%, 11%, or 12%)

Asset Growth Factor .... (i) **5.44**
    Look Up on Plan Aid Table 19, Using Items (g) and (h) above

Preliminary Value of Roth IRA Balances .... (j) $ **27,200**
    Future Value Dollars in Year 1 of Retirement   *(f) x (i)*

Tax Adjustment Percentage .... (k) **70.0** %
    (From item (b), Plan Aid 11a: Example on page 168)

Hypothetical Value of Roth IRA Balances .... (l) $ **38,857**
    Future Value Dollars in Year 1 of Retirement   *(j) ÷ (k)*

For illustration purposes only. Not representative of an actual investment. An individual investors results may vary. All assumptions and computational results are hypothetical in nature. There are no guarantees that you will achieve the results shown. Higher volatility has historically been associated with higher rates of return, and average returns have had a tendency to fluctuate from year to year. You should consult with a financial professional.

After estimating your hypothetical weighted average rate of return, you can use it to help project the hypothetical future value of your Roth IRA balances. Start by rounding it either up or down to the nearest whole percentage, and then enter it as your *Asset Growth Rate Assumption* in box (h) on Plan Aid 18a: Example.

Then, turn to Plan Aid Table 19, and find the column related to your asset growth rate assumption and the row related to the number of years until retirement. Where they intersect in the table, you will find your *Asset Growth Factor*, which should be entered in box (i).

Next, multiply your *Asset Growth Factor* in box (i) by your *Current Roth IRA Balances* in box (f) to compute the *Preliminary Value of Roth IRA Balances* in box (j). This is a "preliminary" value because the amount in your Roth IRAs is actually worth more than the same amount in your regular IRAs, because your Roths provide *tax-free* income in retirement—and you need to account for that.

Plan Aid 19a: Example
Weighted Average Rate of Return
Current Roth IRA Balances

Type of Asset	Asset Value	% of Assets	Expect. Ret.	Wtd. Ret.
Treasury Bonds	$1,750	35.0%	6.0%	2.1%
Large Company Value Stocks	$1,000	20.0%	9.0%	1.8%
International Stocks	$1,750	35.0%	9.0%	3.2%
Small Company Growth Stocks	$250	5.0%	10.0%	0.5%
Mid-Cap Stocks	$250	5.0%	9.0%	0.5%
Tot. Assets & Wtd. Ave. Return	$5,000	100.0%		8.0%

For illustration purposes only. Not representative of an actual investment. An individual investors results may vary. All assumptions and computational results are hypothetical in nature. There are no guarantees that you will achieve the results shown. Higher volatility has historically been associated with higher rates of return, and average returns have had a tendency to fluctuate from year to year. The prices of large company, small company, international, and mid-cap stocks will fluctuate. Investing in international stocks may carry additional risks such as differing securities regulations and more volatile political and economic environments. Treasury Bonds are guaranteed by the U.S. government and, if held to maturity, offer a fixed rate of return and principal value. You should consult with a financial professional.

Plan Aid Table 19:
Tax-Deferred Account Asset Growth Factor Table

Years to Retire	Asset Growth Rate Assumption							
	5.0%	6.0%	7.0%	8.0%	9.0%	10.0%	11.0%	12.0%
1	1.05	1.06	1.07	1.08	1.09	1.10	1.11	1.12
2	1.10	1.12	1.14	1.17	1.19	1.21	1.23	1.25
3	1.16	1.19	1.23	1.26	1.30	1.33	1.37	1.40
4	1.22	1.26	1.31	1.36	1.41	1.46	1.52	1.57
5	1.28	1.34	1.40	1.47	1.54	1.61	1.69	1.76
6	1.34	1.42	1.50	1.59	1.68	1.77	1.87	1.97
7	1.41	1.50	1.61	1.71	1.83	1.95	2.08	2.21
8	1.48	1.59	1.72	1.85	1.99	2.14	2.30	2.48
9	1.55	1.69	1.84	2.00	2.17	2.36	2.56	2.77
10	1.63	1.79	1.97	2.16	2.37	2.59	2.84	3.11
11	1.71	1.90	2.10	2.33	2.58	2.85	3.15	3.48
12	1.80	2.01	2.25	2.52	2.81	3.14	3.50	3.90
13	1.89	2.13	2.41	2.72	3.07	3.45	3.88	4.36
14	1.98	2.26	2.58	2.94	3.34	3.80	4.31	4.89
15	2.08	2.40	2.76	3.17	3.64	4.18	4.78	5.47
16	2.18	2.54	2.95	3.43	3.97	4.59	5.31	6.13
17	2.29	2.69	3.16	3.70	4.33	5.05	5.90	6.87
18	2.41	2.85	3.38	4.00	4.72	5.56	6.54	7.69
19	2.53	3.03	3.62	4.32	5.14	6.12	7.26	8.61
20	2.65	3.21	3.87	4.66	5.60	6.73	8.06	9.65
21	2.79	3.40	4.14	5.03	6.11	7.40	8.95	10.80
22	2.93	3.60	4.43	5.44	6.66	8.14	9.93	12.10
23	3.07	3.82	4.74	5.87	7.26	8.95	11.03	13.55
24	3.23	4.05	5.07	6.34	7.91	9.85	12.24	15.18
25	3.39	4.29	5.43	6.85	8.62	10.83	13.59	17.00
26	3.56	4.55	5.81	7.40	9.40	11.92	15.08	19.04
27	3.73	4.82	6.21	7.99	10.25	13.11	16.74	21.32
28	3.92	5.11	6.65	8.63	11.17	14.42	18.58	23.88
29	4.12	5.42	7.11	9.32	12.17	15.86	20.62	26.75
30	4.32	5.74	7.61	10.06	13.27	17.45	22.89	29.96
31	4.54	6.09	8.15	10.87	14.46	19.19	25.41	33.56
32	4.76	6.45	8.72	11.74	15.76	21.11	28.21	37.58
33	5.00	6.84	9.33	12.68	17.18	23.23	31.31	42.09
34	5.25	7.25	9.98	13.69	18.73	25.55	34.75	47.14
35	5.52	7.69	10.68	14.79	20.41	28.10	38.57	52.80
36	5.79	8.15	11.42	15.97	22.25	30.91	42.82	59.14
37	6.08	8.64	12.22	17.25	24.25	34.00	47.53	66.23
38	6.39	9.15	13.08	18.63	26.44	37.40	52.76	74.18
39	6.70	9.70	13.99	20.12	28.82	41.14	58.56	83.08
40	7.04	10.29	14.97	21.72	31.41	45.26	65.00	93.05
41	7.39	10.90	16.02	23.46	34.24	49.79	72.15	104.22
42	7.76	11.56	17.14	25.34	37.32	54.76	80.09	116.72
43	8.15	12.25	18.34	27.37	40.68	60.24	88.90	130.73
44	8.56	12.99	19.63	29.56	44.34	66.26	98.68	146.42
45	8.99	13.76	21.00	31.92	48.33	72.89	109.53	163.99
46	9.43	14.59	22.47	34.47	52.68	80.18	121.58	183.67
47	9.91	15.47	24.05	37.23	57.42	88.20	134.95	205.71
48	10.40	16.39	25.73	40.21	62.59	97.02	149.80	230.39
49	10.92	17.38	27.53	43.43	68.22	106.72	166.27	258.04
50	11.47	18.42	29.46	46.90	74.36	117.39	184.56	289.00

For illustration purposes only. Not representative of an actual investment. All assumptions and computational results are hypothetical in nature. Higher volatility has historically been associated with higher rates of return, and average returns have had a tendency to fluctuate from year to year.

In Chapter 13: Think About Taxes, we discussed the importance of adjusting the value of certain assets to restate them "as if" they generate *taxable* income from within tax-deferred accounts. Obviously, your Roth IRAs are tax-deferred accounts, so you don't need to revalue them because of that.

However, Roth IRAs *don't* generate *taxable* income, so they need to be adjusted upward to revalue them as if they did. If you don't do this, you will understate their value in terms of their ability to provide income in retirement. Making this adjustment doesn't actually mean that you have more money in the account—it simply means that since these withdrawals are generally not taxable in retirement they may take care of a larger share of your retirement income needs.

So the next step is to make the necessary tax adjustment. To do this, enter your *Tax Adjustment Percentage* in box (k), which is the amount

Plan Aid 18b: Your Plan
Current Roth IRA Balances

Current Roth IRA Balances .... (f) $

Number of Years Until Retirement .... (g)
    (From item (c), Plan Aid 1b: Your Plan on page 13)

Asset Growth Rate Assumption .... (h)   %
    (Use Plan Aid 19b: Your Plan on page 201 to estimate rate of return)
    (Select 5%, 6%, 7%, 8%, 9%, 10%, 11%, or 12%)

Asset Growth Factor .... (i)
    Look Up on Plan Aid Table 19, Using Items (g) and (h) above

Preliminary Value of Roth IRA Balances .... (j) $
    Future Value Dollars in Year 1 of Retirement   *(f) x (i)*

Tax Adjustment Percentage .... (k)   %
    (From item (b), Plan Aid 11b: Your Plan on page 170)

Hypothetical Value of Roth IRA Balances .... (l) $
    Future Value Dollars in Year 1 of Retirement   *(j) ÷ (k)*

For illustration purposes only. Not representative of an actual investment. An individual investors results may vary. All assumptions and computational results are hypothetical in nature. There are no guarantees that you will achieve the results shown. Higher volatility has historically been associated with higher rates of return, and average returns have had a tendency to fluctuate from year to year. You should consult with a financial professional.

Plan Aid 19b: Your Plan
Weighted Average Rate of Return
Current Roth IRA Balances

Type of Asset	Asset Value	% of Assets	Expect. Ret.	Wtd. Ret.
	$	%	%	%
	$	%	%	%
	$	%	%	%
	$	%	%	%
	$	%	%	%
	$	%	%	%
	$	%	%	%
	$	%	%	%
	$	%	%	%
	$	%	%	%
Tot. Assets & Wtd. Ave. Return	$	%		%

For illustration purposes only. Not representative of an actual investment. An individual investors results may vary. All assumptions and computational results are hypothetical in nature. There are no guarantees that you will achieve the results shown. Higher volatility has historically been associated with higher rates of return, and average returns have had a tendency to fluctuate from year to year. You should consult with a financial professional.

you calculated in item (b), Plan Aid 11a: Example on page 168. Then, divide the *Preliminary Value of Roth IRA Balances* in box (j) by your *Tax Adjustment Percentage* in box (k) to compute the *Hypothetical Value of Roth IRA Balances,* and enter it in box (l). This is what your current Roth IRAs might be worth when you stop working, in terms of their ability to provide taxable income in retirement. In a very real sense, this is the part of your final accumulation target that may have already been taken care of by your previous Roth IRA contributions. You don't have this much value in your accounts today, but if you expect your Roth IRAs to keep growing you are calculating what your assets in these accounts might be worth in the future.

After reviewing the example, use Plan Aid 18b: Your Plan to calculate how much you think *your* Roth IRAs might be worth when you decide to stop working. Use Plan Aid 19b: Your Plan to estimate your own hypothetical weighted average rate of return. If you don't have any Roth IRA accounts you can leave this part blank.

18

Annuities

There are many different kinds of annuities, and they offer a wide variety of features and benefits, so you need to get the advice of a knowledgeable financial professional if you want to consider investing in them. Annuities can play a very important role in your overall financial plan, but you have to work with someone who knows what they're doing.

Entire books have been written about annuities, so if you're interested in learning more, there are other resources available. We're only going to scratch the surface of this multifaceted and complicated topic, to help you understand enough about annuities to build them into your own retirement plan.

What Is an Annuity?

As already discussed in Chapter 11, in the simplest terms annuities are investments sold by insurance companies that allow you to invest your money without having to pay income taxes on your investment gains until you take them out during retirement—much like IRAs and retirement plans, although there are significant differences.

There are a few things you should always think about when considering annuities. We have gone through some of this already, but it's important to say it again. First, an investment in a variable annuity involves investment risk, including the possible loss of your principal. Investment returns and principal values will fluctuate, so that upon redemption, your contracts may be worth more or less than their original cost. Annuities are designed for long-term retirement investing, and variable annuities are available by prospectus only. Also, withdrawals of taxable amounts are subject to income tax and, if taken prior to age 59½, a 10 percent federal tax penalty may apply. Early withdrawals may also be subject to withdrawal charges imposed by the issuing company. You should also know that the purchase of a variable annuity is not required for, and cannot be a term of the provision of any banking service or activity, and that an investment in the securities underlying a variable annuity is not guaranteed or endorsed by any bank, is not a deposit or obligation of any bank, and is not federally insured by the FDIC, the Federal Reserve Board, or any other government agency. And finally, any guarantees offered in an annuity contract are only backed by the claims-paying ability of the issuer. Obviously, you should always discuss the appropriateness of annuities with a financial professional.

Keep in mind too that tax-qualified contracts such as IRAs, 401(k) plans, etc. are tax-deferred regardless of whether or not they are funded with an annuity. However, annuities do provide other features and benefits including, but not limited to, a guaranteed death benefit and income options, for which mortality and expense fees are charged.

How to Categorize Annuities

An easy way to bring annuities into focus is to think about them in two different ways. First, how is your money invested? Do you earn a guaranteed fixed interest rate or can you put the money to work in the stock market? Second, when do you expect to start withdrawing money from the contract? Do you need to get income right away, or can you wait until later to take it out?

Fixed and Variable Annuities

A fixed annuity pays a guaranteed rate of interest based on the financial strength of the issuing company for a specific period of time. A variable annuity, on the other hand, allows you to invest in a variety of stock market accounts that are usually managed by different investment managers. With variable annuities, you generally have the same range of investment options that you have with any other type of account, so you should be able to use them to help meet many of your financial objectives. In both cases, the issuing insurance company ultimately pays your money back through a varied choice of withdrawal and/or installment payment options during your retirement years.

Immediate and Deferred Annuities

Another way to look at annuities is to consider whether they are immediate or deferred. Immediate annuities are investment contracts that start paying out income as soon as you buy them. As we discussed in Chapter 11, you will most often use immediate annuities during retirement, because they provide an easy way for you to create your own Income Ladders.

Deferred annuities, on the other hand, are geared more toward long-term accumulation needs, and generally won't be used for income until many years in the future. Although you will probably use them during retirement too, we're most interested in them at this point because they may help you accumulate larger balances for retirement.

Annuities and Your Financial Plan

In some ways annuities are like Roth IRAs, in other ways they're like regular IRAs—and in many ways they're like neither. Because of the unique way annuities are treated for income tax purposes, you have to be careful about how you build them into your financial plan, because they need to be revalued to reflect their special tax treatment.

What Makes Annuities So Different?

One of the most important differences between annuities and IRAs is that there are no legal limits on how much you can put into annuity contracts, although issuing companies can set their own restrictions. So unlike both regular and Roth IRAs, which have income and contribution limits, you can generally put as much as you want into annuities, and you have the flexibility, with some issuer based restrictions, to do it whenever you like.

This is just one of the reasons why people use annuities when they get substantial amounts of money—like when they receive an inheritance or insurance settlement, or when they sell a home or business. Annuity contracts are one of the only ways to get large amounts of money into tax-deferred environments quickly.

How Are Annuities Similar to Roth IRAs?

Like Roth IRAs, the contributions you make into annuities are *not* tax deductible—so all of your deposits are made on an after-tax basis. Also, similar to Roth IRAs, you are never forced under IRS regulations to take money out of your annuity contracts, so you often have a great deal of flexibility when it comes to making withdrawals. However, unlike Roth IRAs, you don't get to take your earnings out of annuities tax-free. In this regard at least, they are more similar to regular IRAs, because you have to pay income tax on at least part of the money you take out.

How Are Annuities Similar to Regular IRAs?

Taking money out of annuities is different than taking money out of regular IRAs, however, because you don't have to pay tax on all of it. Each withdrawal you make is considered to be partially a return of the money you put in, and partially a distribution of taxable earnings in the account. Since you already paid tax on the money you contributed, you're not required to pay it again. As a result, your withdrawals are only *partially* taxed, unlike regular IRAs and 401(k) plans, which almost always generate 100 percent taxable income. This has important consequences for how you value your projected annuity balances.

You also need to remember that you may have to pay a 10 percent penalty on withdrawals taken prior to age 59½, and that the issuing insurance company may impose surrender penalties. So be sure to get the help of your advisors when planning your annuity withdrawals.

Annuities and Financial Planning

Just like regular and Roth IRAs, you have to consider your annuity accounts in two parts. We start by estimating how much your current balances may be worth when you stop working, and later on we project the hypothetical value of future contributions you intend to make. For now, however, to follow *Step #14: Project Annuity Balances*, we will consider only current balances of fixed and variable annuities.

Create Your Own Plan

Follow the steps outlined in Plan Aid 20a: Example to get a feel for how to estimate the hypothetical future value of your annuities. Start with the total current value of all of your annuity contracts, and enter that amount as your *Current Annuity Contract Balances* in box (a). Since there are no limits on the number of annuities you can own, be sure to include all of them in this calculation. Next, enter the *Number of Years Until Retirement* in box (b), which is the same amount you calculated in item (c), Plan Aid 1a: Example on page 13.

Computing Your Weighted Average Rate of Return

Then, use Plan Aid 21a: Example to calculate your hypothetical weighted average asset growth rate assumption for the assets in your existing annuities. This is the average annual rate of return you might plan to earn on your annuity contracts until you retire. If you own any fixed annuity contracts or invest in fixed separate accounts within a variable annuity, you should calculate your hypothetical weighted average rate of return using the guaranteed rates listed in your contract and the dollar amounts for each, separate from any stock market–related investments in your annuities. Also, be advised that all fixed rates of return are based upon the claims-paying ability of the issuer and subject to the terms and conditions of the annuity contract.

After estimating your hypothetical weighted average rate of return, you can project the hypothetical future value of your annuity contracts. Start by rounding the weighted average rate of return either up or down

Plan Aid 20a: Example
Current Annuity Contract Balances

Current Annuity Contract Balances .... (a) $ **5,000**

Number of Years Until Retirement .... (b) **22**
  (From item (c), Plan Aid 1a: Example on page 13)

Asset Growth Rate Assumption .... (c) **8.0** %
  (Use Plan Aid 21a: Example on page 209 to estimate rate of return)
  (Select 5%, 6%, 7%, 8%, 9%, 10%, 11%, or 12%)

Asset Growth Factor .... (d) **5.44**
  Look Up on Plan Aid Table 21a, Using Items (b) and (c) above

Preliminary Value of Annuity Balances .... (e) $ **27,200**
  Future Value Dollars in Year 1 of Retirement   *(a) x (d)*

Amount You Contributed to the Annuity .... (f) $ **2,500**

Exclusion Factor .... (g) **.09**
                                                              (f) ÷ (e)

Combined Tax Rate Assumption .... (h) **30.0** %
  (From item (a), Plan Aid 11a: Example on page 168)

Exclusion Factor Adjustment .... (i) **1.02**
  Look Up on Plan Aid Table 21b, Using Items (g) and (h) above

Hypothetical Value of Annuity Balances .... (j) $ **27,744**
  Future Value Dollars in Year 1 of Retirement   *(e) x (i)*

For illustration purposes only. Not representative of an actual investment. An individual investors results may vary. All assumptions and computational results are hypothetical in nature. Varaiable annuity contracts do have annual fees and expenses that have not been included here in order to simplify the example. If included, the results would be lower. There are no guarantees that you will achieve the results shown. Higher volatility has historically been associated with higher rates of return, and average returns have had a tendency to fluctuate from year to year. You should consult with a financial professional.

Plan Aid 21a: Example
Weighted Average Rate of Return
Current Annuity Contract Balances

Type of Asset	Asset Value	% of Assets	Expect. Ret.	Wtd. Ret.
Treasury Bonds	$1,000	20.0%	6.0%	1.2%
Large Company Value Stocks	$1,750	35.0%	9.0%	3.2%
International Stocks	$1,500	30.0%	9.0%	2.7%
Small Company Growth Stocks	$500	10.0%	10.0%	1.0%
Mid-Cap Stocks	$250	5.0%	9.0%	0.5%
Tot. Assets & Wtd. Ave. Return	$5,000	100.0%		8.5%

For illustration purposes only. Not representative of an actual investment. An individual investors results may vary. All assumptions and computational results are hypothetical in nature. Variable annuity contracts do have annual fees and expenses that have not been included here in order to simplify the example. If included, the results would be lower. There are no guarantees that you will achieve the results shown. Higher volatility has historically been associated with higher rates of return, and average returns have had a tendency to fluctuate from year to year. The prices of large company, small company, international, and mid-cap stocks will fluctuate. Investing in international stocks may carry additional risks such as differing securities regulations and more volatile political and economic environments. Treasury Bonds are guaranteed by the U.S. government and, if held to maturity, offer a fixed rate of return and principal value. You should consult with a financial professional.

to the nearest whole percentage, and then enter it as your *Asset Growth Rate Assumption* in box (c) on Plan Aid 20a: Example.

Then, turn to Plan Aid Table 21a, and find the column related to your asset growth rate assumption and the row related to the number of years until retirement. Where they intersect in the table, you will find your *Asset Growth Factor*, which should be entered in box (d).

Next, multiply your *Asset Growth Factor* in box (d) by your *Current Annuity Contract Balances* in box (a) to compute the *Preliminary Value of Annuity Balances* in box (e). This is a "preliminary" value because the total amount in your annuity contracts may actually be worth more than this, because annuities provide income that is at least *partially tax-free*— so you need to account for the fact that only part of what you take out during retirement will be taxed.

As we've discussed many times, you have to adjust the value of certain assets to restate them as if they are generating *taxable* income from within tax-deferred accounts. Since your annuity contracts are tax-deferred—which is why you probably invested in them in the first place— you obviously don't need to revalue them in that regard.

However, as I said just a moment ago, annuities *don't* generate 100 percent taxable income, so they need to be adjusted upward to revalue them as if they did. If you don't make this adjustment, you will understate their value in terms of their ability to provide income in retirement. Making this adjustment doesn't actually mean that you'll have more money in your annuities—it simply means that the money you do have may be able to take care of a larger share of your retirement income needs.

To make the necessary adjustment, you need to estimate how much of your annuity's hypothetical value at retirement may have come from growth, compared to how much you contributed yourself. To do this, enter the *Amount You Contributed to the Annuity* in box (f). This should be the total amount of your own money invested in all of your annuity contracts.

Next, divide the *Amount You Contributed to the Annuity* in box (f) by the *Preliminary Value of Annuity Balances* in box (e) to compute your *Exclusion Factor*, which should be entered in box (g). This is just a fancy name for the percentage of your hypothetical annuity balance that will

Plan Aid Table 21a:
Tax-Deferred Account Asset Growth Factor Table

Years to Retire	Asset Growth Rate Assumption							
	5.0%	6.0%	7.0%	8.0%	9.0%	10.0%	11.0%	12.0%
1	1.05	1.06	1.07	1.08	1.09	1.10	1.11	1.12
2	1.10	1.12	1.14	1.17	1.19	1.21	1.23	1.25
3	1.16	1.19	1.23	1.26	1.30	1.33	1.37	1.40
4	1.22	1.26	1.31	1.36	1.41	1.46	1.52	1.57
5	1.28	1.34	1.40	1.47	1.54	1.61	1.69	1.76
6	1.34	1.42	1.50	1.59	1.68	1.77	1.87	1.97
7	1.41	1.50	1.61	1.71	1.83	1.95	2.08	2.21
8	1.48	1.59	1.72	1.85	1.99	2.14	2.30	2.48
9	1.55	1.69	1.84	2.00	2.17	2.36	2.56	2.77
10	1.63	1.79	1.97	2.16	2.37	2.59	2.84	3.11
11	1.71	1.90	2.10	2.33	2.58	2.85	3.15	3.48
12	1.80	2.01	2.25	2.52	2.81	3.14	3.50	3.90
13	1.89	2.13	2.41	2.72	3.07	3.45	3.88	4.36
14	1.98	2.26	2.58	2.94	3.34	3.80	4.31	4.89
15	2.08	2.40	2.76	3.17	3.64	4.18	4.78	5.47
16	2.18	2.54	2.95	3.43	3.97	4.59	5.31	6.13
17	2.29	2.69	3.16	3.70	4.33	5.05	5.90	6.87
18	2.41	2.85	3.38	4.00	4.72	5.56	6.54	7.69
19	2.53	3.03	3.62	4.32	5.14	6.12	7.26	8.61
20	2.65	3.21	3.87	4.66	5.60	6.73	8.06	9.65
21	2.79	3.40	4.14	5.03	6.11	7.40	8.95	10.80
22	2.93	3.60	4.43	5.44	6.66	8.14	9.93	12.10
23	3.07	3.82	4.74	5.87	7.26	8.95	11.03	13.55
24	3.23	4.05	5.07	6.34	7.91	9.85	12.24	15.18
25	3.39	4.29	5.43	6.85	8.62	10.83	13.59	17.00
26	3.56	4.55	5.81	7.40	9.40	11.92	15.08	19.04
27	3.73	4.82	6.21	7.99	10.25	13.11	16.74	21.32
28	3.92	5.11	6.65	8.63	11.17	14.42	18.58	23.88
29	4.12	5.42	7.11	9.32	12.17	15.86	20.62	26.75
30	4.32	5.74	7.61	10.06	13.27	17.45	22.89	29.96
31	4.54	6.09	8.15	10.87	14.46	19.19	25.41	33.56
32	4.76	6.45	8.72	11.74	15.76	21.11	28.21	37.58
33	5.00	6.84	9.33	12.68	17.18	23.23	31.31	42.09
34	5.25	7.25	9.98	13.69	18.73	25.55	34.75	47.14
35	5.52	7.69	10.68	14.79	20.41	28.10	38.57	52.80
36	5.79	8.15	11.42	15.97	22.25	30.91	42.82	59.14
37	6.08	8.64	12.22	17.25	24.25	34.00	47.53	66.23
38	6.39	9.15	13.08	18.63	26.44	37.40	52.76	74.18
39	6.70	9.70	13.99	20.12	28.82	41.14	58.56	83.08
40	7.04	10.29	14.97	21.72	31.41	45.26	65.00	93.05
41	7.39	10.90	16.02	23.46	34.24	49.79	72.15	104.22
42	7.76	11.56	17.14	25.34	37.32	54.76	80.09	116.72
43	8.15	12.25	18.34	27.37	40.68	60.24	88.90	130.73
44	8.56	12.99	19.63	29.56	44.34	66.26	98.68	146.42
45	8.99	13.76	21.00	31.92	48.33	72.89	109.53	163.99
46	9.43	14.59	22.47	34.47	52.68	80.18	121.58	183.67
47	9.91	15.47	24.05	37.23	57.42	88.20	134.95	205.71
48	10.40	16.39	25.73	40.21	62.59	97.02	149.80	230.39
49	10.92	17.38	27.53	43.43	68.22	106.72	166.27	258.04
50	11.47	18.42	29.46	46.90	74.36	117.39	184.56	289.00

For illustration purposes only. Not representative of an actual investment. All assumptions and computational results are hypothetical in nature. Higher volatility has historically been associated with higher rates of return, and average returns have had a tendency to fluctuate from year to year.

be made up of your own contributions—and it's an estimate of the percentage of each withdrawal you will eventually make that you should get back tax-free.

The next step is to enter your *Combined Tax Rate Assumption* into box (h), which is the same amount you determined in box (a), Plan Aid 11a: Example on page 168. Then, turn to Plan Aid Table 21b, and find the column related to your combined tax rate assumption and the row related to your exclusion factor—which should be rounded up or down to the nearest 10 percent. Where they intersect in the table, you will find your *Exclusion Factor Adjustment*, which should be entered into box (i).

Finally, multiply the *Preliminary Value of Annuity Balances* in box (e) by your *Exclusion Factor Adjustment* in box (i) to compute the *Hypothetical Value of Annuity Balances* in box (j). This is what you might plan for your current annuity contracts to be worth when you stop working, in terms of their ability to provide income in retirement. In essence, this is the part of your accumulation target that may have already been taken care of by previous contributions into your annuity accounts. You don't have this much value in your accounts today, but if you expect your annuities to keep growing you are calculating what your assets in these accounts might be worth in the future.

After reviewing the example, use Plan Aid 20b: Your Plan to calculate how much you think *your* annuities may be worth when you stop working. Use Plan Aid 21b: Your Plan to estimate your own hypothetical weighted average rate of return. If you don't have any annuity contracts you can leave this part blank.

Plan Aid Table 21b:
Exclusion Factor Adjustment for Annuities

Exclusion Factor	Combined Tax Rate Assumption					
	0%	10%	20%	30%	40%	50%
0.00	1.00	1.00	1.00	1.00	1.00	1.00
0.10	1.00	1.01	1.01	1.02	1.03	1.05
0.20	1.00	1.01	1.03	1.04	1.07	1.10
0.30	1.00	1.02	1.04	1.06	1.10	1.15
0.40	1.00	1.02	1.05	1.09	1.13	1.20
0.50	1.00	1.03	1.06	1.11	1.17	1.25
0.60	1.00	1.03	1.08	1.13	1.20	1.30
0.70	1.00	1.04	1.09	1.15	1.23	1.35
0.80	1.00	1.04	1.10	1.17	1.27	1.40
0.90	1.00	1.05	1.11	1.19	1.30	1.45
1.00	1.00	1.06	1.13	1.21	1.33	1.50

Plan Aid 20b: Your Plan
Current Annuity Contract Balances

Current Annuity Contract Balances ....…........... (a) $ [   ]

Number of Years Until Retirement ....…........... (b) [   ]
(From item (c), Plan Aid 1b: Your Plan on page 13)

Asset Growth Rate Assumption ....…............ (c) [%   ]
(Use Plan Aid 21b: Your Plan on page 215 to estimate rate of return)
(Select 5%, 6%, 7%, 8%, 9%, 10%, 11%, or 12%)

Asset Growth Factor ....………...........…..…...... (d) [   ]
Look Up on Plan Aid Table 21a, Using Items (b) and (c) above

Preliminary Value of Annuity Balances ....…..... (e) $ [   ]
Future Value Dollars in Year 1 of Retirement   *(a) x (d)*

Amount You Contributed to the Annuity ....…..... (f) $ [   ]

Exclusion Factor ....…...........…..…........…...... (g) [   ]
                                                                      (f) ÷ (e)

Combined Tax Rate Assumption ....…............ (h) [%   ]
(From item (a), Plan Aid 11b: Your Plan on page 170)

Exclusion Factor Adjustment ....…................ (i) [   ]
Look Up on Plan Aid Table 21b, Using Items (g) and (h) above

Hypothetical Value of Annuity Balances ....….... (j) $ [   ]
Future Value Dollars in Year 1 of Retirement   *(e) x (i)*

For illustration purposes only. Not representative of an actual investment. An individual investors results may
vary. All assumptions and computational results are hypothetical in nature. Varaiable annuity contracts do have
annual fees and expenses that have not been included here in order to simplify the example. If included, the
results would be lower. There are no guarantees that you will achieve the results shown. Higher volatility has
historically been associated with higher rates of return, and average returns have had a tendency to fluctuate
from year to year. You should consult with a financial professional.

Plan Aid 21b: Your Plan
Weighted Average Rate of Return
Current Annuity Contract Balances

Type of Asset	Asset Value	% of Assets	Expect. Ret.	Wtd. Ret.
	$	%	%	%
	$	%	%	%
	$	%	%	%
	$	%	%	%
	$	%	%	%
	$	%	%	%
	$	%	%	%
	$	%	%	%
	$	%	%	%
	$	%	%	%
Tot. Assets & Wtd. Ave. Return	$	%		%

For illustration purposes only. Not representative of an actual investment. An individual investors results may vary. All assumptions and computational results are hypothetical in nature. Variable annuity contracts do have annual fees and expenses that have not been included here in order to simplify the example. If included, the results would be lower. There are no guarantees that you will achieve the results shown. Higher volatility has historically been associated with higher rates of return, and average returns have had a tendency to fluctuate from year to year. You should consult with a financial professional.

19

Taxable Investments

People invest in taxable accounts for many different reasons. You might be saving for a car, a vacation, or maybe a down payment on a house. But most of the time you don't use taxable accounts for long-term retirement investing—because the tax burden can really inhibit the overall growth you may get. In other words, taxable investments generally lead to smaller account balances, because you give up so much of your return to taxes along the way.

Don't Include Nonretirement Savings in Your Financial Plan

If you're saving for something other than retirement and accumulating money for other needs, you probably shouldn't include those amounts in your long-term retirement plan. Obviously, the money you have earmarked for other purposes isn't going to be available when you retire—so you need to be careful about deciding which assets to build into your plan and which assets to leave out.

You May Use Taxable Investments to Accumulate Money for Retirement

On the other hand, you may have taxable assets that you plan to use for retirement, or at least hope you can use for retirement, which may potentially be used for other purposes instead—like moving, unanticipated home repairs, a child or grandchild's education, or some other unanticipated contingency. If there's a possibility that you'll need the money before you retire, you probably don't want to have it in tax-deferred retirement accounts, because there may be fees, taxes, and/or penalties associated with using it too soon.

However, you may want to build some of these taxable assets into your retirement plan even if you have to take a tax hit to maintain the flexibility you need. For example, many advisors recommend that you have four or five months' worth of living expenses stashed away for a rainy day, and that money will almost certainly be invested in taxable accounts.

If you decide to create an emergency fund, you obviously won't be planning to use the money anytime soon—because it's your safety net. But that doesn't mean that you can tie it up in retirement accounts either, because you may need it on a moment's notice. As a result, you're not going to invest it in an IRA or annuity. Even if you ultimately plan to use it for retirement, you'll probably need to keep the money in a taxable account until you stop working.

Most People Have Taxable Retirement Accounts

Even though they probably won't accumulate as much, you're likely to own at least a few assets that you hope to use for retirement but need to keep invested in taxable accounts. So you have to follow *Step #15: Project Taxable Account Balances* to take them into account when developing your long-term financial plan.

Then, to take it a step further, you also need to evaluate the potential consequences of moving those taxable assets into tax-deferred accounts when you get to retirement—if it turns out that you don't need them beforehand. This is an important consideration, because you may be able to get more income during retirement if you transfer them into tax-deferred accounts than if you leave them in taxable accounts.

What Is a Taxable Account?

Taxable accounts are simply investments that don't include provisions for the deferral or elimination of income taxes. Examples are certificates of deposit, mutual funds, individual stocks and bonds, savings accounts, and anything else you invest in outside of your regular and Roth IRAs, retirement plans, and annuity contracts.

Your Own Tax Situation

Different investments come with different tax characteristics and different tax consequences—depending upon your overall tax rate, income, investment activity, and many other variables. We can't possibly address all of these issues, and certainly not on an individual basis—which is just another reason to work with a financial professional. The main thing to remember now is that for planning purposes, we assume that you will be paying taxes every year on the growth in your taxable accounts, based upon the tax rate you may be subject to.

Taxable Accounts and Your Financial Plan

Your taxable accounts have to be treated differently than your retirement plans, regular and Roth IRAs, and annuities. The fact that your earnings will be taxed every year means that you may accumulate less in these accounts over time—which is the price you pay for maintaining flexibility. But there are other differences too.

Taxable Accounts Provide "After-Tax" Income

Because we assume that you're going to pay taxes each year on the earnings in your taxable accounts, by the time you get to retirement you may have less than if you invested the same amount in a tax-deferred vehicle like an IRA or annuity. However, although the balances may be lower, they might also be worth more, because income taxes on the growth in these accounts will often have already been paid—so they may be able to generate more "after-tax" income during retirement.

In other words, you won't have to pay income tax again on most of the money coming out of your taxable accounts during retirement, because you may already have paid it—and since you're planning for the amount of *pretax* income you need, you have to adjust these accounts upward to reflect the enhanced values.

You May Not Be Managing Inside of Tax-Deferred Accounts

There is also something else you need to be aware of. If you don't transfer your taxable assets into tax-deferred accounts at retirement time, you may end up suffering significant tax consequences.

Because you will generally be selling stock market investments throughout retirement to periodically set aside the assets you need for income, you will typically want these sales transactions to take place within tax-deferred accounts if at all possible. That way, you can defer paying income taxes until you actually take money out of the accounts, as we discussed in Chapter 11.

Avoiding Liquidity Taxes

If you stay invested in taxable accounts, you'll probably have to pay what I call liquidity taxes every time you sell stocks during retirement, which may significantly reduce the amount of income you are likely to get out of your portfolio. Protecting yourself against these liquidity taxes is one of the most important reasons to take advantage of tax-deferred accounts in retirement.

If you don't plan to avoid the liquidity taxes, you will need to *reduce* the value of the assets you plan to leave in taxable accounts during retirement. If, however, you *do* plan to avoid the liquidity taxes, by moving your assets into tax-deferred accounts, you should be able to *increase* the hypothetical value of the assets to reflect the possibility that they may generate more income than if they were left in taxable accounts.

Two Kinds of Adjustments to Revalue Taxable Accounts

There are two kinds of adjustments you may need to make to your taxable accounts. First, you have to revalue them upward to account for the fact that you may not have to pay taxes on most of the income you take out during retirement. And second, you have to revalue them either *up* or *down*, depending upon whether or not you move the assets into tax-deferred accounts when you stop working. The tax adjustment factors we use in this chapter take both of these adjustments into account.

Taxable Accounts and Financial Planning

Just like the rest of your accounts, you need to consider your taxable assets in two separate pieces. We start by estimating how much your current account balances may be worth when you stop working, and then we project the hypothetical value of future contributions a little later. For now, we'll take *Step #15: Project Taxable Account Balances*, by considering only your existing assets.

Create Your Own Plan

Let's go through the steps outlined in Plan Aid 22a: Example to see how to estimate the hypothetical future value of your taxable accounts. Start with the total current value of all your taxable accounts, and enter that amount as your *Current Taxable Account Balances* in box (a). Since there are no limits on the number of taxable accounts you can have, be sure to include all of them in this calculation. Next, enter the *Number of Years Until Retirement* in box (b), which is the same amount you calculated in item (c), Plan Aid 1a: Example on page 13.

Plan Aid 22a: Example
Taxable Accounts

Current Taxable Account Balances .... | (a) $ | **5,000**

Number of Years Until Retirement .... | (b) | **22**
(From item (c), Plan Aid 1a: Example on page 13)

Asset Growth Rate Assumption .... | (c) | **8.0** %
(Use Plan Aid 23a: Example on page 223 to estimate rate of return)
(Select 5%, 6%, 7%, 8%, 9%, 10%, 11%, or 12%)

Combined Tax Rate Assumption .... | (d) | **30.0** %
(From item (a), Plan Aid 11a: Example on page 168)

Lookup Table for Appropriate Tax Rate .... | (e) | **Table 23d**
Select lookup table for appropriate tax rate below | *From Index Table below*

Asset Growth Factor .... | (f) | **3.32**
Look Up on Table Noted in Item (e) above, Using Items (b) and (c) above

Preliminary Value of Taxable Accounts .... | (g) $ | **16,600**
Future Value Dollars in Year 1 of Retirement | *(a) x (f)*

IF TAXABLE ASSETS REMAIN IN TAXABLE ACCOUNTS

Taxable Account Adjustment Factor .... | (h) | **.97**
(From item (c), Plan Aid 11a: Example on page 168)

Hypothetical Value of Taxable Accounts .... | (i) $ | **16,102**
Future Value Dollars in Year 1 of Retirement | *(g) x (h)*

IF TAXABLE ASSETS PUT INTO TAX-DEFERRED ACCOUNTS

Tax-Deferred Account Adjustment Factor .... | (j) | **1.21**
(From item (d), Plan Aid 11a: Example on page 168)

Hypothetical Value of Taxable Accounts .... | (k) $ | **20,086**
Future Value Dollars in Year 1 of Retirement | *(g) x (j)*

SELECTED VALUE (TAXABLE OR TAX-DEFERRED)

Hypothetical Value of Current Taxable Accounts ..... | (l) $ | **20,086**
Future Value Dollars in Year 1 of Retirement | *Select item (i) or (k) above*

INDEX FOR TAX RATE TABLES
Use tax rate in item (d) above to select appropriate lookup table below

Total Tax Rate	0%	....	Plan Aid Table 23a
Total Tax Rate	10%	....	Plan Aid Table 23b
Total Tax Rate	20%	....	Plan Aid Table 23c
Total Tax Rate	30%	....	Plan Aid Table 23d
Total Tax Rate	40%	....	Plan Aid Table 23e
Total Tax Rate	50%	....	Plan Aid Table 23f

Computing Your Weighted Average Rate of Return

Then, using Plan Aid 23a: Example, calculate a hypothetical weighted average rate of return for the assets in your taxable accounts. This is the average annual pretax rate of return you might plan to earn on the accounts until you retire.

Next, round the weighted average rate of return either up or down to the nearest whole percentage, and enter it as your *Asset Growth Rate Assumption* in box (c) on Plan Aid 22a: Example.

After estimating your hypothetical weighted average rate of return, you are almost ready to project the hypothetical future value of your taxable accounts. But first you have to consider your tax situation—because it has a direct bearing on how much you will be able to accumulate. Obviously, the higher your estimated tax rate, the lower your projected account balance when you get to retirement. So the next step is to enter your *Combined Tax Rate Assumption* into box (d), which is the same amount you used in box (a), Plan Aid 11a: Example on page 168.

Then, to determine which lookup table to use in estimating the hypothetical future value of your accounts, look down to the Index for Tax Rate Tables at the bottom of the page, and find the table that relates to your combined tax rate assumption in box (d). Note which table you are going to use in box (e), *Lookup Table for Appropriate Tax Rate*. This table will provide an asset growth factor that helps you to project your taxable account balances based upon your own tax rate assumption.

Once you know which table to use, locate it in pages 224 through 229, and find the column related to your asset growth rate assumption and the row related to the number of years until retirement. Where they intersect in the table, you will find your *Asset Growth Factor*, which should be entered in box (f).

Next, multiply your *Asset Growth Factor* in box (f) by your *Current Taxable Account Balances* in box (a) to compute the *Preliminary Value of Taxable Accounts,* which should be entered into box (g). This is a preliminary value because in order to determine what it may actually be worth, it has to be revalued to reflect the fact that it will generate primarily after-tax income, and because you have to decide whether you're going to keep the money in a taxable account during retirement or move

Plan Aid 23a: Example
Weighted Average Rate of Return
Taxable Accounts

Type of Asset	Asset Value	% of Assets	Expect. Ret.	Wtd. Ret.
Treasury Bonds	$1,000	20.0%	5.0%	1.0%
Large Company Value Stocks	$1,750	35.0%	9.0%	3.2%
International Stocks	$1,500	30.0%	9.0%	2.7%
Small Company Growth Stocks	$500	10.0%	9.0%	0.9%
Mid-Cap Stocks	$250	5.0%	9.0%	0.5%
Tot. Assets & Wtd. Ave. Return	$5,000	100.0%		8.2%

For illustration purposes only. Not representative of an actual investment. An individual investors results may vary. All assumptions and computational results are hypothetical in nature. There are no guarantees that you will achieve the results shown. Higher volatility has historically been associated with higher rates of return, and average returns have had a tendency to fluctuate from year to year. The prices of large company, small company, international, and mid-cap stocks will fluctuate. Investing in international stocks may carry additional risks such as differing securities regulations and more volatile political and economic environments. Treasury Bonds are guaranteed by the U.S. government and, if held to maturity, offer a fixed rate of return and principal value. You should consult with a financial professional.

Plan Aid Table 23a:
Taxable Account Asset Growth Factor Table
(Total Tax Rate = 0%)

Years to Retire	Asset Growth Rate							
	5.0%	6.0%	7.0%	8.0%	9.0%	10.0%	11.0%	12.0%
1	1.05	1.06	1.07	1.08	1.09	1.10	1.11	1.12
2	1.10	1.12	1.14	1.17	1.19	1.21	1.23	1.25
3	1.16	1.19	1.23	1.26	1.30	1.33	1.37	1.40
4	1.22	1.26	1.31	1.36	1.41	1.46	1.52	1.57
5	1.28	1.34	1.40	1.47	1.54	1.61	1.69	1.76
6	1.34	1.42	1.50	1.59	1.68	1.77	1.87	1.97
7	1.41	1.50	1.61	1.71	1.83	1.95	2.08	2.21
8	1.48	1.59	1.72	1.85	1.99	2.14	2.30	2.48
9	1.55	1.69	1.84	2.00	2.17	2.36	2.56	2.77
10	1.63	1.79	1.97	2.16	2.37	2.59	2.84	3.11
11	1.71	1.90	2.10	2.33	2.58	2.85	3.15	3.48
12	1.80	2.01	2.25	2.52	2.81	3.14	3.50	3.90
13	1.89	2.13	2.41	2.72	3.07	3.45	3.88	4.36
14	1.98	2.26	2.58	2.94	3.34	3.80	4.31	4.89
15	2.08	2.40	2.76	3.17	3.64	4.18	4.78	5.47
16	2.18	2.54	2.95	3.43	3.97	4.59	5.31	6.13
17	2.29	2.69	3.16	3.70	4.33	5.05	5.90	6.87
18	2.41	2.85	3.38	4.00	4.72	5.56	6.54	7.69
19	2.53	3.03	3.62	4.32	5.14	6.12	7.26	8.61
20	2.65	3.21	3.87	4.66	5.60	6.73	8.06	9.65
21	2.79	3.40	4.14	5.03	6.11	7.40	8.95	10.80
22	2.93	3.60	4.43	5.44	6.66	8.14	9.93	12.10
23	3.07	3.82	4.74	5.87	7.26	8.95	11.03	13.55
24	3.23	4.05	5.07	6.34	7.91	9.85	12.24	15.18
25	3.39	4.29	5.43	6.85	8.62	10.83	13.59	17.00
26	3.56	4.55	5.81	7.40	9.40	11.92	15.08	19.04
27	3.73	4.82	6.21	7.99	10.25	13.11	16.74	21.32
28	3.92	5.11	6.65	8.63	11.17	14.42	18.58	23.88
29	4.12	5.42	7.11	9.32	12.17	15.86	20.62	26.75
30	4.32	5.74	7.61	10.06	13.27	17.45	22.89	29.96
31	4.54	6.09	8.15	10.87	14.46	19.19	25.41	33.56
32	4.76	6.45	8.72	11.74	15.76	21.11	28.21	37.58
33	5.00	6.84	9.33	12.68	17.18	23.23	31.31	42.09
34	5.25	7.25	9.98	13.69	18.73	25.55	34.75	47.14
35	5.52	7.69	10.68	14.79	20.41	28.10	38.57	52.80
36	5.79	8.15	11.42	15.97	22.25	30.91	42.82	59.14
37	6.08	8.64	12.22	17.25	24.25	34.00	47.53	66.23
38	6.39	9.15	13.08	18.63	26.44	37.40	52.76	74.18
39	6.70	9.70	13.99	20.12	28.82	41.14	58.56	83.08
40	7.04	10.29	14.97	21.72	31.41	45.26	65.00	93.05
41	7.39	10.90	16.02	23.46	34.24	49.79	72.15	104.22
42	7.76	11.56	17.14	25.34	37.32	54.76	80.09	116.72
43	8.15	12.25	18.34	27.37	40.68	60.24	88.90	130.73
44	8.56	12.99	19.63	29.56	44.34	66.26	98.68	146.42
45	8.99	13.76	21.00	31.92	48.33	72.89	109.53	163.99
46	9.43	14.59	22.47	34.47	52.68	80.18	121.58	183.67
47	9.91	15.47	24.05	37.23	57.42	88.20	134.95	205.71
48	10.40	16.39	25.73	40.21	62.59	97.02	149.80	230.39
49	10.92	17.38	27.53	43.43	68.22	106.72	166.27	258.04
50	11.47	18.42	29.46	46.90	74.36	117.39	184.56	289.00

For illustration purposes only. Not representative of an actual investment. All assumptions and computational results are hypothetical in nature. Higher volatility has historically been associated with higher rates of return, and average returns have had a tendency to fluctuate from year to year.

Plan Aid Table 23b:
Taxable Account Asset Growth Factor Table
(Total Tax Rate = 10%)

Years to Retire	Asset Growth Rate							
	5.0%	6.0%	7.0%	8.0%	9.0%	10.0%	11.0%	12.0%
1	1.05	1.05	1.06	1.07	1.08	1.09	1.10	1.11
2	1.09	1.11	1.13	1.15	1.17	1.19	1.21	1.23
3	1.14	1.17	1.20	1.23	1.26	1.30	1.33	1.36
4	1.19	1.23	1.28	1.32	1.37	1.41	1.46	1.51
5	1.25	1.30	1.36	1.42	1.48	1.54	1.60	1.67
6	1.30	1.37	1.44	1.52	1.60	1.68	1.76	1.85
7	1.36	1.45	1.53	1.63	1.72	1.83	1.94	2.05
8	1.42	1.52	1.63	1.74	1.86	1.99	2.13	2.27
9	1.49	1.61	1.73	1.87	2.02	2.17	2.34	2.52
10	1.55	1.69	1.84	2.00	2.18	2.37	2.57	2.79
11	1.62	1.78	1.96	2.15	2.36	2.58	2.82	3.09
12	1.70	1.88	2.08	2.30	2.55	2.81	3.10	3.42
13	1.77	1.98	2.21	2.47	2.75	3.07	3.41	3.79
14	1.85	2.09	2.35	2.65	2.98	3.34	3.75	4.20
15	1.94	2.20	2.50	2.84	3.22	3.64	4.12	4.66
16	2.02	2.32	2.66	3.04	3.48	3.97	4.53	5.16
17	2.11	2.45	2.83	3.26	3.76	4.33	4.98	5.72
18	2.21	2.58	3.00	3.50	4.06	4.72	5.47	6.33
19	2.31	2.72	3.19	3.75	4.39	5.14	6.01	7.02
20	2.41	2.86	3.39	4.02	4.75	5.60	6.61	7.78
21	2.52	3.02	3.61	4.31	5.13	6.11	7.26	8.62
22	2.63	3.18	3.83	4.62	5.55	6.66	7.98	9.55
23	2.75	3.35	4.08	4.95	6.00	7.26	8.77	10.58
24	2.88	3.53	4.33	5.30	6.48	7.91	9.64	11.72
25	3.01	3.72	4.61	5.69	7.01	8.62	10.59	12.99
26	3.14	3.93	4.90	6.10	7.58	9.40	11.64	14.39
27	3.28	4.14	5.20	6.54	8.19	10.25	12.79	15.94
28	3.43	4.36	5.53	7.01	8.85	11.17	14.06	17.66
29	3.58	4.60	5.88	7.51	9.57	12.17	15.45	19.57
30	3.75	4.84	6.25	8.05	10.35	13.27	16.98	21.69
31	3.91	5.11	6.65	8.63	11.18	14.46	18.66	24.03
32	4.09	5.38	7.06	9.25	12.09	15.76	20.51	26.62
33	4.27	5.67	7.51	9.92	13.07	17.18	22.54	29.50
34	4.47	5.98	7.98	10.63	14.13	18.73	24.77	32.69
35	4.67	6.30	8.49	11.40	15.27	20.41	27.22	36.22
36	4.88	6.64	9.02	12.22	16.51	22.25	29.92	40.13
37	5.10	7.00	9.59	13.10	17.85	24.25	32.88	44.46
38	5.33	7.38	10.19	14.04	19.29	26.44	36.13	49.26
39	5.57	7.78	10.83	15.05	20.85	28.82	39.71	54.58
40	5.82	8.20	11.52	16.14	22.54	31.41	43.64	60.48
41	6.08	8.64	12.24	17.30	24.37	34.24	47.96	67.01
42	6.35	9.11	13.01	18.54	26.34	37.32	52.71	74.25
43	6.64	9.60	13.83	19.88	28.48	40.68	57.93	82.26
44	6.94	10.12	14.70	21.31	30.78	44.34	63.66	91.15
45	7.25	10.66	15.63	22.84	33.28	48.33	69.97	100.99
46	7.57	11.24	16.62	24.49	35.97	52.68	76.89	111.90
47	7.92	11.84	17.66	26.25	38.89	57.42	84.51	123.98
48	8.27	12.48	18.78	28.14	42.04	62.59	92.87	137.38
49	8.64	13.16	19.96	30.17	45.44	68.22	102.07	152.21
50	9.03	13.87	21.22	32.34	49.12	74.36	112.17	168.65

For illustration purposes only. Not representative of an actual investment. All assumptions and computational results are hypothetical in nature. Higher volatility has historically been associated with higher rates of return, and average returns have had a tendency to fluctuate from year to year.

Plan Aid Table 23c:
Taxable Account Asset Growth Factor Table
(Total Tax Rate = 20%)

Years to Retire	Asset Growth Rate							
	5.0%	6.0%	7.0%	8.0%	9.0%	10.0%	11.0%	12.0%
1	1.04	1.05	1.06	1.06	1.07	1.08	1.09	1.10
2	1.08	1.10	1.12	1.13	1.15	1.17	1.18	1.20
3	1.12	1.15	1.18	1.20	1.23	1.26	1.29	1.32
4	1.17	1.21	1.24	1.28	1.32	1.36	1.40	1.44
5	1.22	1.26	1.31	1.36	1.42	1.47	1.52	1.58
6	1.27	1.32	1.39	1.45	1.52	1.59	1.66	1.73
7	1.32	1.39	1.46	1.54	1.63	1.71	1.80	1.90
8	1.37	1.46	1.55	1.64	1.74	1.85	1.96	2.08
9	1.42	1.52	1.63	1.75	1.87	2.00	2.14	2.28
10	1.48	1.60	1.72	1.86	2.00	2.16	2.32	2.50
11	1.54	1.67	1.82	1.98	2.15	2.33	2.53	2.74
12	1.60	1.76	1.92	2.11	2.30	2.52	2.75	3.00
13	1.67	1.84	2.03	2.24	2.47	2.72	2.99	3.29
14	1.73	1.93	2.14	2.38	2.65	2.94	3.26	3.61
15	1.80	2.02	2.26	2.54	2.84	3.17	3.54	3.96
16	1.87	2.12	2.39	2.70	3.04	3.43	3.86	4.33
17	1.95	2.22	2.53	2.87	3.26	3.70	4.19	4.75
18	2.03	2.33	2.67	3.05	3.50	4.00	4.56	5.21
19	2.11	2.44	2.82	3.25	3.75	4.32	4.97	5.71
20	2.19	2.55	2.97	3.46	4.02	4.66	5.40	6.25
21	2.28	2.68	3.14	3.68	4.31	5.03	5.88	6.86
22	2.37	2.81	3.32	3.91	4.62	5.44	6.39	7.51
23	2.46	2.94	3.50	4.17	4.95	5.87	6.96	8.23
24	2.56	3.08	3.70	4.43	5.30	6.34	7.57	9.03
25	2.67	3.23	3.90	4.72	5.69	6.85	8.24	9.89
26	2.77	3.38	4.12	5.02	6.10	7.40	8.96	10.84
27	2.88	3.55	4.35	5.34	6.54	7.99	9.75	11.88
28	3.00	3.72	4.60	5.68	7.01	8.63	10.61	13.02
29	3.12	3.89	4.86	6.04	7.51	9.32	11.54	14.27
30	3.24	4.08	5.13	6.43	8.05	10.06	12.56	15.64
31	3.37	4.28	5.41	6.84	8.63	10.87	13.66	17.14
32	3.51	4.48	5.72	7.28	9.25	11.74	14.86	18.79
33	3.65	4.70	6.04	7.75	9.92	12.68	16.17	20.59
34	3.79	4.92	6.38	8.24	10.63	13.69	17.59	22.57
35	3.95	5.16	6.73	8.77	11.40	14.79	19.14	24.74
36	4.10	5.41	7.11	9.33	12.22	15.97	20.83	27.11
37	4.27	5.67	7.51	9.93	13.10	17.25	22.66	29.72
38	4.44	5.94	7.93	10.56	14.04	18.63	24.65	32.57
39	4.62	6.22	8.37	11.24	15.05	20.12	26.82	35.70
40	4.80	6.52	8.84	11.96	16.14	21.72	29.18	39.12
41	4.99	6.84	9.34	12.72	17.30	23.46	31.75	42.88
42	5.19	7.16	9.86	13.54	18.54	25.34	34.55	46.99
43	5.40	7.51	10.41	14.40	19.88	27.37	37.59	51.51
44	5.62	7.87	11.00	15.33	21.31	29.56	40.90	56.45
45	5.84	8.25	11.61	16.31	22.84	31.92	44.49	61.87
46	6.07	8.64	12.26	17.35	24.49	34.47	48.41	67.81
47	6.32	9.06	12.95	18.46	26.25	37.23	52.67	74.32
48	6.57	9.49	13.67	19.64	28.14	40.21	57.30	81.45
49	6.83	9.95	14.44	20.90	30.17	43.43	62.35	89.27
50	7.11	10.42	15.25	22.24	32.34	46.90	67.83	97.84

For illustration purposes only. Not representative of an actual investment. All assumptions and computational results are hypothetical in nature. Higher volatility has historically been associated with higher rates of return, and average returns have had a tendency to fluctuate from year to year.

Plan Aid Table 23d:
Taxable Account Asset Growth Factor Table
(Total Tax Rate = 30%)

Years to Retire	Asset Growth Rate							
	5.0%	6.0%	7.0%	8.0%	9.0%	10.0%	11.0%	12.0%
1	1.04	1.04	1.05	1.06	1.06	1.07	1.08	1.08
2	1.07	1.09	1.10	1.12	1.13	1.14	1.16	1.18
3	1.11	1.13	1.15	1.18	1.20	1.23	1.25	1.27
4	1.15	1.18	1.21	1.24	1.28	1.31	1.35	1.38
5	1.19	1.23	1.27	1.31	1.36	1.40	1.45	1.50
6	1.23	1.28	1.33	1.39	1.44	1.50	1.56	1.62
7	1.27	1.33	1.40	1.46	1.53	1.61	1.68	1.76
8	1.32	1.39	1.47	1.55	1.63	1.72	1.81	1.91
9	1.36	1.45	1.54	1.63	1.73	1.84	1.95	2.07
10	1.41	1.51	1.61	1.72	1.84	1.97	2.10	2.24
11	1.46	1.57	1.69	1.82	1.96	2.10	2.26	2.43
12	1.51	1.64	1.78	1.92	2.08	2.25	2.44	2.63
13	1.56	1.71	1.86	2.03	2.21	2.41	2.62	2.85
14	1.62	1.78	1.95	2.14	2.35	2.58	2.83	3.09
15	1.68	1.85	2.05	2.26	2.50	2.76	3.04	3.35
16	1.73	1.93	2.15	2.39	2.66	2.95	3.28	3.63
17	1.79	2.01	2.26	2.53	2.83	3.16	3.53	3.94
18	1.86	2.10	2.37	2.67	3.00	3.38	3.80	4.27
19	1.92	2.19	2.48	2.82	3.19	3.62	4.09	4.63
20	1.99	2.28	2.60	2.97	3.39	3.87	4.41	5.02
21	2.06	2.37	2.73	3.14	3.61	4.14	4.75	5.44
22	2.13	2.47	2.86	3.32	3.83	4.43	5.11	5.90
23	2.21	2.58	3.00	3.50	4.08	4.74	5.51	6.39
24	2.28	2.68	3.15	3.70	4.33	5.07	5.93	6.93
25	2.36	2.80	3.31	3.90	4.61	5.43	6.39	7.51
26	2.45	2.91	3.47	4.12	4.90	5.81	6.88	8.14
27	2.53	3.04	3.64	4.35	5.20	6.21	7.41	8.83
28	2.62	3.16	3.82	4.60	5.53	6.65	7.98	9.57
29	2.71	3.30	4.00	4.86	5.88	7.11	8.60	10.37
30	2.81	3.44	4.20	5.13	6.25	7.61	9.26	11.24
31	2.91	3.58	4.41	5.41	6.65	8.15	9.97	12.19
32	3.01	3.73	4.62	5.72	7.06	8.72	10.74	13.21
33	3.11	3.89	4.85	6.04	7.51	9.33	11.56	14.32
34	3.22	4.05	5.09	6.38	7.98	9.98	12.45	15.52
35	3.33	4.22	5.34	6.73	8.49	10.68	13.41	16.83
36	3.45	4.40	5.60	7.11	9.02	11.42	14.45	18.24
37	3.57	4.58	5.87	7.51	9.59	12.22	15.56	19.77
38	3.70	4.77	6.16	7.93	10.19	13.08	16.76	21.43
39	3.83	4.98	6.46	8.37	10.83	13.99	18.05	23.23
40	3.96	5.18	6.78	8.84	11.52	14.97	19.44	25.19
41	4.10	5.40	7.11	9.34	12.24	16.02	20.93	27.30
42	4.24	5.63	7.46	9.86	13.01	17.14	22.55	29.60
43	4.39	5.87	7.82	10.41	13.83	18.34	24.28	32.08
44	4.54	6.11	8.21	11.00	14.70	19.63	26.15	34.78
45	4.70	6.37	8.61	11.61	15.63	21.00	28.16	37.70
46	4.87	6.64	9.03	12.26	16.62	22.47	30.33	40.86
47	5.04	6.91	9.47	12.95	17.66	24.05	32.67	44.30
48	5.21	7.21	9.94	13.67	18.78	25.73	35.18	48.02
49	5.40	7.51	10.42	14.44	19.96	27.53	37.89	52.05
50	5.58	7.82	10.93	15.25	21.22	29.46	40.81	56.42

For illustration purposes only. Not representative of an actual investment. All assumptions and computational results are hypothetical in nature. Higher volatility has historically been associated with higher rates of return, and average returns have had a tendency to fluctuate from year to year.

Plan Aid Table 23e:
Taxable Account Asset Growth Factor Table
(Total Tax Rate = 40%)

Years to Retire	Asset Growth Rate							
	5.0%	6.0%	7.0%	8.0%	9.0%	10.0%	11.0%	12.0%
1	1.03	1.04	1.04	1.05	1.05	1.06	1.07	1.07
2	1.06	1.07	1.09	1.10	1.11	1.12	1.14	1.15
3	1.09	1.11	1.13	1.15	1.17	1.19	1.21	1.23
4	1.13	1.15	1.18	1.21	1.23	1.26	1.29	1.32
5	1.16	1.19	1.23	1.26	1.30	1.34	1.38	1.42
6	1.19	1.24	1.28	1.32	1.37	1.42	1.47	1.52
7	1.23	1.28	1.33	1.39	1.45	1.50	1.56	1.63
8	1.27	1.33	1.39	1.46	1.52	1.59	1.67	1.74
9	1.30	1.37	1.45	1.52	1.61	1.69	1.78	1.87
10	1.34	1.42	1.51	1.60	1.69	1.79	1.89	2.00
11	1.38	1.48	1.57	1.67	1.78	1.90	2.02	2.15
12	1.43	1.53	1.64	1.76	1.88	2.01	2.15	2.30
13	1.47	1.58	1.71	1.84	1.98	2.13	2.30	2.47
14	1.51	1.64	1.78	1.93	2.09	2.26	2.45	2.65
15	1.56	1.70	1.85	2.02	2.20	2.40	2.61	2.84
16	1.60	1.76	1.93	2.12	2.32	2.54	2.78	3.04
17	1.65	1.82	2.01	2.22	2.45	2.69	2.96	3.26
18	1.70	1.89	2.10	2.33	2.58	2.85	3.16	3.50
19	1.75	1.96	2.19	2.44	2.72	3.03	3.37	3.75
20	1.81	2.03	2.28	2.55	2.86	3.21	3.59	4.02
21	1.86	2.10	2.37	2.68	3.02	3.40	3.83	4.31
22	1.92	2.18	2.47	2.81	3.18	3.60	4.08	4.62
23	1.97	2.26	2.58	2.94	3.35	3.82	4.35	4.95
24	2.03	2.34	2.68	3.08	3.53	4.05	4.64	5.30
25	2.09	2.42	2.80	3.23	3.72	4.29	4.94	5.69
26	2.16	2.51	2.91	3.38	3.93	4.55	5.27	6.10
27	2.22	2.60	3.04	3.55	4.14	4.82	5.62	6.54
28	2.29	2.69	3.16	3.72	4.36	5.11	5.99	7.01
29	2.36	2.79	3.30	3.89	4.60	5.42	6.38	7.51
30	2.43	2.89	3.44	4.08	4.84	5.74	6.80	8.05
31	2.50	2.99	3.58	4.28	5.11	6.09	7.25	8.63
32	2.58	3.10	3.73	4.48	5.38	6.45	7.73	9.25
33	2.65	3.21	3.89	4.70	5.67	6.84	8.24	9.92
34	2.73	3.33	4.05	4.92	5.98	7.25	8.79	10.63
35	2.81	3.45	4.22	5.16	6.30	7.69	9.36	11.40
36	2.90	3.57	4.40	5.41	6.64	8.15	9.98	12.22
37	2.99	3.70	4.58	5.67	7.00	8.64	10.64	13.10
38	3.07	3.83	4.77	5.94	7.38	9.15	11.34	14.04
39	3.17	3.97	4.98	6.22	7.78	9.70	12.09	15.05
40	3.26	4.12	5.18	6.52	8.20	10.29	12.89	16.14
41	3.36	4.26	5.40	6.84	8.64	10.90	13.74	17.30
42	3.46	4.42	5.63	7.16	9.11	11.56	14.65	18.54
43	3.56	4.58	5.87	7.51	9.60	12.25	15.62	19.88
44	3.67	4.74	6.11	7.87	10.12	12.99	16.65	21.31
45	3.78	4.91	6.37	8.25	10.66	13.76	17.74	22.84
46	3.90	5.09	6.64	8.64	11.24	14.59	18.92	24.49
47	4.01	5.27	6.91	9.06	11.84	15.47	20.16	26.25
48	4.13	5.46	7.21	9.49	12.48	16.39	21.50	28.14
49	4.26	5.66	7.51	9.95	13.16	17.38	22.91	30.17
50	4.38	5.86	7.82	10.42	13.87	18.42	24.43	32.34

For illustration purposes only. Not representative of an actual investment. All assumptions and computational results are hypothetical in nature. Higher volatility has historically been associated with higher rates of return, and average returns have had a tendency to fluctuate from year to year.

Plan Aid Table 23f:
Taxable Account Asset Growth Factor Table
(Total Tax Rate = 50%)

Years to Retire	Asset Growth Rate							
	5.0%	6.0%	7.0%	8.0%	9.0%	10.0%	11.0%	12.0%
1	1.03	1.03	1.04	1.04	1.05	1.05	1.06	1.06
2	1.05	1.06	1.07	1.08	1.09	1.10	1.11	1.12
3	1.08	1.09	1.11	1.12	1.14	1.16	1.17	1.19
4	1.10	1.13	1.15	1.17	1.19	1.22	1.24	1.26
5	1.13	1.16	1.19	1.22	1.25	1.28	1.31	1.34
6	1.16	1.19	1.23	1.27	1.30	1.34	1.38	1.42
7	1.19	1.23	1.27	1.32	1.36	1.41	1.45	1.50
8	1.22	1.27	1.32	1.37	1.42	1.48	1.53	1.59
9	1.25	1.30	1.36	1.42	1.49	1.55	1.62	1.69
10	1.28	1.34	1.41	1.48	1.55	1.63	1.71	1.79
11	1.31	1.38	1.46	1.54	1.62	1.71	1.80	1.90
12	1.34	1.43	1.51	1.60	1.70	1.80	1.90	2.01
13	1.38	1.47	1.56	1.67	1.77	1.89	2.01	2.13
14	1.41	1.51	1.62	1.73	1.85	1.98	2.12	2.26
15	1.45	1.56	1.68	1.80	1.94	2.08	2.23	2.40
16	1.48	1.60	1.73	1.87	2.02	2.18	2.36	2.54
17	1.52	1.65	1.79	1.95	2.11	2.29	2.48	2.69
18	1.56	1.70	1.86	2.03	2.21	2.41	2.62	2.85
19	1.60	1.75	1.92	2.11	2.31	2.53	2.77	3.03
20	1.64	1.81	1.99	2.19	2.41	2.65	2.92	3.21
21	1.68	1.86	2.06	2.28	2.52	2.79	3.08	3.40
22	1.72	1.92	2.13	2.37	2.63	2.93	3.25	3.60
23	1.76	1.97	2.21	2.46	2.75	3.07	3.43	3.82
24	1.81	2.03	2.28	2.56	2.88	3.23	3.61	4.05
25	1.85	2.09	2.36	2.67	3.01	3.39	3.81	4.29
26	1.90	2.16	2.45	2.77	3.14	3.56	4.02	4.55
27	1.95	2.22	2.53	2.88	3.28	3.73	4.24	4.82
28	2.00	2.29	2.62	3.00	3.43	3.92	4.48	5.11
29	2.05	2.36	2.71	3.12	3.58	4.12	4.72	5.42
30	2.10	2.43	2.81	3.24	3.75	4.32	4.98	5.74
31	2.15	2.50	2.91	3.37	3.91	4.54	5.26	6.09
32	2.20	2.58	3.01	3.51	4.09	4.76	5.55	6.45
33	2.26	2.65	3.11	3.65	4.27	5.00	5.85	6.84
34	2.32	2.73	3.22	3.79	4.47	5.25	6.17	7.25
35	2.37	2.81	3.33	3.95	4.67	5.52	6.51	7.69
36	2.43	2.90	3.45	4.10	4.88	5.79	6.87	8.15
37	2.49	2.99	3.57	4.27	5.10	6.08	7.25	8.64
38	2.56	3.07	3.70	4.44	5.33	6.39	7.65	9.15
39	2.62	3.17	3.83	4.62	5.57	6.70	8.07	9.70
40	2.69	3.26	3.96	4.80	5.82	7.04	8.51	10.29
41	2.75	3.36	4.10	4.99	6.08	7.39	8.98	10.90
42	2.82	3.46	4.24	5.19	6.35	7.76	9.48	11.56
43	2.89	3.56	4.39	5.40	6.64	8.15	10.00	12.25
44	2.96	3.67	4.54	5.62	6.94	8.56	10.55	12.99
45	3.04	3.78	4.70	5.84	7.25	8.99	11.13	13.76
46	3.11	3.90	4.87	6.07	7.57	9.43	11.74	14.59
47	3.19	4.01	5.04	6.32	7.92	9.91	12.38	15.47
48	3.27	4.13	5.21	6.57	8.27	10.40	13.07	16.39
49	3.35	4.26	5.40	6.83	8.64	10.92	13.78	17.38
50	3.44	4.38	5.58	7.11	9.03	11.47	14.54	18.42

it into a tax-deferred vehicle. Remember, all of your assets need to be valued as if they generate 100 percent *pretax* income from within *tax-deferred* accounts.

You Need to Consider Both Strategies

You need to look at the consequences of keeping your assets in taxable accounts, as well as the impact of moving them into tax-deferred vehicles. Ultimately, you have to decide which value to use in your plan—but you need to start by figuring out what those values are.

If Your Assets Remain in Taxable Accounts Throughout Retirement

If you decide to leave your assets in taxable accounts, you need to revalue them *downward*, to reflect the fact that you will not be managing them inside of tax-deferred accounts, and are therefore likely to get less income throughout retirement.

To make this adjustment, enter your *Taxable Account Adjustment Factor* in box (h). This is the same amount you determined in item (c), Plan Aid 11a: Example on page 168. Then, simply multiply that amount by the *Preliminary Value of Taxable Accounts* in box (g) to determine the *Hypothetical Value of Taxable Accounts*, which should be entered in box (i). This is what you might plan for your current taxable accounts to be worth when you stop working, in terms of their ability to take care of your lifestyle in retirement—**if you decide to leave them in a taxable account.**

If You Move Your Assets into Tax-Deferred Accounts

However, if you decide to move your assets into tax-deferred accounts when you get to retirement, you will need to revalue them *upward*, to reflect the fact that you may get more income by managing them inside of tax-deferred accounts than if you don't.

To make this adjustment, enter your *Tax-Deferred Account Adjustment Factor* in box (j). This is the same amount you determined in item (d), Plan Aid 11a: Example on page 168. Then, multiply that amount by your *Preliminary Value of Taxable Accounts* in box (g) to determine the second *Hypothetical Value of Taxable Accounts,* which should be entered in box (k). This is what your current taxable accounts might be worth when you stop working, in terms of their ability to take care of your lifestyle in retirement—**if you decide to transfer them into tax-deferred accounts** when you stop working.

You Get More Value in Tax-Deferred Accounts

As you can see, your taxable assets may be worth more if you move them into tax-deferred accounts. This doesn't necessarily mean that you will always do it this way—because there may be good reasons not to. You have to discuss this with your financial advisors. But generally speaking, if income is your most pressing concern, you will probably want to move your taxable assets into tax-deferred accounts at retirement time.

Keep in mind that none of the adjustments we're talking about will actually change the amount of money you have in your taxable accounts. They simply help you determine how much those assets may be worth in terms of their ability to support your lifestyle when you get to retirement.

Selecting a Value

The final step is to decide which way you think you will go. Select either the lower taxable account value in box (i) or the higher tax-deferred account value in box (k), and enter it in box (l), *Hypothetical Value of Current Taxable Accounts.* This is what your current taxable accounts might be worth when you stop working, in terms of their ability to support your lifestyle in retirement. In essence, this is the part of your accumulation target that may have already been taken care of by previous investments in taxable accounts. You don't have this much value in the accounts today, but if you expect them to keep growing, you are calculating what your assets in these accounts might be worth in the future.

After reviewing the example, use Plan Aid 22b: Your Plan to calculate how much you think *your* taxable accounts may be worth when you stop working. Use Plan Aid 23b: Your Plan to estimate your own hypothetical weighted average rate of return. If you don't have any taxable retirement accounts you can leave this part blank.

Plan Aid 22b: Your Plan
Taxable Accounts

Current Taxable Account Balances .... (a) $ _____

Number of Years Until Retirement .... (b) _____
    (From item (c), Plan Aid 1b: Your Plan on page 13)

Asset Growth Rate Assumption .... (c) _____ %
    (Use Plan Aid 23b: Your Plan, on page 233 to estimate rate of return)
    (Select 5%, 6%, 7%, 8%, 9%, 10%, 11%, or 12%)

Combined Tax Rate Assumption .... (d) _____ %
    (From item (a), Plan Aid 11b: Your Plan, on page 170)

Lookup Table for Appropriate Tax Rate .... (e) _____
    Select lookup table for appropriate tax rate below   *From Index Table below*

Asset Growth Factor .... (f) _____
    Look Up on Table Noted in Item (e) above, Using Items (b) and (c) above

Preliminary Value of Taxable Accounts .... (g) $ _____
    Future Value Dollars in Year 1 of Retirement   *(a) x (f)*

IF TAXABLE ASSETS REMAIN IN TAXABLE ACCOUNTS

Taxable Account Adjustment Factor .... (h) _____
    (From item (c), Plan Aid 11b: Your Plan, on page 170)

Hypothetical Value of Taxable Accounts .... (i) $ _____
    Future Value Dollars in Year 1 of Retirement   *(g) x (h)*

IF TAXABLE ASSETS PUT INTO TAX-DEFERRED ACCOUNTS

Tax-Deferred Account Adjustment Factor .... (j) _____
    (From item (d), Plan Aid 11b: Your Plan, on page 170)

Hypothetical Value of Taxable Accounts .... (k) $ _____
    Future Value Dollars in Year 1 of Retirement   *(g) x (j)*

SELECTED VALUE (TAXABLE OR TAX-DEFERRED)

Hypothetical Value of Current Taxable Accounts ..... (l) $ _____
    Future Value Dollars in Year 1 of Retirement   *Select item (i) or (k) above*

INDEX FOR TAX RATE TABLES
Use tax rate in item (d) above to select appropriate lookup table below

Total Tax Rate	0%	Plan Aid Table 23a
Total Tax Rate	10%	Plan Aid Table 23b
Total Tax Rate	20%	Plan Aid Table 23c
Total Tax Rate	30%	Plan Aid Table 23d
Total Tax Rate	40%	Plan Aid Table 23e
Total Tax Rate	50%	Plan Aid Table 23f

Plan Aid 23b: Your Plan
Weighted Average Rate of Return
Taxable Accounts

Type of Asset	Asset Value	% of Assets	Expect. Ret.	Wtd. Ret.
	$	%	%	%
	$	%	%	%
	$	%	%	%
	$	%	%	%
	$	%	%	%
	$	%	%	%
	$	%	%	%
	$	%	%	%
	$	%	%	%
	$	%	%	%
Tot. Assets & Wtd. Ave. Return	$	%		%

For illustration purposes only. Not representative of an actual investment. An individual investors results may vary. All assumptions and computational results are hypothetical in nature. There are no guarantees that you will achieve the results shown. Higher volatility has historically been associated with higher rates of return, and average returns have had a tendency to fluctuate from year to year. You should consult with a financial professional.

Future Taxable Lump-Sum Amounts

Some people may also be expecting to get lump-sum amounts before retirement. For example, you might be expecting an inheritance, be planning to sell a home or business, or have rental property that you intend to sell. Although you probably can't say for sure when these things will occur, you may want to build them into your plan if you think they are likely to happen.

The easiest way to do this is to ask yourself how much you think each of these amounts will be worth by the time you get to retirement, and then add them all up and include them in your plan as a single lump sum. We assume that all of the taxes will have been paid on these amounts by the time you get to retirement, so just like your current taxable accounts, they'll provide primarily after-tax income, and therefore need to be revalued accordingly.

Also, because these amounts will be in taxable accounts, you have to decide whether to leave them in a taxable environment during retirement or move them into tax-deferred accounts before you can determine their ultimate value for planning purposes.

Calculating the Value of Taxable Lump-Sum Amounts

To project the value of your expected taxable lump-sum amounts, start on Plan Aid 24a: Example, by entering your *Preliminary Value of Taxable Lump-Sums* in box (a). This is the total value of all the lump-sum amounts you expect to get prior to retirement, and is "preliminary" because in order to determine what it might be worth, it has to be revalued to reflect the fact that it will generate primarily after-tax income, and because you need to decide whether or not you're going to keep it in taxable accounts during retirement. Remember, you need to value all of your assets as if they generate 100 percent *pretax* income from within a *tax-deferred* account.

Plan Aid 24a: Example
Future Taxable Lump-Sum Amounts

Preliminary Value of Taxable Lump-Sum .... (a) $ **25,000**

IF LUMP-SUM ASSETS REMAIN IN TAXABLE ACCOUNTS

Taxable Account Adjustment Factor .... (b) **.97**
(From item (c), Plan Aid 11a: Example on page 168)

Hypothetical Value of Taxable Lump-Sum .... (c) $ **24,250**
Future Value Dollars in Year 1 of Retirement — (a) x (b)

IF LUMP-SUM ASSETS PUT INTO TAX-DEFERRED ACCOUNTS

Tax-Deferred Account Adjustment Factor .... (d) **1.21**
(From item (d), Plan Aid 11a: Example on page 168)

Hypothetical Value of Taxable Lump-Sum .... (e) $ **30,250**
Future Value Dollars in Year 1 of Retirement — (a) x (d)

SELECTED VALUE (TAXABLE OR TAX-DEFERRED)

Hypothetical Value of Future Lump-Sum .... (f) $ **24,250**
Future Value Dollars in Year 1 of Retirement — Select item (c) or (e) above

For illustration purposes only. Not representative of an actual investment. An individual investor's results may vary. All assumptions and computational results are hypothetical in nature. There are no guarantees that you will achieve the results shown. You should consult with a financial professional.

You Need to Consider Both Strategies

You need to look at the consequences of keeping the assets in taxable accounts throughout retirement, as well as the impact of moving them into tax-deferred accounts.

If Your Lump-Sum Assets Remain in Taxable Accounts Throughout Retirement

If you decide to leave the assets in taxable accounts, you need to revalue them *downward* to reflect the fact that you will not be managing them inside of tax-deferred accounts, and are therefore likely to get less income throughout retirement.

To make this adjustment, enter your *Taxable Account Adjustment Factor* in box (b). This is the same amount you determined in item (c),

Plan Aid 11a: Example on page 168. Then, simply multiply that amount by your *Preliminary Value of Taxable Lump-Sum* in box (a) to determine the *Hypothetical Value of Taxable Lump-Sum* which should be entered in box (c). This is what you might plan for your taxable lump-sum amounts to be worth when you stop working, in terms of their ability to take care of your lifestyle in retirement—**if you decide to leave them in a taxable account.**

If You Move Your Lump-Sum Assets into Tax-Deferred Accounts

However, if you decide to move the assets into tax-deferred accounts when you get to retirement, you need to revalue them *upward* to reflect the fact that you may get more income by managing them inside of tax-deferred accounts than if you leave them in taxable accounts.

To make this adjustment, enter your *Tax-Deferred Account Adjustment Factor* in box (d). This is the same amount you determined in item (d), Plan Aid 11a: Example on page 168. Then, multiply that amount by your *Preliminary Value of Taxable Lump-Sum* in box (a) to determine the second *Hypothetical Value of Taxable Lump-Sum*, which should be entered in box (e). This is what your taxable lump-sum accounts might be worth when you stop working—**if you decide to transfer them into tax-deferred accounts.**

You Get More Value in Tax-Deferred Accounts

As you can see, the taxable lump-sum assets may be worth more if you move them into tax-deferred accounts. This doesn't necessarily mean that you will do it this way—because there may be good reasons not to. Again, you have to talk with your financial advisors. But generally speaking, if income is your biggest concern, you will probably want to move your lump-sum assets into tax-deferred accounts at retirement time—even though we decided not to do it in the example.

Keep in mind that none of these adjustments actually change the amounts of money you're expecting to get as taxable lump-sums. They simply help you determine how much those assets may be worth in terms of their ability to support your lifestyle in retirement.

Selecting a Value

The final step is to decide which way you think you will go. Select either the lower taxable account value in box (c) or the higher tax-deferred account value in box (e), and enter it in box (f), *Hypothetical Value of Future Lump-Sum*. This is what your taxable lump-sum amounts might be worth when you stop working. In essence, this is the part of your accumulation target that may be taken care of by the future lump-sum amounts you hope to receive.

After reviewing the example, use Plan Aid 24b: Your Plan to calculate how much you think *your* hypothetical taxable lump-sum amounts may be worth when you stop working. If you are not expecting to receive any lump-sum amounts, you can leave this part blank.

Plan Aid 24b: Your Plan
Future Taxable Lump-Sum Amounts

Preliminary Value of Taxable Lump-Sum .... (a) $

IF LUMP-SUM ASSETS REMAIN IN TAXABLE ACCOUNTS

Taxable Account Adjustment Factor .... (b)
  (From item (c), Plan Aid 11b: Your Plan on page 170)

Hypothetical Value of Taxable Lump-Sum .... (c) $
  Future Value Dollars in Year 1 of Retirement   *(a) x (b)*

IF LUMP-SUM ASSETS PUT INTO TAX-DEFERRED ACCOUNTS

Tax-Deferred Account Adjustment Factor .... (d)
  (From item (d), Plan Aid 11b: Your Plan on page 170)

Hypothetical Value of Taxable Lump-Sum .... (e) $
  Future Value Dollars in Year 1 of Retirement   *(a) x (d)*

SELECTED VALUE (TAXABLE OR TAX-DEFERRED)

Hypothetical Value of Future Lump-Sum .... (f) $
  Future Value Dollars in Year 1 of Retirement   *Select item (c) or (e) above*

For illustration purposes only. Not representative of an actual investment. An individual investors results may vary. All assumptions and computational results are hypothetical in nature. There are no guarantees that you will achieve the results shown. You should consult with a financial professional.

Setting Your "Missing Money" Accumulation Target

The final step in this part of the process is to figure out how much you may still need to accumulate for retirement.

A Quick Review

Back in Chapter 12 you got the ball rolling by setting your hypothetical total retirement accumulation target. To do that, you determined how much income you think you will need when you stop working, and then you subtracted the amount you think you will get from sources like Social Security and pension plans. That left you with the amount of income that you may have to provide for *yourself* throughout retirement.

Then, with that amount in mind, you learned how to manage your money during retirement, and used that strategy to set a hypothetical total accumulation target—which is the amount *you* may need to accumulate to provide the income that you think *you* are going to be responsible for.

Taking Stock of What You Already Have

In the last six chapters you considered the hypothetical future values of the assets you've already saved for retirement. You looked at pension plans, retirement plans at work, regular and Roth IRAs, annuities, and the value of your taxable investments. Since you projected how much these assets might be worth when you retire, you can now subtract them from the total amount you have to accumulate to determine how much more you may *still* need to pull together.

In a very real sense, the hypothetical future value of these investments takes care of a portion of the assets you need to accumulate. By subtracting them from your overall target amount, you establish what I call the "missing money." This is the amount that you may *still* need to accumulate by the time you get to retirement. It's the amount you have to take care of in the future, with contributions into all of your various retirement accounts.

Deciding What to Do Next

After figuring out how much more you may need to accumulate, you can start thinking about the future contributions you'll have to make. In the next section of the book, you will consider all of your future contributions and then develop a savings and investment plan to help you reach your goals. But before you do, you have to first follow *Step #16: Measure the "Missing Money."*

Create Your Own Plan

To figure out how much more you may need to save and invest for retirement, start with Plan Aid 25a: Example, and add up the hypothetical future value of all your existing accounts. This is the amount of your total accumulation target that may have already been taken care of by your previous savings, contributions, and investments.

In box (g), enter your *Hypothetical Value of Annual Pensions*, which comes from item (g), Plan Aid 12a: Example on page 176. Then, in box (h), enter your *Hypothetical Lump-Sum Pension Benefit*, which comes from item (h), Plan Aid 13a: Example on page 179. Then, in box (i), enter your *Hypothetical Value of Retirement Plan Balances*, which comes from item (m), Plan Aid 14a: Example on page 181. Then, in box (j), enter your *Hypothetical Value of IRA Balances,* which comes from item (e), Plan Aid 16a: Example on page 189. Then, in box (k), enter your *Hypothetical Value of Roth IRA Balances,* which comes from item (l), Plan Aid 18a: Example on page 197. Then, in box (l), enter your *Hypothetical Value of Annuity Balances,* which comes from item (j), Plan Aid 20a: Example on page 208. Then, in box (m), enter your *Hypothetical Value of Current Taxable Accounts,* which comes from item (l), Plan Aid 22a: Example on page 221. Then, in box (n), enter your *Hypothetical Value of Future Lump-Sum,* which comes from item (f), Plan Aid 24a: Example on page 235. And finally, add boxes (g) through (n) to determine the *Hypothetical Value of* **All Current Assets,** which should be entered into box (o). This is the total hypothetical value of your existing assets.

Plan Aid 25a: Example
Future Value of Current Assets (Summary)

Hypothetical Value of Annual Pension .... (g) $ **93,484**
(From item (g), Plan Aid 12a: Example on page 176)

Hypothetical Lump-Sum Pension Benefit .... (h) $ **50,000**
(From item (h), Plan Aid 13a: Example on page 179)

Hypothetical Value of Retirement Plan Balances ..... (i) $ **272,000**
(From item (m), Plan Aid 14a: Example on page 181)

Hypothetical Value of IRA Balances .... (j) $ **27,200**
(From item (e), Plan Aid 16a: Example on page 189)

Hypothetical Value of Roth IRA Balances .... (k) $ **38,857**
(From item (l), Plan Aid 18a: Example on page 197)

Hypothetical Value of Annuity Balances .... (l) $ **27,744**
(From item (j), Plan Aid 20a: Example on page 208)

Hypothetical Value of Current Taxable Accounts ..... (m) $ **20,086**
(From item (l), Plan Aid 22a: Example on page 221)

Hypothetical Value of Future Lump-Sum .... (n) $ **24,250**
(From item (f), Plan Aid 24a: Example on page 235)

Hypothetical Value of **All Current Assets** .... (o) $ **553,621**
Future Value Dollars in Year 1 of Retirement   *Total of (g) through (n)*

Using Your Own Numbers

After reviewing the example, fill in Plan Aid 25b: Your Plan now to determine how much your own assets are likely to be worth at retirement.

Plan Aid 25b: Your Plan
Future Value of Current Assets (Summary)

Hypothetical Value of Annual Pension .... (g) $ _____
(From item (g), Plan Aid 12b: Your Plan on page 178)

Hypothetical Lump-Sum Pension Benefit .... (h) $ _____
(From item (h), Plan Aid 13b: Your Plan on page 179)

Hypothetical Value of Retirement Plan Balances ..... (i) $ _____
(From item (m), Plan Aid 14b: Your Plan on page 185)

Hypothetical Value of IRA Balances .... (j) $ _____
(From item (e), Plan Aid 16b: Your Plan on page 193)

Hypothetical Value of Roth IRA Balances .... (k) $ _____
(From item (l), Plan Aid 18b: Your Plan on page 200)

Hypothetical Value of Annuity Balances .... (l) $ _____
(From item (j), Plan Aid 20b: Your Plan on page 214)

Hypothetical Value of Current Taxable Accounts ..... (m) $ _____
(From item (l), Plan Aid 22b: Your Plan on page 232)

Hypothetical Value of Future Lump-Sum .... (n) $ _____
(From item (f), Plan Aid 24b: Your Plan on page 237)

Hypothetical Value of **All Current Assets** .... (o) $ _____
    Future Value Dollars in Year 1 of Retirement   *Total of (g) through (n)*

For illustration purposes only. Not representative of an actual investment. An individual investors results may vary. All assumptions and computational results are hypothetical in nature. There are no guarantees that you will achieve the results shown. You should consult with a financial professional.

Setting Your "Missing Money" Accumulation Target

Now that you know the hypothetical future value of your existing assets, you can calculate how much more you may *still* need to accumulate. To do this, turn to Plan Aid 26a: Example and enter your *Hypothetical Total Accumulation Target* into box (a). This is the amount you determined in item (e), Plan Aid 10a: Example on page 160.

Plan Aid 26a: Example
Setting Your "Missing Money" Accumulation Target

Hypothetical Total Accumulation Target .... (a) $ **1,763,850**
　　(From item (e), Plan Aid 10a: Example on page 160)

Hypothetical Value of **All Current Assets** .... (b) $ **553,621**
　　(From item (o), Plan Aid 25a: Example on page 240)

Hypothetical "Missing Money" Target .... (c) $ **1,210,229**
　　Future Value Dollars in Year 1 of Retirement　　　　*(a) - (b)*

For illustration purposes only. Not representative of an actual investment. An individual investors results may vary. All assumptions and computational results are hypothetical in nature. There are no guarantees that you will achieve the results shown. You should consult with a financial professional.

Then, enter your *Hypothetical Value of* **All Current Assets** into box (b), which is the amount you just determined in box (o) on Plan Aid 25a: Example on page 240. This is the total hypothetical value of your existing assets. The final step is to subtract the future value of your current assets in box (b) from your total accumulation target in box (a) to determine your *Hypothetical "Missing Money" Target*, which should be entered into box (c). This is the amount of money you may still need to accumulate for retirement.

Using Your Own Numbers

After reviewing the example, fill in Plan Aid 26b: Your Plan now to determine your own hypothetical "missing money" target, and to figure out how much you may still need to accumulate by the time you get to retirement.

If your *Hypothetical "Missing Money" Target* in box (c) is **equal to or less than zero,** it means that you may have already saved enough to meet your overall retirement objectives—given the assumptions you have made so far. Obviously, you don't want to stop saving and investing for

Plan Aid 26b: Your Plan
Setting Your "Missing Money" Accumulation Target

Hypothetical Total Accumulation Target .... (a) $
  (From item (e), Plan Aid 10b: Your Plan on page 161)

Hypothetical Value of **All Current Assets** .... (b) $
  (From item (o), Plan Aid 25b: Your Plan on page 241)

Hypothetical "Missing Money" Target .... (c) $
  Future Value Dollars in Year 1 of Retirement   (a) - (b)

For illustration purposes only. Not representative of an actual investment. An individual investors results may vary. All assumptions and computational results are hypothetical in nature. There are no guarantees that you will achieve the results shown. You should consult with a financial professional.

retirement, so at this point, if you came up with a negative number, you should go back to the beginning and change some of your planning variables to give yourself a higher goal to shoot for.

For example, you could plan to retire earlier, plan to maintain a higher percentage of your preretirement income during retirement, or reduce the rates of return you estimated for some of your existing assets. The important thing is to keep building on what you've accomplished so far, no matter how much ahead of expectations you think you are—because you never know what may happen in the future.

PART FIVE

Projecting the Value of Future Investments

In this section, we cover:

> *Step #17: Value IRA Contributions;*
>
> *Step #18: Value Roth IRA Contributions;*
>
> *Step #19: Value Annuity Contributions;*
>
> *Step #20: Value Your Savings in Taxable Accounts; and*
>
> *Step #21: Establish a Retirement Plan Accumulation Target.*

After completing this part of the book, you should have learned about the benefits of dollar cost averaging, determined the hypothetical future value of contributions you plan to make into various investment vehicles, and figured out how much *more* you might need to accumulate in your retirement plans at work.

Take Advantage of
Dollar Cost Averaging

One of the most important ideas for younger people to understand is the concept of dollar cost averaging. It's one of the reasons that time is so beneficial for investors with a long-term financial perspective.

We saw in Chapter 11 that dollar cost averaging *out* of the stock market, or what I call "dollar price erosion," can be very hazardous during retirement. On the other hand, dollar cost averaging *into* the stock market before you retire may be one of the smartest things you can do. And best of all, it happens automatically if you have a strategy to keep adding to your accounts on a routine basis.

The Benefits of Dollar Cost Averaging

Dollar cost averaging may be very beneficial when you add money into your accounts on a regular basis—like when you're saving and investing for retirement.

For example, let's say you're going to put $100 per month into a large company stock mutual fund for thirty years. If you invest the same amount each month, dollar cost averaging will cause you to buy more shares when the market goes down, because they cost less.

On the other hand, when markets go up, you buy fewer shares, because they'll cost more. So you always end up buying more shares when they're cheap, and fewer shares when they're expensive, which is a smart thing to do. And, as a result, you always own shares that have an average cost that is lower than the average price in the market. Keep in mind that a program of regular investment cannot assure a profit or protect from a loss in a declining market, but it does offer these potential benefits. Also, since such a program involves continuous investments regardless of fluctuating market conditions, you should consider your ability to continue a systematic investment program through all market cycles.

Dollar Cost Averaging: An Example

If a mutual fund share costs $1.00 today, and you invest $100, you can buy 100 shares. If, at the beginning of next month, the price of a share drops to $.50, you can buy 200 shares with your $100. However, if the price goes up to $2.00 per share, rather than dropping to $.50, you will only be able to buy 50 shares with the same $100. Again, when the price goes down, the number of shares you buy goes up, and when the price goes up, the number of shares you buy goes down.

Remember that mutual funds are an investment that fluctuates with market conditions, and when redeemed your shares may be worth more or less than their original cost. Mutual funds are sold by prospectus only and you should contact a financial professional or the mutual fund directly for a copy of the prospectus. Please read it carefully before you invest or send money.

But think about this on an average basis. If the price goes down to $.50 per share, after two months you'll own 300 shares costing a total of $200, for an average cost per share of about $.67 each. However, the average price in the market during this period of time is $.75. You bought one batch at $1.00 per share, and another batch at $.50 per share, for an average market price of $.75.

In this example, because of dollar cost averaging, you end up owning all of your shares at an average cost of $.67, during a period of time in which the market was pricing them at an average of $.75. And it always works this way. With dollar cost averaging you always get into the market at a lower average cost than the average price over the same period of time.

Dollar Cost Averaging: Another Example

But what if the price does go up to $2.00 per share in the second month? You would probably be excited. However, in that case, during the same two-month period, you would only be able to purchase 150 shares with your $200, which would lead to an average cost of about $1.33 per share. Of course, as I said a moment ago, the average price in the market during this period should be even higher.

You bought one batch when they sold for $1.00 per share, and another batch when they sold for $2.00 per share, for an average market price of $1.50. So even if the price goes up, you still own your shares at a lower average cost than the average price in the market.

Dollar Cost Averaging Always Works This Way

The beauty of dollar cost averaging is that it always works this way. The same process goes on and on throughout any accumulation period. If you invest the same amount on a periodic basis, you can be confident that you will always buy more shares when the price is down, and fewer shares when the price is up—which is a good way to do it. This is why dollar cost averaging may be so beneficial for younger investors.

An Actual Thirty-Year Investment Period

Illustration 30 is an example of dollar cost averaging using actual return data for large company stocks during the thirty years between 1969 and 1998. It compares the average cost to the average price of a share in a hypothetical large company stock mutual fund.

Buy More Shares When They Cost Less
and Fewer When They Cost More

If you invested $100 per year between 1969 and 1998 you would have experienced a typical, random pattern of gains and losses. The price of a share would have increased from $10 at the beginning of 1969 to $358 at the end of 1998, a 12.7 percent compound average annual rate of return—but you would have had a roller-coaster ride of ups and downs along the way. The best year delivered a return of 37.4 percent in 1995, while the worst year lost 26.5 percent in 1974.

The important thing to notice, however, is that after each good year in the market, you purchased fewer shares the following year—because they cost more—while after each losing year you were able to purchase more shares the next year—because they cost less. As a result, you always bought more shares when they were down, and fewer shares when they were up—which led to a lower average cost per share.

The Average Cost Is Always Lower Than the Average Price

If you compare the average cost per share with the average price per share in the example, you will see that the average cost is always lower. While the average cost increased from $10 in 1969 to about $21 in 1998, the average price per share went up from $10 in 1969 to over $58 in 1998—a substantial difference.

It's easy to calculate the average cost by dividing the total amount invested at the end of each year by the total number of shares owned at that time, while the average price is calculated by simply adding up all the annual share prices and dividing by the number of years you've been investing. The important thing is that by the end of the thirty-year period, you would have owned more than 142 shares that cost on average slightly more than $21 per share, while the market price of those same shares averaged more than $58.

Investing Routinely over the Long Term Is a Great Idea

This is why younger investors need to get on a program of periodic investing—and then stay with it. Even when markets go down, you shouldn't stop putting money into your accounts. In fact, it's generally a great time to invest when markets go down, because you'll be getting more shares for your money. Investing when markets are going up, when everyone else is getting excited, is usually not the best time to buy. You still have to do it, because you don't want to deviate from your plan, but you obviously won't be getting as many shares for your money.

Illustration 30: Dollar Cost Averaging
Actual 30-Year Investment Period from 1969 to 1998
Large Company Stock Returns

Year Bal.	Ann. Invest.	Tot. Invest.	Ann. Return	Ann. Share Price $10.00	Ann. Shares Bought	Tot. Shares Owned	Ave. Share Cost	Ave. Market Price
1969	$100	$100	-8.5%	$9.15	10.00	10.00	$10.00	$10.00
1970	$100	$200	4.0%	$9.52	10.93	20.93	$9.56	$9.58
1971	$100	$300	14.3%	$10.88	10.51	31.44	$9.54	$9.56
1972	$100	$400	19.0%	$12.94	9.19	40.63	$9.85	$9.89
1973	$100	$500	-14.7%	$11.05	7.73	48.35	$10.34	$10.50
1974	$100	$600	-26.5%	$8.12	9.05	57.41	$10.45	$10.59
1975	$100	$700	37.2%	$11.14	12.31	69.72	$10.04	$10.24
1976	$100	$800	23.8%	$13.80	8.97	78.69	$10.17	$10.35
1977	$100	$900	-7.2%	$12.81	7.25	85.94	$10.47	$10.73
1978	$100	$1,000	6.6%	$13.65	7.81	93.75	$10.67	$10.94
1979	$100	$1,100	18.4%	$16.17	7.33	101.07	$10.88	$11.19
1980	$100	$1,200	32.4%	$21.41	6.19	107.26	$11.19	$11.60
1981	$100	$1,300	-4.9%	$20.36	4.67	111.93	$11.61	$12.36
1982	$100	$1,400	21.4%	$24.72	4.91	116.84	$11.98	$12.93
1983	$100	$1,500	22.5%	$30.28	4.05	120.89	$12.41	$13.71
1984	$100	$1,600	6.3%	$32.18	3.30	124.19	$12.88	$14.75
1985	$100	$1,700	32.2%	$42.53	3.11	127.30	$13.35	$15.77
1986	$100	$1,800	18.5%	$50.38	2.35	129.65	$13.88	$17.26
1987	$100	$1,900	5.2%	$53.01	1.98	131.63	$14.43	$19.00
1988	$100	$2,000	16.8%	$61.93	1.89	133.52	$14.98	$20.70
1989	$100	$2,100	31.5%	$81.43	1.61	135.14	$15.54	$22.67
1990	$100	$2,200	-3.2%	$78.85	1.23	136.36	$16.13	$25.34
1991	$100	$2,300	30.6%	$102.93	1.27	137.63	$16.71	$27.66
1992	$100	$2,400	7.7%	$110.83	0.97	138.60	$17.32	$30.80
1993	$100	$2,500	10.0%	$121.90	0.90	139.51	$17.92	$34.00
1994	$100	$2,600	1.3%	$123.50	0.82	140.33	$18.53	$37.38
1995	$100	$2,700	37.4%	$169.72	0.81	141.14	$19.13	$40.57
1996	$100	$2,800	23.1%	$208.88	0.59	141.73	$19.76	$45.18
1997	$100	$2,900	33.4%	$278.56	0.48	142.20	$20.39	$50.83
1998	$100	$3,000	28.6%	$358.17	0.36	142.56	$21.04	$58.42

Don't Panic When the Markets Go Down

Of course, when you think about it, this makes as much sense in the world of investing as it does in the rest of your life. We've learned since we were children that it's almost always better to buy when things are on sale than when they're not. That captures the essence and spirit of dollar cost averaging pretty well.

As younger investors, you shouldn't get too alarmed when markets go down. Many people panic when the markets take a dip, because they experience a drop in the current value of their portfolio. But the next time this happens, just remember, savvy investors know that temporary market dips provide buying opportunities—and, like them, you should probably take advantage of those opportunities. Over the long haul, investing on a routine basis and staying the course no matter what will help you do that.

Individual Retirement Account (IRA) Contributions

In Chapter 16 we talked about the importance of IRA accounts in your overall financial plan, and considered the potential value of assets that you may have already accumulated in your IRAs. It's time now to consider the hypothetical value of *future* contributions you intend to make into your Individual Retirement Accounts.

There Are Limitations on the Contributions You Can Make

The amounts you can contribute to your IRAs in any given year are subject to income, contribution, and other limitations that you need to review periodically with your advisors. The rules change from time to time, so it's important to get professional advice in this area.

Making Contributions into Your IRAs

Individual Retirement Accounts are a great way to save for retirement because you may get a tax deduction for your contributions and your money grows tax-free. Since you don't have to pay taxes on your accounts until you use the money for retirement, IRAs can lead to larger balances.

Tax-Deferred Versus Taxable Investments: An Example

Saving in tax-deferred vehicles like IRAs can help you accumulate more money in two ways. To begin with, if you don't have to pay taxes on the money you invest, you can save more in the first place. Then, if you don't have to pay taxes on the growth in your account, you can compound more for retirement too.

Let's say you earn $3,000 per year for thirty-five years and want to save it all for retirement. If you put $250 a month into an IRA, you will contribute the entire $3,000 per year, get it all invested, and earn tax-deferred returns until you take it out. If you invest the assets in a combination of large and small company stock mutual funds and earn a hypothetical return of 11 percent, you will have slightly more than $1,075,000 in your account after thirty-five years.

However, if you decide to invest the $250 per month in a taxable mutual fund and are in a 30 percent tax bracket, the results will be considerably different. First, you'll have to pay taxes on the $250 before you invest it—so you'll only be able to sock away about $175 per month. Then, you will have to pay taxes on the earnings each year too, which will also make a big difference. In this scenario, by the time you get to retirement, you may only have about $350,000 in your account.

Please take note that these examples are for illustrative purposes only and do not represent an actual investment. Your results may vary. Also remember that mutual funds are investments that fluctuate with market conditions and do involve risk. As such, your shares may be worth more or less than original cost when they are redeemed. Mutual funds include fees and expenses which have not been included here to simplify the example. If such fees and expenses had been included, the results would be lower.

You Tend to Accumulate More in IRAs

In the previous example, you accumulated more than three times as much in the IRA as in the taxable account. That's why most advisors will tell you that if you're trying to accumulate more money for retirement over long periods of time, it's a good idea to save and invest in tax-deferred accounts whenever possible. IRAs are obviously one of the best ways to do that.

But remember, the rules surrounding the use of IRAs can be a little complicated, and we're not getting into all of the fine print. However, it's important to note that non-qualified IRA withdrawals prior to age 59½ will be subject to a 10 percent penalty and ordinary income taxes, so it's important to get the facts. Before you decide to contribute to an IRA, or any other type of investment, please seek the advice of a knowledgeable advisor. Good advice is almost always cheaper than expensive mistakes.

IRA Contributions and Financial Planning

IRAs will probably be an important part of your ongoing financial efforts—so you have to follow *Step #17: Value IRA Contributions*. You need to know how much your future contributions may be worth when you get to retirement.

Create Your Own Plan

Follow along in Plan Aid 27a: Example as we calculate the hypothetical value of future *monthly* contributions into an IRA account. You could look at it on an annual basis too, which is the way many people think about IRAs. However, in this book, we consider everything on a monthly basis. It's the way most people budget, and it's the way they think about their retirement plan contributions at work.

So, we'll start with the *monthly* amount you plan to contribute into IRA accounts for the rest of your working life, and enter that amount as your *Monthly IRA Contributions* in box (a). Next, enter the *Number of Years Until Retirement* in box (b), which is the same amount you calculated in item (c), Plan Aid 1a: Example on page 13.

Plan Aid 27a: Example
Monthly IRA Contributions

Monthly IRA Contributions .... (a) $ **100**

Number of Years Until Retirement .... (b)   **22**
   (From item (c), Plan Aid 1a: Example on page 13)

Asset Growth Rate Assumption .... (c)   **8.0** %
   (Use Plan Aid 28a: Example on page 257 to estimate rate of return)
   (Select 5%, 6%, 7%, 8%, 9%, 10%, 11%, or 12%)

Asset Growth Factor .... (d)   **690**
   Look Up on Plan Aid Table 28, Using Items (b) and (c) above

Hypothetical Value of IRA Contributions .... (e) $ **69,000**
   Future Value Dollars in Year 1 of Retirement   *(a) x (d)*

For illustration purposes only. Not representative of an actual investment. An individual investors results may vary. All assumptions and computational results are hypothetical in nature. There are no guarantees that you will achieve the results shown. Higher volatility has historically been associated with higher rates of return, and average returns have had a tendency to fluctuate from year to year. You should consult with a financial professional.

Computing Your Weighted Average Rate of Return

Then, use Plan Aid 28a: Example to calculate your hypothetical weighted average asset growth rate assumption for the money you plan to contribute to your IRAs. This is the average annual rate of return you might plan to earn on all future contributions into your IRA accounts. Since you may contribute to a number of different IRAs, and because they will probably be invested in different assets and mutual funds, you should compute a hypothetical weighted average rate of return that you can apply to all the contributions you plan to make.

As you can see, calculating an average annual rate of return for future monthly contributions isn't any different than calculating an average annual rate of return for existing account balances. We've gone through the process many times, so we won't do it again. Just review the example to see where the hypothetical rate of return is coming from.

After estimating your hypothetical weighted average rate of return, you can use it to project the hypothetical value of your future IRA contributions. Start by rounding the weighted average rate of return either up or down to the nearest whole percentage, and then enter it as your

Plan Aid 28a: Example
Weighted Average Rate of Return
Monthly IRA Contributions

Type of Asset	Asset Value	% of Assets	Expect. Ret.	Wtd. Ret.
Treasury Bonds	$25	25.0%	5.0%	1.3%
Large Company Value Stocks	$50	50.0%	9.0%	4.5%
Small Company Growth Stocks	$25	25.0%	10.0%	2.5%
Tot. Assets & Wtd. Ave. Return	$100	100.0%		8.3%

For illustration purposes only. Not representative of an actual investment. An individual investors results may vary. All assumptions and computational results are hypothetical in nature. There are no guarantees that you will achieve the results shown. Higher volatility has historically been associated with higher rates of return, and average returns have had a tendency to fluctuate from year to year. The prices of large company stocks and small company stocks will fluctuate. Treasury Bonds are guaranteed by the U.S. government and, if held to maturity, offer a fixed rate of return and principal value. You should consult with a financial professional.

Plan Aid Table 28:
Tax-Deferred Account Asset Growth Factor Table
for Monthly Contributions

Years to Retire	Asset Growth Rate							
	5.0%	6.0%	7.0%	8.0%	9.0%	10.0%	11.0%	12.0%
1	12	12	12	12	12	13	13	13
2	25	25	26	26	26	26	27	27
3	39	39	40	40	41	42	42	43
4	53	54	55	56	57	58	59	60
5	68	69	71	73	75	77	78	80
6	83	86	89	91	94	97	100	103
7	100	103	107	111	115	119	123	128
8	117	122	127	132	138	143	149	156
9	135	142	148	155	163	170	178	187
10	154	162	171	180	190	200	211	222
11	174	185	195	207	219	232	246	261
12	195	208	221	236	252	268	286	305
13	217	233	249	267	287	308	330	354
14	241	259	279	301	325	351	379	410
15	265	287	311	338	367	398	433	471
16	290	316	345	377	412	451	494	541
17	317	348	382	420	462	508	560	618
18	345	381	421	466	516	572	635	705
19	375	416	463	515	575	642	717	802
20	406	453	508	569	639	718	809	911
21	438	493	555	627	709	803	910	1,033
22	473	535	607	690	785	895	1,023	1,170
23	508	579	662	757	868	998	1,148	1,323
24	546	626	720	830	959	1,110	1,287	1,494
25	586	676	783	909	1,058	1,233	1,441	1,686
26	627	729	850	994	1,165	1,369	1,612	1,901
27	671	785	922	1,086	1,283	1,519	1,802	2,142
28	717	845	999	1,185	1,411	1,683	2,013	2,412
29	765	908	1,081	1,293	1,550	1,864	2,247	2,714
30	815	975	1,169	1,409	1,702	2,063	2,506	3,052
31	868	1,045	1,264	1,534	1,868	2,282	2,795	3,431
32	924	1,120	1,365	1,669	2,048	2,522	3,115	3,855
33	983	1,200	1,472	1,815	2,245	2,787	3,470	4,331
34	1,044	1,284	1,588	1,972	2,460	3,078	3,864	4,863
35	1,108	1,374	1,711	2,143	2,694	3,399	4,302	5,459
36	1,176	1,468	1,844	2,326	2,949	3,751	4,788	6,127
37	1,247	1,569	1,985	2,525	3,226	4,139	5,327	6,875
38	1,322	1,675	2,136	2,739	3,529	4,565	5,925	7,712
39	1,400	1,788	2,298	2,971	3,859	5,034	6,590	8,650
40	1,483	1,908	2,472	3,221	4,219	5,550	7,327	9,701
41	1,569	2,034	2,657	3,491	4,611	6,118	8,146	10,878
42	1,660	2,169	2,855	3,783	5,039	6,742	9,055	12,196
43	1,755	2,311	3,068	4,098	5,505	7,429	10,063	13,672
44	1,855	2,462	3,295	4,438	6,013	8,184	11,183	15,325
45	1,960	2,622	3,538	4,806	6,567	9,015	12,425	17,177
46	2,070	2,792	3,798	5,203	7,170	9,930	13,805	19,251
47	2,186	2,972	4,076	5,631	7,828	10,935	15,336	21,573
48	2,308	3,163	4,374	6,094	8,545	12,041	17,035	24,175
49	2,435	3,365	4,692	6,594	9,326	13,258	18,922	27,089
50	2,569	3,579	5,033	7,134	10,178	14,596	21,016	30,352

For illustration purposes only. Not representative of an actual investment. All Assumptions and computational results are hypotheticcal in nature. Higher volatility has historically been associated with higher rates of return, and average returns have had a tendency to fluctuate form year to year.

Asset Growth Rate Assumption in box (c) on Plan Aid 27a: Example. As always, if you want to be on the conservative side you can round it down, and if you want to be a little more aggressive you can round it up.

Then, turn to Plan Aid Table 28, and find the column related to your asset growth rate assumption and the row related to the number of years until retirement. Where they intersect in the table, you will find your *Asset Growth Factor*, which should be entered in box (d).

The final step is to multiply your *Asset Growth Factor* in box (d) by your *Monthly IRA Contributions* in box (a) to compute the *Hypothetical Value of IRA Contributions* in box (e). This is the amount your future IRA contributions might be worth when you retire. In a very real sense, it's the part of your "missing money" accumulation target that could be taken care of by *future* IRA contributions you intend to make.

After reviewing the example, use Plan Aid 27b: Your Plan to calculate what you think *your* IRA contributions may be worth when you stop working. Use Plan Aid 28b: Your Plan to estimate your own hypothetical weighted average rate of return. If you don't plan to contribute to IRAs in the future you can leave this part blank.

Plan Aid 27b: Your Plan
Monthly IRA Contributions

Monthly IRA Contributions .... (a) $

Number of Years Until Retirement .... (b)
    (From item (c), Plan Aid 1b: Your Plan on page 13)

Asset Growth Rate Assumption .... (c)   %
    (Use Plan Aid 28b: Your Plan on page 260 to estimate rate of return)
    (Select 5%, 6%, 7%, 8%, 9%, 10%, 11%, or 12%)

Asset Growth Factor .... (d)
    Look up on Plan Aid Table 28, Using Items (b) and (c) above

Hypothetical Value of IRA Contributions .... (e) $
    Future Value Dollars in Year 1 of Retirement   *(a) x (d)*

Plan Aid 28b: Your Plan
Weighted Average Rate of Return
Monthly IRA Contributions

Type of Asset	Asset Value	% of Assets	Expect. Ret.	Wtd. Ret.
	$	%	%	%
	$	%	%	%
	$	%	%	%
	$	%	%	%
	$	%	%	%
	$	%	%	%
	$	%	%	%
	$	%	%	%
	$	%	%	%
	$	%	%	%
Tot. Assets & Wtd. Ave. Return	$	%		%

For illustration purposes only. Not representative of an actual investment. An individual investors results may vary. All assumptions and computational results are hypothetical in nature. There are no guarantees that you will achieve the results shown. Higher volatility has historically been associated with higher rates of return, and average returns have had a tendency to fluctuate from year to year. You should consult with a financial professional.

Roth IRA Contributions

As you know, Roth IRAs are both similar to and different from regular IRAs. You will often have to decide which one to put your money into—and the answer is never clear cut. As with most other investment decisions, it depends upon your own circumstances and expectations.

Roth IRAs Versus Regular IRAs

The decision about which type of IRA account to use often boils down to three key issues: First, do you need the tax deduction of a regular IRA to put enough away in the first place? Remember, Roth IRAs are not tax deductible, so you have to pay taxes on the money you invest in them.

Second, you need to decide if you would rather pay taxes now or later. You have to pay taxes on the money you put into a Roth IRA before you make the contribution, but then you never have to pay taxes again—on either the contributions or the growth in your account. Keep in mind though, that to get this benefit, Roth IRAs must be held for at least five years. Otherwise, any withdrawals of earnings prior to the end of the five-year period and prior to the age of 59½ will be subject to a 10 percent penalty and ordinary income tax.

With regular IRAs, however, you don't pay any taxes going in, but you have to pay taxes on both your contributions and growth when you take your money out. There are a lot of reasons you might prefer to pay taxes sooner or later, and they're different for everyone. You have to consider your own circumstances.

Finally, you also need to decide how important it is to have more flexibility when it comes to taking money out of your accounts. Remember, you are forced to start withdrawals from your regular IRAs when you reach age 70½, whereas you never have to take money out of your Roth IRAs. Based upon your overall retirement situation and estate planning objectives, you may, as a result, prefer one kind over the other.

You Need Good Advice in This Area

Because Roth IRAs have many unique attributes and can be powerful investment vehicles, you may decide to take advantage of them at some point in your life—so you need to know how to follow *Step #18: Value Roth IRA Contributions*. We haven't even scratched the surface of the rules and regulations surrounding the use of Roth IRAs, however, so as with all other investments, you should get the advice of a competent financial professional. There are many issues and limitations concerning when you can use them and how much you can contribute each year—and the rules seem to change frequently.

Roth IRA Contributions and Financial Planning

In Chapter 17, we estimated the hypothetical value of your existing Roth IRA accounts. Now, it's time to consider what your *future* Roth IRA contributions may be worth when you retire.

Create Your Own Plan

You can follow Plan Aid 29a: Example to learn how to estimate the hypothetical value of your future contributions. Start with the *monthly* amount you plan to contribute, and enter it as your *Monthly Roth IRA Contributions* in box (f). Next, enter the *Number of Years Until Retirement* in box (g), which is the same amount you calculated in item (c), Plan Aid 1a: Example on page 13.

Plan Aid 29a: Example
Monthly Roth IRA Contributions

Monthly Roth IRA Contributions .... (f) $ **100**

Number of Years Until Retirement .... (g) **22**
   (From item (c), Plan Aid 1a: Example on page 13)

Asset Growth Rate Assumption .... (h) **8.0** %
   (Use Plan Aid 30a: Example on page 264 to estimate rate of return)
   (Select 5%, 6%, 7%, 8%, 9%, 10%, 11%, or 12%)

Asset Growth Factor .... (i) **690**
   Look Up on Plan Aid Table 30, Using Items (g) and (h) above

Preliminary Value of Roth IRA Contributions .... (j) $ **69,000**
   Future Value Dollars in Year 1 of Retirement   *(f) x (i)*

Tax Adjustment Percentage .... (k) **70.0** %
   (From item (b), Plan Aid 11a: Example on page 168)

Hypothetical Value of Roth IRA Contributions .... (l) $ **98,571**
   Future Value Dollars in Year 1 of Retirement   *(j) ÷ (k)*

For illustration purposes only. Not representative of an actual investment. An individual investors results may vary. All assumptions and computational results are hypothetical in nature. There are no guarantees that you will achieve the results shown. Higher volatility has historically been associated with higher rates of return, and average returns have had a tendency to fluctuate from year to year. You should consult with a financial professional.

Computing Your Weighted Average Rate of Return

Then, use Plan Aid 30a: Example to calculate your hypothetical weighted average asset growth rate assumption for the money you plan to contribute to your Roth IRAs. This is the average annual rate of return you might plan to earn on future contributions into all your Roth IRA accounts.

Calculating an average annual rate of return for your Roth IRA accounts is exactly the same as calculating an average annual rate of return for your regular IRA contributions. Review the example to get a feel for where the hypothetical rate of return is coming from.

After estimating your hypothetical weighted average rate of return, you can project the hypothetical value of your future Roth IRA contributions. Start by rounding the weighted average rate of return either up or

Plan Aid 30a: Example
Weighted Average Rate of Return
Monthly Roth IRA Contributions

Type of Asset	Asset Value	% of Assets	Expect. Ret.	Wtd. Ret.
Treasury Bonds	$50	50.0%	5.0%	2.5%
Large Company Value Stocks	$25	25.0%	10.0%	2.5%
Small Company Growth Stocks	$25	25.0%	12.0%	3.0%
Tot. Assets & Wtd. Ave. Return	$100	100.0%		8.0%

For illustration purposes only. Not representative of an actual investment. An individual investors results may vary. All assumptions and computational results are hypothetical in nature. There are no guarantees that you will achieve the results shown. Higher volatility has historically been associated with higher rates of return, and average returns have had a tendency to fluctuate from year to year. The prices of large company stocks and small company stocks will fluctuate. Treasury Bonds are guaranteed by the U.S. government and, if held to maturity, offer a fixed rate of return and principal value. You should consult with a financial professional.

down to the nearest whole percentage, and then enter it as your *Asset Growth Rate Assumption* in box (h) on Plan Aid 29a: Example.

Then, turn to Plan Aid Table 30, and find the column related to your asset growth rate assumption and the row related to the number of years until retirement. Where they intersect in the table, you will find your *Asset Growth Factor,* which should be entered in box (i).

Next, multiply your *Asset Growth Factor* in box (i) by your *Monthly Roth IRA Contributions* in box (f) to compute the *Preliminary Value of Roth IRA Contributions* in box (j). This is a "preliminary" value because as you know, the amount in your Roth IRAs is actually worth more than the same amount in your regular IRAs, because your Roth IRAs provide *tax-free* income during retirement—and you need to account for that.

We've already discussed the importance of adjusting the value of certain assets to restate them as if they generate *taxable* income from within tax-deferred accounts. Since Roth IRAs are tax-deferred accounts to begin with, you don't need to revalue the contributions because of that.

However, since they *don't* generate *taxable* income, the hypothetical future value of your contributions does have to be adjusted upward to revalue them as if they did. If you don't do that, you will understate their value in terms of their ability to provide pretax income in retirement. Making this adjustment doesn't mean that you're going to have more money in the account—it simply means that the money you do have may take care of a bigger piece of your retirement income need.

So the next step is to make the tax adjustment—just like you did to your current Roth IRA balances in Chapter 17. Start by entering your *Tax Adjustment Percentage* in box (k), which is the amount you calculated in item (b), Plan Aid 11a: Example on page 168. Then, divide the *Preliminary Value of Roth IRA Contributions* in box (j) by your *Tax Adjustment Percentage* in box (k) to compute your *Hypothetical Value of Roth IRA Contributions,* and enter it in box (l). This is what your future Roth IRA contributions might be worth when you stop working, in terms of their ability to provide taxable income in retirement. In a very real sense, this is the part of your "missing money" accumulation target that may be taken care of by the *future* Roth IRA contributions you intend to make.

After reviewing the example, use Plan Aid 29b: Your Plan to estimate

Plan Aid Table 30:
Tax-Deferred Account Asset Growth Factor Table
for Monthly Contributions

Years to Retire	Asset Growth Rate							
	5.0%	6.0%	7.0%	8.0%	9.0%	10.0%	11.0%	12.0%
1	12	12	12	12	12	13	13	13
2	25	25	26	26	26	26	27	27
3	39	39	40	40	41	42	42	43
4	53	54	55	56	57	58	59	60
5	68	69	71	73	75	77	78	80
6	83	86	89	91	94	97	100	103
7	100	103	107	111	115	119	123	128
8	117	122	127	132	138	143	149	156
9	135	142	148	155	163	170	178	187
10	154	162	171	180	190	200	211	222
11	174	185	195	207	219	232	246	261
12	195	208	221	236	252	268	286	305
13	217	233	249	267	287	308	330	354
14	241	259	279	301	325	351	379	410
15	265	287	311	338	367	398	433	471
16	290	316	345	377	412	451	494	541
17	317	348	382	420	462	508	560	618
18	345	381	421	466	516	572	635	705
19	375	416	463	515	575	642	717	802
20	406	453	508	569	639	718	809	911
21	438	493	555	627	709	803	910	1,033
22	473	535	607	690	785	895	1,023	1,170
23	508	579	662	757	868	998	1,148	1,323
24	546	626	720	830	959	1,110	1,287	1,494
25	586	676	783	909	1,058	1,233	1,441	1,686
26	627	729	850	994	1,165	1,369	1,612	1,901
27	671	785	922	1,086	1,283	1,519	1,802	2,142
28	717	845	999	1,185	1,411	1,683	2,013	2,412
29	765	908	1,081	1,293	1,550	1,864	2,247	2,714
30	815	975	1,169	1,409	1,702	2,063	2,506	3,052
31	868	1,045	1,264	1,534	1,868	2,282	2,795	3,431
32	924	1,120	1,365	1,669	2,048	2,522	3,115	3,855
33	983	1,200	1,472	1,815	2,245	2,787	3,470	4,331
34	1,044	1,284	1,588	1,972	2,460	3,078	3,864	4,863
35	1,108	1,374	1,711	2,143	2,694	3,399	4,302	5,459
36	1,176	1,468	1,844	2,326	2,949	3,751	4,788	6,127
37	1,247	1,569	1,985	2,525	3,226	4,139	5,327	6,875
38	1,322	1,675	2,136	2,739	3,529	4,565	5,925	7,712
39	1,400	1,788	2,298	2,971	3,859	5,034	6,590	8,650
40	1,483	1,908	2,472	3,221	4,219	5,550	7,327	9,701
41	1,569	2,034	2,657	3,491	4,611	6,118	8,146	10,878
42	1,660	2,169	2,855	3,783	5,039	6,742	9,055	12,196
43	1,755	2,311	3,068	4,098	5,505	7,429	10,063	13,672
44	1,855	2,462	3,295	4,438	6,013	8,184	11,183	15,325
45	1,960	2,622	3,538	4,806	6,567	9,015	12,425	17,177
46	2,070	2,792	3,798	5,203	7,170	9,930	13,805	19,251
47	2,186	2,972	4,076	5,631	7,828	10,935	15,336	21,573
48	2,308	3,163	4,374	6,094	8,545	12,041	17,035	24,175
49	2,435	3,365	4,692	6,594	9,326	13,258	18,922	27,089
50	2,569	3,579	5,033	7,134	10,178	14,596	21,016	30,352

For illustration purposes only. Not representative of an actual investment. All assumptions and computational results are hypothetical in nature. Higher volatility has historically been associated with higher rates of return, and average returns have had a tendency to fluctuate from year to year.

how much your Roth IRA contributions may be worth at retirement. Use Plan Aid 30b: Your Plan to estimate your own hypothetical weighted average rate of return. If you don't intent to contribute to Roth IRAs in the future you can leave this part blank.

Plan Aid 29b: Your Plan
Monthly Roth IRA Contributions

Monthly Roth IRA Contributions .... (f) $

Number of Years Until Retirement .... (g)
    (From item (c), Plan Aid 1b: Your Plan on page 13)

Asset Growth Rate Assumption .... (h)   %
    (Use Plan Aid 30b: Your Plan on page 268 to estimate rate of return)
    (Select 5%, 6%, 7%, 8%, 9%, 10%, 11%, or 12%)

Asset Growth Factor .... (i)
    Look Up on Plan Aid Table 30, Using Items (g) and (h) above

Preliminary Value of Roth IRA Contributions .... (j) $
    Future Value Dollars in Year 1 of Retirement   *(f) x (i)*

Tax Adjustment Percentage .... (k)   %
    (From item (b), Plan Aid 11b: Your Plan on page 170)

Hypothetical Value of Roth IRA Contributions .... (l) $
    Future Value Dollars in Year 1 of Retirement   *(j) + (k)*

For illustration purposes only. Not representative of an actual investment. An individual investors results may vary. All assumptions and computational results are hypothetical in nature. There are no guarantees that you will achieve the results shown. Higher volatility has historically been associated with higher rates of return, and average returns have had a tendency to fluctuate from year to year. You should consult with a financial professional.

Plan Aid 30b: Your Plan
Weighted Average Rate of Return
Monthly Roth IRA Contributions

Type of Asset	Asset Value	% of Assets	Expect. Ret.	Wtd. Ret.
	$	%	%	%
	$	%	%	%
	$	%	%	%
	$	%	%	%
	$	%	%	%
	$	%	%	%
	$	%	%	%
	$	%	%	%
	$	%	%	%
	$	%	%	%
Tot. Assets & Wtd. Ave. Return	$	%		%

For illustration purposes only. Not representative of an actual investment. An individual investors results may vary. All assumptions and computational results are hypothetical in nature. There are no guarantees that you will achieve the results shown. Higher volatility has historically been associated with higher rates of return, and average returns have had a tendency to fluctuate from year to year. You should consult with a financial professional.

Investments in Annuity Contracts

After saving as much as you can in your IRAs and retirement plans at work, you may want to set aside even more money in tax-deferred accounts. Annuities are a very common solution to this problem, which is why we consider them in *Step #19: Value Annuity Contributions*. Annuities, like Roth IRAs, are usually funded with after-tax dollars, and allow you to get tax-deferred growth until you take your money out—which means that you should be able to accumulate larger balances over the long run. And, like Roth IRAs and regular IRAs, early withdrawals prior to age 59½ are subject to a 10 percent penalty and ordinary income taxes. Penalties for early withdrawal may also be imposed by the issuer, as defined in the contract.

Get the Help You Need

Annuities can play an important role in accumulating money for retirement, but you want to work with someone who understands them. There are many different kinds and they offer a variety of features and benefits, so a knowledgeable professional can be very helpful. In Chapter 18 we touched on a few important details about annuities, and we're not going to go any deeper here—there are plenty of other books for that. Suffice it to say that you should be prepared to use these versatile financial tools in appropriate circumstances and that you should only pay for the features and benefits you really need.

Investing in Annuities and Your Financial Plan

We've already considered the hypothetical value of your existing annuity contracts—now it's time to estimate the hypothetical value of *future* investments you intend to make.

Remember, unlike regular and Roth IRAs, you can generally put as much as you want into your annuities, and you can do it as often as you like, so you usually have a great deal of flexibility when it comes to deciding how much and when to invest. That's why people often use them when they receive large amounts of money, because annuities are one of the only ways to get a lot of money into a tax-deferred environment fast. At the same time, however, they are also a great way to invest systematically over longer investment periods.

Create Your Own Plan

Follow the steps outlined in Plan Aid 31a: Example to get a feel for how to estimate the hypothetical value of your *future* annuity investments. Start with the *monthly* amount you plan to invest in new or existing annuity contracts, and enter it as your *Monthly Annuity Contract Contributions* in box (a). Next, enter the *Number of Years Until Retirement* in box (b), which is the same amount you calculated in item (c), Plan Aid 1a: Example on page 13.

Computing Your Weighted Average Rate of Return

Then, use Plan Aid 32a: Example to calculate your hypothetical weighted average asset growth rate assumption for the assets you expect to purchase in your annuities. This is the average annual rate of return you might plan to earn on future annuity investments until you retire.

After estimating your hypothetical weighted average rate of return, you can project the hypothetical value of your future annuity invest-

Plan Aid 31a: Example
Monthly Annuity Contract Contributions

Monthly Annuity Contract Contributions ......…......... (a) $ **100**

Number of Years Until Retirement ....…............ (b) **22**
    (From item (c), Plan Aid 1a: Example on page 13)

Asset Growth Rate Assumption ....…............... (c) **8.0** %
       (Use Plan Aid 32a: Example on page 272 to estimate rate of return)
       (Select 5%, 6%, 7%, 8%, 9%, 10%, 11%, or 12%)

Asset Growth Factor ....…...................…........ (d) **690**
    Look Up on Plan Aid Table 32a, Using Items (b) and (c) above

Preliminary Value of Annuity Contributions ..….......... (e) $ **69,000**
    Future Value Dollars in Year 1 of Retirement   *(a) x (d)*

Amount You Contributed to the Annuity ....…........ (f) $ **26,400**
                                       (a) x (b) x 12

Exclusion Factor ....…..............…................ (g) **.383**
                                       (f) ÷ (e)

Combined Tax Rate Assumption ....…............. (h) **30.0** %
    (From item (a), Plan Aid 11a: Example on page 168)

Exclusion Factor Adjustment ....…................. (i) **1.09**
    Look Up on Plan Aid Table 32b, Using Items (g) and (h) above

Hypothetical Value of Annuity Contributions ......…..... (j) $ **75,210**
    Future Value Dollars in Year 1 of Retirement   *(e) x (i)*

Plan Aid 32a: Example
Weighted Average Rate of Return
Monthly Annuity Contract Contributions

Type of Asset	Asset Value	% of Assets	Expect. Ret.	Wtd. Ret.
Treasury Bonds	$60	60.0%	5.5%	3.3%
Large Company Value Stocks	$25	25.0%	11.0%	2.8%
Small Company Growth Stocks	$15	15.0%	12.0%	1.8%
Tot. Assets & Wtd. Ave. Return	$100	100.0%		7.9%

For illustration purposes only. Not representative of an actual investment. An individual investors results may vary. All assumptions and computational results are hypothetical in nature. Variable annuity contracts do have annual fees and expenses that have not been included here in order to simplify the example. If included, the results would be lower. There are no guarantees that you will achieve the results shown. Higher volatility has historically been associated with higher rates of return, and average returns have had a tendency to fluctuate from year to year. The prices of large company stocks and small company stocks will fluctuate. Treasury Bonds are guaranteed by the U.S. government and, if held to maturity, offer a fixed rate of return and principal value. You should consult with a financial professional.

ments. Start by rounding the hypothetical rate of return either up or down to the nearest whole percentage, and then enter it as your *Asset Growth Rate Assumption* in box (c) on Plan Aid 31a: Example.

Then, turn to Plan Aid Table 32a, and find the column related to your asset growth rate assumption and the row related to the number of years until retirement. Where they intersect in the table, you will find your *Asset Growth Factor*, which should be entered in box (d).

Next, multiply your *Asset Growth Factor* in box (d) by your *Monthly Annuity Contract Contributions* in box (a) to compute the *Preliminary Value of Annuity Contributions* in box (e). This is a "preliminary" value because as you know, the total amount in your annuity contracts may actually be worth more than this, since annuities provide income that is at least *partially tax-free*—so you need to account for the fact that only part of what you take out during retirement will be taxed.

As we've discussed, you have to adjust the value of certain assets to restate them as if they generate *taxable* income from within tax-deferred accounts. Since your annuity contracts are tax-deferred—which is why you're probably investing in them in the first place—you obviously don't need to revalue them in that regard.

However, your annuities *won't* generate 100 percent *taxable* income, so you need to adjust them upward to revalue them as if they did. If you don't make this adjustment, you may understate their value in terms of their ability to provide taxable income in retirement. Making this adjustment doesn't mean that you'll have more money in your annuities—it just means that the money you do have may take care of a larger share of your retirement income needs.

To make the necessary adjustment, you have to figure out how much of the hypothetical value at retirement will come from growth in your accounts, and how much you will contribute yourself. To do this, you can compute the *Amount You Contributed to the Annuity* by multiplying your *Monthly Annuity Contract Contributions* in box (a) by the *Number of Years Until Retirement* in box (b), and then multiplying that amount by twelve. The answer should be entered into box (f). This is the total amount you plan to invest in all of your annuity contracts by the time you retire.

Next, divide the *Amount You Contributed to the Annuity* in box (f)

Plan Aid Table 32a:
Tax-Deferred Account Asset Growth Factor Table for Monthly Contributions

Years to Retire	Asset Growth Rate							
	5.0%	6.0%	7.0%	8.0%	9.0%	10.0%	11.0%	12.0%
1	12	12	12	12	12	13	13	13
2	25	25	26	26	26	26	27	27
3	39	39	40	40	41	42	42	43
4	53	54	55	56	57	58	59	60
5	68	69	71	73	75	77	78	80
6	83	86	89	91	94	97	100	103
7	100	103	107	111	115	119	123	128
8	117	122	127	132	138	143	149	156
9	135	142	148	155	163	170	178	187
10	154	162	171	180	190	200	211	222
11	174	185	195	207	219	232	246	261
12	195	208	221	236	252	268	286	305
13	217	233	249	267	287	308	330	354
14	241	259	279	301	325	351	379	410
15	265	287	311	338	367	398	433	471
16	290	316	345	377	412	451	494	541
17	317	348	382	420	462	508	560	618
18	345	381	421	466	516	572	635	705
19	375	416	463	515	575	642	717	802
20	406	453	508	569	639	718	809	911
21	438	493	555	627	709	803	910	1,033
22	473	535	607	690	785	895	1,023	1,170
23	508	579	662	757	868	998	1,148	1,323
24	546	626	720	830	959	1,110	1,287	1,494
25	586	676	783	909	1,058	1,233	1,441	1,686
26	627	729	850	994	1,165	1,369	1,612	1,901
27	671	785	922	1,086	1,283	1,519	1,802	2,142
28	717	845	999	1,185	1,411	1,683	2,013	2,412
29	765	908	1,081	1,293	1,550	1,864	2,247	2,714
30	815	975	1,169	1,409	1,702	2,063	2,506	3,052
31	868	1,045	1,264	1,534	1,868	2,282	2,795	3,431
32	924	1,120	1,365	1,669	2,048	2,522	3,115	3,855
33	983	1,200	1,472	1,815	2,245	2,787	3,470	4,331
34	1,044	1,284	1,588	1,972	2,460	3,078	3,864	4,863
35	1,108	1,374	1,711	2,143	2,694	3,399	4,302	5,459
36	1,176	1,468	1,844	2,326	2,949	3,751	4,788	6,127
37	1,247	1,569	1,985	2,525	3,226	4,139	5,327	6,875
38	1,322	1,675	2,136	2,739	3,529	4,565	5,925	7,712
39	1,400	1,788	2,298	2,971	3,859	5,034	6,590	8,650
40	1,483	1,908	2,472	3,221	4,219	5,550	7,327	9,701
41	1,569	2,034	2,657	3,491	4,611	6,118	8,146	10,878
42	1,660	2,169	2,855	3,783	5,039	6,742	9,055	12,196
43	1,755	2,311	3,068	4,098	5,505	7,429	10,063	13,672
44	1,855	2,462	3,295	4,438	6,013	8,184	11,183	15,325
45	1,960	2,622	3,538	4,806	6,567	9,015	12,425	17,177
46	2,070	2,792	3,798	5,203	7,170	9,930	13,805	19,251
47	2,186	2,972	4,076	5,631	7,828	10,935	15,336	21,573
48	2,308	3,163	4,374	6,094	8,545	12,041	17,035	24,175
49	2,435	3,365	4,692	6,594	9,326	13,258	18,922	27,089
50	2,569	3,579	5,033	7,134	10,178	14,596	21,016	30,352

by the *Preliminary Value of Annuity Contributions* in box (e) to compute your *Exclusion Factor*, which should be entered in box (g). This is just a fancy name for the percentage of your expected annuity balance that will be made up of your own contributions—and it's an estimate of the percentage of each withdrawal you eventually make that you should get back tax-free.

The next step is to enter your *Combined Tax Rate Assumption* into box (h), which is the amount you determined in box (a), Plan Aid 11a: Example on page 168. Then, turn to Plan Aid Table 32b, and find the column related to your combined tax rate assumption and the row related to your exclusion factor—which should be rounded up or down to the nearest 10 percent. Where the row and column intersect in the table, you will find your *Exclusion Factor Adjustment*, which should be entered in box (i).

Finally, multiply the *Preliminary Value of Annuity Contributions* in box (e) by your *Exclusion Factor Adjustment* in box (i) to compute the *Hypothetical Value of Annuity Contributions* in box (j). This is what your *future* annuity investments might be worth when you stop working, in terms of their ability to provide *taxable* income in retirement. In essence, this is the part of your "missing money" accumulation target that may be taken care of by the *future* contributions you plan to make into your annuity contracts.

After reviewing the example, use Plan Aid 31b: Your Plan to calculate how much you think *your* annuities will be worth when you stop working. Use Plan Aid 32b: Your Plan to estimate your own hypothetical weighted average rate of return. If you don't plan to contribute to annuity contracts you can leave this part blank.

Plan Aid Table 32b:
Exclusion Factor Adjustment for Annuities

Exclusion Factor	Combined Tax Rate Assumption					
	0%	10%	20%	30%	40%	50%
0.00	1.00	1.00	1.00	1.00	1.00	1.00
0.10	1.00	1.01	1.01	1.02	1.03	1.05
0.20	1.00	1.01	1.03	1.04	1.07	1.10
0.30	1.00	1.02	1.04	1.06	1.10	1.15
0.40	1.00	1.02	1.05	1.09	1.13	1.20
0.50	1.00	1.03	1.06	1.11	1.17	1.25
0.60	1.00	1.03	1.08	1.13	1.20	1.30
0.70	1.00	1.04	1.09	1.15	1.23	1.35
0.80	1.00	1.04	1.10	1.17	1.27	1.40
0.90	1.00	1.05	1.11	1.19	1.30	1.45
1.00	1.00	1.06	1.13	1.21	1.33	1.50

Plan Aid 31b: Your Plan
Monthly Annuity Contract Contributions

Monthly Annuity Contract Contributions ……………..…… (a) $ [   ]

Number of Years Until Retirement ……………………… (b) [   ]
   (From item (c), Plan Aid 1b: Your Plan on page 13)

Asset Growth Rate Assumption ……………………….… (c) [%   ]
   (Use Plan Aid 32b: Your Plan on page 278 to estimate rate of return)
   (Select 5%, 6%, 7%, 8%, 9%, 10%, 11%, or 12%)

Asset Growth Factor ……………………………..……… (d) [   ]
   Look Up on Plan Aid Table 32a, Using Items (b) and (c) above

Preliminary Value of Annuity Contributions …………. (e) $ [   ]
   Future Value Dollars in Year 1 of Retirement   *(a) x (d)*

Amount You Contributed to the Annuity …………….… (f) $ [   ]
                                              (a) x (b) x 12

Exclusion Factor …………………………………..………… (g) [   ]
                                              (f) ÷ (e)

Combined Tax Rate Assumption ……………………… (h) [%   ]
   (From item (a), Plan Aid 11b: Your Plan on page 170)

Exclusion Factor Adjustment ………………………… (i) [   ]
   Look Up on Plan Aid Table 32b, Using Items (g) and (h) above

Hypothetical Value of Annuity Contributions ……….. (j) $ [   ]
   Future Value Dollars in Year 1 of Retirement   *(e) x (i)*

Plan Aid 32b: Your Plan
Weighted Average Rate of Return
Monthly Annuity Contract Contributions

Type of Asset	Asset Value	% of Assets	Expect. Ret.	Wtd. Ret.
	$	%	%	%
	$	%	%	%
	$	%	%	%
	$	%	%	%
	$	%	%	%
	$	%	%	%
	$	%	%	%
	$	%	%	%
	$	%	%	%
	$	%	%	%
Tot. Assets & Wtd. Ave. Return	$	%		%

For illustration purposes only. Not representative of an actual investment. An individual investors results may vary. All assumptions and computational results are hypothetical in nature. Variable annuity contracts do have annual fees and expenses that have not been included here in order to simplify the example. If included, the results would be lower. There are no guarantees that you will achieve the results shown. Higher volatility has historically been associated with higher rates of return, and average returns have had a tendency to fluctuate from year to year. You should consult with a financial professional.

25

Investments in Taxable Accounts

If you're investing for retirement, taxable accounts are probably the last place you want to put your money. They're fine if you're saving for a new car or vacation, but they generally don't get you very far when you're shooting for retirement—because the taxes along the way can take such a big bite out of the growth in your accounts.

Investing in Taxable Accounts Versus Annuity Contracts

Saving in tax-deferred vehicles like annuities may help you accumulate more for retirement because you don't have to pay taxes on the growth in your accounts, and can therefore compound larger balances. That's why many advisors will tell you that if you're trying to accumulate more money for retirement over a long period of time, it's often better to save and invest in tax-deferred accounts.

For example, let's say you want to save $6,000 per year, or $500 a month, for thirty years. If you put the $500 per month into an annuity, you can earn tax-deferred returns until you take it out in retirement. If you invest in a combination of large and small company stock accounts within the contract, and earn a hypothetical average annual rate of return of 11 percent, you should have about $1,253,000 after thirty years.

However, if you decide to invest the $500 per month in taxable mutual funds, and are in a 30 percent tax bracket, by the time you get to retirement you may only have about $666,000. So the annuity might allow you to accumulate more than twice as much as a taxable account. Although this is only a hypothetical example, it is meant to illustrate how the tax-deferral features available in an annuity may allow you to accumulate more than in a taxable account. It's important to note that fees and expenses have not been included here to simplify the example. If included, the results would have been lower. As we've discussed before, there are penalties for early withdrawals in annuities that may not be imposed in mutual funds and you should consider them in your overall plan prior to investing in annuities or other tax-deferred vehicles.

What About the Extra Fees in Annuities?

As we've already discussed, there are a variety of fees and expenses associated with the use of annuity contracts, most of which are related to the insurance features and death benefits they provide. People often point to these fees as a reason not to invest in annuities—but this may be an oversimplification of the issue.

For example, let's say an annuity contract charges 1 percent more per year than a comparable mutual fund, assuming that both the annuity and mutual fund have the same underlying asset management fees. If you grow your $500 per month at 10 percent rather than 11 percent to take the extra fees into account, you may end up with about $1,031,000 after thirty years—or $365,000 more than in the taxable account.

At a 9 percent rate of return, which is equivalent to an extra 2 percent annuity charge, you might still end up with $851,000—or about 28 percent more than the comparable taxable investment. So the fees have to become quite large to narrow the gap—and we haven't even accounted for the potential value of the benefits you would be paying for in the first place.

As with all other examples in this book, please keep in mind that the rates used and results obtained in the previous examples are hypothetical in nature and not representative of any particular investment—and of course, your results may vary.

All of this is not to say that the fees and expenses in annuities are unimportant. Like everything else you buy, you should always shop around to get the best product for the best price. That's why it pays to get some help in sorting through the options.

Nonretirement Savings

As I said earlier, if you are saving for things other than retirement—and most people are—don't make the mistake of building those amounts into your retirement plan. In other words, if you don't expect the money to be available when you retire, don't add it into your retirement assets.

Taxable Investments You May Want to Include

However, you may be setting aside some money every month for a rainy day or an emergency fund, hoping that you'll eventually be able to use it for retirement. If you're confident that you won't use it except in emergencies, you may want to go ahead and build it into your plan—it's up to you. At any rate, if you think you will be saving in taxable accounts, and ultimately plan to use the money for retirement, you need to consider *Step #20: Value Your Savings in Taxable Accounts.*

Accounting for the Value of "After-Tax" Income

Since they're taxed every year, your taxable investments may not accumulate as much as other kinds of accounts. However, although the balances might be lower, they may also be "worth" more. Since the taxes have often already been paid, these investments should provide substantially "after-tax" income in retirement. Therefore, you need to adjust their value *upward* to reflect that enhanced value.

Taxable Accounts at Retirement Time

If you decide to save for retirement in taxable vehicles, you will want to investigate the potential benefit of moving those assets into tax-deferred accounts when you stop working, just like you did in Chapter 19 with your existing taxable assets. For the same reasons discussed there, your future taxable savings may be able to generate more income in tax-deferred accounts, so you'll need to revalue them *upward* if you plan to transfer them into tax-deferred vehicles.

Liquidity Taxes

If you don't transfer your taxable assets into tax-deferred accounts at retirement, however, you may end up paying liquidity taxes every time you sell stocks during retirement, which can significantly reduce the amount of income you're likely to get out of your portfolio. If you don't plan to avoid the liquidity taxes, you'll need to *reduce* the value of the assets you plan to leave in taxable accounts.

Adjusting the Value of Future Taxable Investments

Just like your existing taxable assets in Chapter 19, you have to make two kinds of adjustments to the hypothetical future value of your taxable account investments. You have to revalue them *upward* because they provide essentially after-tax income during retirement, and you have to revalue them either *up* or *down* depending upon whether or not you plan to move them into tax-deferred accounts when you stop working. The tax adjustment factors we use in this chapter take both of these adjustments into account.

Considering Taxes

Different investments have different tax consequences, and you may plan to invest in a variety of different accounts. We can't possibly address all of the tax issues related to your own investments and financial situation. The key thing to remember at this stage is that for planning purposes, we assume that you will be paying taxes every year on the growth in your taxable accounts, based upon the tax rate you may be subject to.

Create Your Own Plan

Let's go through the steps outlined in Plan Aid 33a: Example to see how to estimate the hypothetical value of the future monthly investments you plan to make into your taxable accounts. Start with the amount you intend to invest each month, and enter it as your *Monthly Taxable Account Contributions* in box (a). Next, enter the *Number of Years Until Retirement* in box (b), which is the same amount you calculated in item (c), Plan Aid 1a: Example on page 13.

Computing Your Weighted Average Rate of Return

Then, using Plan Aid 34a: Example, calculate a hypothetical weighted average rate of return for the assets you plan to invest in. This is the average annual pretax rate of return you might expect to earn on the accounts until you retire.

Next, round the hypothetical weighted average rate of return either up or down to the nearest whole percentage, and enter it as your *Asset Growth Rate Assumption* in box (c) on Plan Aid 33a: Example.

After estimating your hypothetical weighted average rate of return, you are almost ready to project the hypothetical value of your future taxable investments. But first you have to consider your tax situation—because it has a direct bearing on how much you will be able to accumulate. The higher your estimated tax rate, the lower your projected account balance will be. So the next step is to enter your *Combined Tax Rate Assumption* into box (d), which is the same amount you used in item (a), Plan Aid 11a: Example on page 168.

Then, to determine which lookup table to use in estimating the hypothetical future value of your contributions, look down to the Index for Tax Rate Tables at the bottom of page 284, and find the table that relates to your combined tax rate assumption in box (d). Note which table you are going to use in box (e), *Lookup Table for Appropriate Tax Rate*. This table will provide an asset growth factor that may help you project the value of your taxable investments based upon your own tax rate assumptions.

Once you know which table to use, locate it in pages 287 through

Plan Aid 33a: Example
Monthly Taxable Account Contributions

Monthly Taxable Account Contributions .... | (a) $ | **100**

Number of Years Until Retirement .... | (b) | **22**
(From item (c), Plan Aid 1a: Example on page 13)

Asset Growth Rate Assumption .... | (c) | **8.0** %
(Use Plan Aid 34a: Example on page 285 to estimate rate of return)
(Select 5%, 6%, 7%, 8%, 9%, 10%, 11%, or 12%)

Combined Tax Rate Assumption .... | (d) | **30.0** %
(From item (a), Plan Aid 11a: Example on page 168)

Lookup Table for Appropriate Tax Rate .... | (e) | **Table 34d**
Select look up table for appropriate tax rate below | *From Index Table below*

Asset Growth Factor .... | (f) | **509**
Look Up on Table Noted in Item (e) above, Using Items (b) and (c) above

Preliminary Value of Tax Account Contributions ...... | (g) $ | **50,900**
Future Value Dollars in Year 1 of Retirement | *(a) x (f)*

IF TAXABLE ASSETS REMAIN IN TAXABLE ACCOUNTS

Taxable Account Adjustment Factor .... | (h) | **.97**
(From item (c), Plan Aid 11a: Example on page 168)

Hypothetical Value of Tax Account Contributions ..... | (i) $ | **49,373**
Future Value Dollars in Year 1 of Retirement | *(g) x (h)*

IF TAXABLE ASSETS PUT INTO TAX-DEFERRED ACCOUNTS

Tax-Deferred Account Adjustment Factor .... | (j) | **1.21**
(From item (d), Plan Aid 11a: Example on page 168)

Hypothetical Value of Tax Account Contributions .... | (k) $ | **61,589**
Future Value Dollars in Year 1 of Retirement | *(g) x (j)*

SELECTED VALUE (TAXABLE OR TAX-DEFERRED)

Hypothetical Value of Tax Account Contributions ..... | (l) $ | **61,589**
Future Value Dollars in Year 1 of Retirement | *Select item (i) or (k) above*

INDEX FOR TAX RATE TABLES
Use tax rate in item (d) above to select appropriate lookup table below

Total Tax Rate	0%	Table 34a
Total Tax Rate	10%	Table 34b
Total Tax Rate	20%	Table 34c
Total Tax Rate	30%	Table 34d
Total Tax Rate	40%	Table 34e
Total Tax Rate	50%	Table 34f

Plan Aid 34a: Example
Weighted Average Rate of Return
Monthly Taxable Account Contributions

Type of Asset	Asset Value	% of Assets	Expect. Ret.	Wtd. Ret.
Treasury Bonds	$40	40.0%	4.5%	1.8%
Large Company Value Stocks	$50	50.0%	10.0%	5.0%
Small Company Growth Stocks	$10	10.0%	10.5%	1.1%
Tot. Assets & Wtd. Ave. Return	$100	100.0%		7.9%

For illustration purposes only. Not representative of an actual investment. An individual investors results may vary. All assumptions and computational results are hypothetical in nature. There are no guarantees that you will achieve the results shown. Higher volatility has historically been associated with higher rates of return, and average returns have had a tendency to fluctuate from year to year. The prices of large company stocks and small company stocks will fluctuate. Treasury Bonds are guaranteed by the U.S. government and, if held to maturity, offer a fixed rate of return and principal value. You should consult with a financial professional.

292, and find the column related to your asset growth rate assumption and the row related to the number of years until retirement. Where they intersect in the table, you will find your *Asset Growth Factor*, which should be entered in box (f).

Next, multiply your *Asset Growth Factor* in box (f) by your *Monthly Taxable Account Contributions* in box (a) to compute the *Preliminary Value of Tax Account Contributions*, which should be entered in box (g). This is a preliminary value because in order to determine what it may actually be worth, you have to revalue it to reflect the fact that it will generate primarily after-tax income, and because you have to decide whether or not you're going to keep the money in a taxable account during retirement or move it into a tax-deferred vehicle such as a variable annuity. Remember, all of your assets need to be valued as if they generate 100 percent *pretax* income from within *tax-deferred* accounts.

You Need to Consider Both Strategies

You need to look at the consequences of keeping your assets in taxable accounts, as well as the impact of moving them into tax-deferred vehicles. Ultimately, you will need to decide which value to use in your plan—but you have to start by figuring out what each of those values might be.

If Your Assets Remain in Taxable Accounts Throughout Retirement

If you plan to leave your assets in taxable accounts, they need to be revalued *downward* to reflect the fact that you're not going to be managing them inside of tax-deferred accounts, and due to liquidity taxes you are therefore likely to get less income in retirement.

To make this adjustment, enter your *Taxable Account Adjustment Factor* in box (h). This is the same amount you determined in item (c), Plan Aid 11a: Example on page 168. Then, simply multiply that amount by your *Preliminary Value of Tax Account Contributions* in box (g) to determine the *Hypothetical Value of Tax Account Contributions*, which should be entered in box (i). This is what your future taxable investments might be worth when you stop working, in terms of their ability to take

Plan Aid Table 34a:
Taxable Account Asset Growth Factor Table
for Monthly Contributions
(Total Tax Rate = 0%)

Years to Retire	Asset Growth Rate							
	5.0%	6.0%	7.0%	8.0%	9.0%	10.0%	11.0%	12.0%
1	12	12	12	12	12	13	13	13
2	25	25	26	26	26	26	27	27
3	39	39	40	40	41	42	42	43
4	53	54	55	56	57	58	59	60
5	68	69	71	73	75	77	78	80
6	83	86	89	91	94	97	100	103
7	100	103	107	111	115	119	123	128
8	117	122	127	132	138	143	149	156
9	135	142	148	155	163	170	178	187
10	154	162	171	180	190	200	211	222
11	174	185	195	207	219	232	246	261
12	195	208	221	236	252	268	286	305
13	217	233	249	267	287	308	330	354
14	241	259	279	301	325	351	379	410
15	265	287	311	338	367	398	433	471
16	290	316	345	377	412	451	494	541
17	317	348	382	420	462	508	560	618
18	345	381	421	466	516	572	635	705
19	375	416	463	515	575	642	717	802
20	406	453	508	569	639	718	809	911
21	438	493	555	627	709	803	910	1,033
22	473	535	607	690	785	895	1,023	1,170
23	508	579	662	757	868	998	1,148	1,323
24	546	626	720	830	959	1,110	1,287	1,494
25	586	676	783	909	1,058	1,233	1,441	1,686
26	627	729	850	994	1,165	1,369	1,612	1,901
27	671	785	922	1,086	1,283	1,519	1,802	2,142
28	717	845	999	1,185	1,411	1,683	2,013	2,412
29	765	908	1,081	1,293	1,550	1,864	2,247	2,714
30	815	975	1,169	1,409	1,702	2,063	2,506	3,052
31	868	1,045	1,264	1,534	1,868	2,282	2,795	3,431
32	924	1,120	1,365	1,669	2,048	2,522	3,115	3,855
33	983	1,200	1,472	1,815	2,245	2,787	3,470	4,331
34	1,044	1,284	1,588	1,972	2,460	3,078	3,864	4,863
35	1,108	1,374	1,711	2,143	2,694	3,399	4,302	5,459
36	1,176	1,468	1,844	2,326	2,949	3,751	4,788	6,127
37	1,247	1,569	1,985	2,525	3,226	4,139	5,327	6,875
38	1,322	1,675	2,136	2,739	3,529	4,565	5,925	7,712
39	1,400	1,788	2,298	2,971	3,859	5,034	6,590	8,650
40	1,483	1,908	2,472	3,221	4,219	5,550	7,327	9,701
41	1,569	2,034	2,657	3,491	4,611	6,118	8,146	10,878
42	1,660	2,169	2,855	3,783	5,039	6,742	9,055	12,196
43	1,755	2,311	3,068	4,098	5,505	7,429	10,063	13,672
44	1,855	2,462	3,295	4,438	6,013	8,184	11,183	15,325
45	1,960	2,622	3,538	4,806	6,567	9,015	12,425	17,177
46	2,070	2,792	3,798	5,203	7,170	9,930	13,805	19,251
47	2,186	2,972	4,076	5,631	7,828	10,935	15,336	21,573
48	2,308	3,163	4,374	6,094	8,545	12,041	17,035	24,175
49	2,435	3,365	4,692	6,594	9,326	13,258	18,922	27,089
50	2,569	3,579	5,033	7,134	10,178	14,596	21,016	30,352

For illustration purposes only. Not representative of an actual investment. All assumptions and computational results are hypothetical in nature. Higher volatility has historically been associated with higher rates of return, and average returns have had a tendency to fluctuate from year to year.

Plan Aid Table 34b:
Taxable Account Asset Growth Factor Table
for Monthly Contributions
(Total Tax Rate = 10%)

Years to Retire	Asset Growth Rate							
	5.0%	6.0%	7.0%	8.0%	9.0%	10.0%	11.0%	12.0%
1	12	12	12	12	12	12	13	13
2	25	25	25	26	26	26	26	27
3	38	39	39	40	40	41	41	42
4	52	53	54	55	56	57	58	59
5	67	68	70	72	73	75	76	78
6	82	84	87	89	91	94	96	99
7	98	101	105	108	111	115	119	122
8	115	119	123	128	133	138	143	148
9	132	138	144	150	156	163	170	177
10	150	158	165	173	181	190	199	208
11	169	178	188	198	208	219	231	243
12	189	200	212	224	237	252	266	282
13	210	223	238	253	269	287	305	325
14	232	248	265	283	303	325	348	373
15	255	273	294	316	340	367	395	426
16	278	300	325	351	380	412	447	485
17	303	329	358	389	424	462	504	550
18	329	359	392	429	470	516	566	622
19	356	391	430	473	521	575	635	701
20	384	424	469	519	576	639	710	790
21	414	459	511	569	635	709	793	887
22	445	496	555	622	698	785	884	996
23	477	536	603	680	768	868	984	1,116
24	511	577	653	741	842	959	1,094	1,249
25	546	620	706	807	923	1,058	1,214	1,397
26	583	666	763	877	1,010	1,165	1,347	1,560
27	621	714	824	953	1,104	1,283	1,493	1,741
28	661	765	888	1,034	1,206	1,411	1,653	1,942
29	703	819	956	1,120	1,316	1,550	1,830	2,164
30	747	875	1,029	1,213	1,435	1,702	2,023	2,410
31	793	935	1,106	1,313	1,564	1,868	2,236	2,683
32	841	998	1,188	1,420	1,703	2,048	2,470	2,985
33	891	1,064	1,275	1,535	1,853	2,245	2,727	3,320
34	943	1,133	1,368	1,658	2,016	2,460	3,010	3,692
35	998	1,207	1,466	1,789	2,192	2,694	3,320	4,103
36	1,055	1,284	1,571	1,931	2,382	2,949	3,661	4,559
37	1,115	1,366	1,683	2,082	2,587	3,226	4,036	5,064
38	1,177	1,452	1,801	2,244	2,809	3,529	4,449	5,623
39	1,242	1,543	1,927	2,418	3,049	3,859	4,902	6,243
40	1,311	1,638	2,060	2,605	3,309	4,219	5,399	6,930
41	1,382	1,739	2,203	2,805	3,589	4,611	5,946	7,691
42	1,456	1,845	2,354	3,019	3,892	5,039	6,548	8,534
43	1,534	1,957	2,514	3,249	4,220	5,505	7,208	9,468
44	1,615	2,075	2,685	3,495	4,574	6,013	7,934	10,503
45	1,700	2,200	2,867	3,759	4,957	6,567	8,733	11,650
46	1,789	2,331	3,059	4,042	5,371	7,170	9,610	12,921
47	1,882	2,469	3,265	4,346	5,818	7,828	10,573	14,329
48	1,979	2,615	3,483	4,671	6,302	8,545	11,633	15,889
49	2,080	2,768	3,714	5,020	6,825	9,326	12,797	17,618
50	2,186	2,930	3,961	5,394	7,390	10,178	14,076	19,533

For illustration purposes only. Not representative of an actual investment. All assumptions and computational results are hypothetical in nature. Higher volatility has historically been associated with higher rates of return, and average returns have had a tendency to fluctuate from year to year.

Plan Aid Table 34c:
Taxable Account Asset Growth Factor Table
for Monthly Contributions
(Total Tax Rate = 20%)

Years to Retire	Asset Growth Rate							
	5.0%	6.0%	7.0%	8.0%	9.0%	10.0%	11.0%	12.0%
1	12	12	12	12	12	12	12	13
2	25	25	25	25	26	26	26	26
3	38	39	39	39	40	40	41	41
4	52	53	54	54	55	56	57	58
5	66	67	69	70	72	73	74	76
6	81	83	85	87	89	91	93	96
7	97	99	102	105	108	111	114	117
8	113	116	120	124	128	132	137	141
9	129	134	139	144	150	155	161	167
10	147	153	159	166	173	180	188	196
11	165	172	180	189	198	207	217	227
12	184	193	203	213	224	236	248	261
13	203	214	226	239	253	267	283	299
14	223	237	251	267	283	301	320	340
15	245	261	278	296	316	338	361	385
16	267	285	306	328	351	377	405	435
17	290	311	335	361	389	420	453	489
18	313	339	366	396	429	466	505	549
19	338	367	399	434	473	515	562	614
20	364	397	434	474	519	569	624	685
21	391	428	470	517	569	627	692	764
22	418	461	509	562	622	690	765	849
23	447	496	550	611	680	757	845	943
24	478	532	593	662	741	830	931	1,047
25	509	569	638	717	807	909	1,026	1,160
26	541	609	686	775	877	994	1,129	1,283
27	575	650	737	837	953	1,086	1,240	1,419
28	611	694	791	903	1,034	1,185	1,362	1,568
29	647	739	847	973	1,120	1,293	1,494	1,731
30	685	787	907	1,048	1,213	1,409	1,638	1,910
31	725	837	970	1,127	1,313	1,534	1,795	2,105
32	766	890	1,037	1,212	1,420	1,669	1,966	2,320
33	809	945	1,107	1,302	1,535	1,815	2,151	2,555
34	854	1,002	1,181	1,397	1,658	1,972	2,353	2,813
35	900	1,063	1,260	1,499	1,789	2,143	2,572	3,096
36	948	1,126	1,343	1,607	1,931	2,326	2,811	3,405
37	998	1,192	1,430	1,722	2,082	2,525	3,071	3,745
38	1,050	1,262	1,523	1,845	2,244	2,739	3,354	4,117
39	1,105	1,335	1,620	1,975	2,418	2,971	3,661	4,525
40	1,161	1,411	1,723	2,114	2,605	3,221	3,996	4,971
41	1,220	1,491	1,832	2,262	2,805	3,491	4,360	5,461
42	1,281	1,575	1,947	2,419	3,019	3,783	4,756	5,998
43	1,344	1,663	2,068	2,586	3,249	4,098	5,187	6,586
44	1,410	1,755	2,196	2,764	3,495	4,438	5,656	7,231
45	1,479	1,851	2,332	2,953	3,759	4,806	6,167	7,938
46	1,550	1,952	2,474	3,155	4,042	5,203	6,722	8,712
47	1,624	2,058	2,625	3,369	4,346	5,631	7,326	9,561
48	1,702	2,169	2,785	3,597	4,671	6,094	7,983	10,492
49	1,782	2,286	2,953	3,839	5,020	6,594	8,698	11,512
50	1,865	2,408	3,131	4,097	5,394	7,134	9,476	12,629

Plan Aid Table 34d:
Taxable Account Asset Growth Factor Table
for Monthly Contributions
(Total Tax Rate = 30%)

Years to Retire	Asset Growth Rate							
	5.0%	6.0%	7.0%	8.0%	9.0%	10.0%	11.0%	12.0%
1	12	12	12	12	12	12	12	12
2	25	25	25	25	25	26	26	26
3	38	38	39	39	39	40	40	41
4	51	52	53	54	54	55	56	56
5	65	67	68	69	70	71	72	74
6	80	82	83	85	87	89	90	92
7	95	97	100	102	105	107	110	113
8	110	113	117	120	123	127	131	134
9	126	130	135	139	144	148	153	158
10	143	148	154	159	165	171	177	184
11	160	167	173	180	188	195	203	212
12	178	186	194	203	212	221	232	242
13	196	206	216	226	238	249	262	275
14	216	227	239	251	265	279	294	310
15	235	249	263	278	294	311	329	349
16	256	271	288	306	325	345	367	391
17	277	295	314	335	358	382	408	436
18	299	319	342	366	392	421	452	485
19	321	345	371	399	430	463	499	538
20	345	372	401	434	469	508	550	596
21	369	400	433	470	511	555	604	658
22	394	429	467	509	555	607	663	726
23	420	459	502	550	603	662	727	800
24	447	490	539	593	653	720	795	879
25	475	523	577	638	706	783	869	966
26	504	557	618	686	763	850	948	1,059
27	533	593	661	737	824	922	1,034	1,160
28	564	630	705	791	888	999	1,126	1,270
29	596	669	752	847	956	1,081	1,225	1,390
30	629	709	801	907	1,029	1,169	1,332	1,519
31	664	751	853	970	1,106	1,264	1,447	1,659
32	699	795	907	1,037	1,188	1,365	1,570	1,811
33	736	841	963	1,107	1,275	1,472	1,704	1,975
34	774	888	1,023	1,181	1,368	1,588	1,847	2,154
35	813	938	1,085	1,260	1,466	1,711	2,002	2,347
36	853	989	1,151	1,343	1,571	1,844	2,169	2,556
37	896	1,043	1,219	1,430	1,683	1,985	2,348	2,784
38	939	1,099	1,291	1,523	1,801	2,136	2,541	3,030
39	984	1,158	1,367	1,620	1,927	2,298	2,749	3,297
40	1,031	1,218	1,446	1,723	2,060	2,472	2,973	3,586
41	1,079	1,282	1,529	1,832	2,203	2,657	3,215	3,900
42	1,129	1,348	1,617	1,947	2,354	2,855	3,475	4,240
43	1,181	1,417	1,708	2,068	2,514	3,068	3,755	4,609
44	1,234	1,488	1,804	2,196	2,685	3,295	4,056	5,008
45	1,290	1,563	1,905	2,332	2,867	3,538	4,381	5,441
46	1,347	1,641	2,010	2,474	3,059	3,798	4,731	5,911
47	1,406	1,722	2,121	2,625	3,265	4,076	5,107	6,420
48	1,468	1,807	2,237	2,785	3,483	4,374	5,513	6,972
49	1,531	1,895	2,359	2,953	3,714	4,692	5,950	7,570
50	1,597	1,987	2,487	3,131	3,961	5,033	6,420	8,218

For illustration purposes only. Not representative of an actual investment. All assumptions and computational results are hypothetical in nature. Higher volatility has historically been associated with higher rates of return, and average returns have had a tendency to fluctuate from year to year.

Plan Aid Table 34e:
Taxable Account Asset Growth Factor Table
for Monthly Contributions
(Total Tax Rate = 40%)

Years to Retire	Asset Growth Rate							
	5.0%	6.0%	7.0%	8.0%	9.0%	10.0%	11.0%	12.0%
1	12	12	12	12	12	12	12	12
2	25	25	25	25	25	25	26	26
3	38	38	38	39	39	39	40	40
4	51	51	52	53	53	54	55	55
5	65	66	67	67	68	69	71	72
6	79	80	82	83	84	86	88	89
7	93	95	97	99	101	103	106	108
8	108	111	113	116	119	122	125	128
9	124	127	130	134	138	142	146	150
10	139	144	148	153	158	162	168	173
11	156	161	167	172	178	185	191	198
12	173	179	186	193	200	208	216	224
13	190	198	206	214	223	233	243	253
14	208	217	227	237	248	259	271	283
15	226	237	249	261	273	287	301	316
16	245	258	271	285	300	316	333	351
17	265	279	295	311	329	348	368	389
18	285	302	319	339	359	381	404	429
19	306	325	345	367	391	416	443	473
20	327	348	372	397	424	453	485	519
21	349	373	400	428	459	493	529	569
22	371	399	429	461	496	535	577	622
23	395	425	459	496	536	579	627	680
24	419	453	490	532	577	626	681	741
25	443	481	523	569	620	676	738	807
26	469	511	557	609	666	729	799	877
27	495	542	593	650	714	785	864	953
28	522	573	630	694	765	845	934	1,034
29	550	606	669	739	819	908	1,008	1,120
30	579	640	709	787	875	975	1,087	1,213
31	608	675	751	837	935	1,045	1,171	1,313
32	639	712	795	890	998	1,120	1,260	1,420
33	670	750	841	945	1,064	1,200	1,356	1,535
34	702	789	888	1,002	1,133	1,284	1,458	1,658
35	735	829	938	1,063	1,207	1,374	1,566	1,789
36	770	871	989	1,126	1,284	1,468	1,682	1,931
37	805	915	1,043	1,192	1,366	1,569	1,805	2,082
38	841	960	1,099	1,262	1,452	1,675	1,937	2,244
39	879	1,007	1,158	1,335	1,543	1,788	2,077	2,418
40	917	1,055	1,218	1,411	1,638	1,908	2,227	2,605
41	957	1,106	1,282	1,491	1,739	2,034	2,386	2,805
42	998	1,158	1,348	1,575	1,845	2,169	2,556	3,019
43	1,040	1,211	1,417	1,663	1,957	2,311	2,737	3,249
44	1,083	1,267	1,488	1,755	2,075	2,462	2,930	3,495
45	1,128	1,325	1,563	1,851	2,200	2,622	3,136	3,759
46	1,174	1,385	1,641	1,952	2,331	2,792	3,355	4,042
47	1,221	1,447	1,722	2,058	2,469	2,972	3,589	4,346
48	1,270	1,511	1,807	2,169	2,615	3,163	3,838	4,671
49	1,320	1,578	1,895	2,286	2,768	3,365	4,104	5,020
50	1,372	1,647	1,987	2,408	2,930	3,579	4,387	5,394

For illustration purposes only. Not representative of an actual investment. All assumptions and computational results are hypothetical in nature. Higher volatility has historically been associated with higher rates of return, and average returns have had a tendency to fluctuate from year to year.

Plan Aid Table 34f:
Taxable Account Asset Growth Factor Table
for Monthly Contributions
(Total Tax Rate = 50%)

Years to Retire	Asset Growth Rate							
	5.0%	6.0%	7.0%	8.0%	9.0%	10.0%	11.0%	12.0%
1	12	12	12	12	12	12	12	12
2	25	25	25	25	25	25	25	25
3	37	38	38	38	38	39	39	39
4	50	51	51	52	52	53	53	54
5	64	65	65	66	67	68	69	69
6	78	79	80	81	82	83	85	86
7	92	93	95	97	98	100	102	103
8	106	108	110	113	115	117	120	122
9	121	124	126	129	132	135	138	142
10	136	139	143	147	150	154	158	162
11	152	156	160	165	169	174	179	185
12	167	173	178	184	189	195	202	208
13	184	190	196	203	210	217	225	233
14	200	208	216	223	232	241	250	259
15	218	226	235	245	255	265	276	287
16	235	245	256	267	278	290	303	316
17	253	265	277	290	303	317	332	348
18	272	285	299	313	329	345	363	381
19	291	306	321	338	356	375	395	416
20	310	327	345	364	384	406	429	453
21	330	349	369	391	414	438	465	493
22	350	371	394	418	445	473	503	535
23	371	395	420	447	477	508	543	579
24	393	419	447	478	511	546	585	626
25	415	443	475	509	546	586	629	676
26	437	469	504	541	583	627	676	729
27	460	495	533	575	621	671	726	785
28	484	522	564	611	661	717	778	845
29	508	550	596	647	703	765	833	908
30	533	579	629	685	747	815	891	975
31	558	608	664	725	793	868	952	1,045
32	584	639	699	766	841	924	1,017	1,120
33	611	670	736	809	891	983	1,085	1,200
34	639	702	774	854	943	1,044	1,157	1,284
35	667	735	813	900	998	1,108	1,233	1,374
36	695	770	853	948	1,055	1,176	1,313	1,468
37	725	805	896	998	1,115	1,247	1,398	1,569
38	755	841	939	1,050	1,177	1,322	1,487	1,675
39	786	879	984	1,105	1,242	1,400	1,581	1,788
40	818	917	1,031	1,161	1,311	1,483	1,680	1,908
41	851	957	1,079	1,220	1,382	1,569	1,785	2,034
42	884	998	1,129	1,281	1,456	1,660	1,895	2,169
43	918	1,040	1,181	1,344	1,534	1,755	2,012	2,311
44	953	1,083	1,234	1,410	1,615	1,855	2,135	2,462
45	989	1,128	1,290	1,479	1,700	1,960	2,265	2,622
46	1,026	1,174	1,347	1,550	1,789	2,070	2,401	2,792
47	1,064	1,221	1,406	1,624	1,882	2,186	2,546	2,972
48	1,103	1,270	1,468	1,702	1,979	2,308	2,698	3,163
49	1,142	1,320	1,531	1,782	2,080	2,435	2,859	3,365
50	1,183	1,372	1,597	1,865	2,186	2,569	3,028	3,579

For illustration purposes only. Not representative of an actual investment. All assumptions and computational results are hypothetical in nature. Higher volatility has historically been associated with higher rates of return, and average returns have had a tendency to fluctuate from year to year.

care of your lifestyle in retirement—**if you decide to leave them in a taxable account.**

If You Move Your Assets into Tax-Deferred Accounts

However, if you plan to move your assets into tax-deferred accounts when you get to retirement, you will need to revalue them *upward*, to reflect the fact that you will probably get more income by managing them inside of tax-deferred accounts than if you don't.

To make this adjustment, enter your *Tax-Deferred Account Adjustment Factor* in box (j). This is the same amount you determined in item (d), Plan Aid 11a: Example on page 168. Then, multiply that amount by your *Preliminary Value of Tax Account Contributions* in box (g) to determine the second *Hypothetical Value of Tax Account Contributions*, which should be entered in box (k). This is what your future taxable investments might be worth when you stop working—**if you decide to transfer them into tax-deferred accounts.**

You Get More Value in Tax-Deferred Accounts

As you can see, your taxable assets are likely to be worth more if you move them into tax-deferred accounts. This doesn't necessarily mean that you will do it this way—because there may be good reasons not to. But generally speaking, if income is your biggest concern, you will probably want to move your assets into tax-deferred accounts at retirement time.

Keep in mind that none of the adjustments we've been talking about will actually change the amount of money you have in your taxable accounts. They simply help you determine how much those assets may be worth in terms of their ability to support your lifestyle when you get to retirement.

Selecting a Value

The final step is to decide which way you think you will go. Select either the lower taxable account value in box (i) or the higher tax-deferred account value in box (k), and enter it in box (l), *Hypothetical Value of Tax Account Contributions*. This is what you might plan for your *future* investments in taxable accounts to be worth when you stop working, in terms of their ability to support your lifestyle in retirement. In essence, this is the part of your "missing money" accumulation target that may be taken care of by *future* investments in your taxable accounts.

After reviewing the example, use Plan Aid 33b: Your Plan to calculate how much your taxable accounts may be worth when you stop working. Use Plan Aid 34b: Your Plan to estimate a hypothetical weighted average rate of return. If you don't plan to save for retirement in taxable accounts you can leave this part blank.

Plan Aid 33b: Your Plan
Monthly Taxable Account Contributions

Monthly Taxable Account Contributions .... (a) $ [   ]

Number of Years Until Retirement .... (b) [   ]
  (From item (c), Plan Aid 1b: Your Plan on page 13)

Asset Growth Rate Assumption .... (c) [%]
  (Use Plan Aid 34b: Your Plan on page 296 to estimate rate of return)
  (Select 5%, 6%, 7%, 8%, 9%, 10%, 11%, or 12%)

Combined Tax Rate Assumption .... (d) [%]
  (From item (a), Plan Aid 11b: Your Plan on page 170)

Lookup Table for Appropriate Tax Rate .... (e) [   ]
  Select lookup table for appropriate tax rate below   *From Index Table below*

Asset Growth Factor .... (f) [   ]
  Look Up on Table Noted in Item (e) above, using Items (b) and (c) above

Preliminary Value of Tax Account Contributions ...... (g) $ [   ]
  Future Value Dollars in Year 1 of Retirement   *(a) x (f)*

IF TAXABLE ASSETS REMAIN IN TAXABLE ACCOUNTS

Taxable Account Adjustment Factor .... (h) [   ]
  (From item (c), Plan Aid 11b: Your Plan on page 170)

Hypothetical Value of Tax Account Contributions ..... (i) $ [   ]
  Future Value Dollars in Year 1 of Retirement   *(g) x (h)*

IF TAXABLE ASSETS PUT INTO TAX-DEFERRED ACCOUNTS

Tax-Deferred Account Adjustment Factor .... (j) [   ]
  (From item (d), Plan Aid 11b: Your Plan on page 170)

Hypothetical Value of Tax Account Contributions .... (k) $ [   ]
  Future Value Dollars in Year 1 of Retirement   *(g) x (j)*

SELECTED VALUE (TAXABLE OR TAX-DEFERRED)

Hypothetical Value of Tax Account Contributions ..... (l) $ [   ]
  Future Value Dollars in Year 1 of Retirement   *Select item (i) or (k) above*

INDEX FOR TAX RATE TABLES
Use tax rate in item (d) above to select appropriate lookup table below

Total Tax Rate 0%	Table 34a
Total Tax Rate 10%	Table 34b
Total Tax Rate 20%	Table 34c
Total Tax Rate 30%	Table 34d
Total Tax Rate 40%	Table 34e
Total Tax Rate 50%	Table 34f

Plan Aid 34b: Your Plan
Weighted Average Rate of Return
Monthly Taxable Account Contributions

Type of Asset	Asset Value	% of Assets	Expect. Ret.	Wtd. Ret.
	$	%	%	%
	$	%	%	%
	$	%	%	%
	$	%	%	%
	$	%	%	%
	$	%	%	%
	$	%	%	%
	$	%	%	%
	$	%	%	%
	$	%	%	%
Tot. Assets & Wtd. Ave. Return	$	%		%

For illustration purposes only. Not representative of an actual investment. An individual investors results may vary. All assumptions and computational results are hypothetical in nature. There are no guarantees that you will achieve the results shown. Higher volatility has historically been associated with higher rates of return, and average returns have had a tendency to fluctuate from year to year. You should consult with a financial professional.

26

Setting Your Retirement Plan Accumulation Target

The final step in this part of the process is to figure out how much you may still need to accumulate in your retirement plans at work. For most people, their 401(k) plans, 403(b) plans, SEP, SIMPLE and other employee savings accounts will make up the bulk of their retirement resources—so you need to know how much to save and how to invest it to achieve your ultimate goals and objectives.

A Quick Review

Back in Chapter 20 you established your hypothetical "missing money" accumulation target. To do that, you subtracted the hypothetical future value of your existing retirement accounts from the total retirement accumulation target you set in Chapter 12. This helped you to figure out how much more you needed to accumulate.

Taking Stock of What You Plan to Save in the Future

In the last four chapters you projected the hypothetical future value of the additional investments and contributions you plan to make into your regular and Roth IRAs, annuities, and taxable investments. Since you calculated how much these assets may be worth when you get to retirement, you can now subtract them from the "missing money" target you established earlier, to determine how much you may still need to accumulate in your retirement plans at work.

Deciding What to Do in Your Retirement Plans at Work

After calculating how much more you may need to accumulate, you can also figure out how much you may have to contribute each month into your retirement plans at work to reach your objective. In the next section of the book we'll consider the contributions you may have to make, as well as the contributions that might be made for you by your employer.

Many retirement plans include provisions for employers to make matching contributions and/or outright deposits into participant accounts, so you need to determine how much *you* may have to contribute and how much *your employer* might kick in for you—and then how to invest all of it. To do that, however, you have to start with *Step #21: Establish a Retirement Plan Accumulation Target.*

Create Your Own Plan

To figure out how much you may need to save and invest in your retirement plans at work, start with Plan Aid 35a: Example, and add up the hypothetical values of all the future contributions you intend to make into your various retirement accounts. This is the amount of your hypothetical "missing money" accumulation target that should be taken care of by the future contributions you plan to make.

In box (a), enter your *Hypothetical Value of IRA Contributions*, which comes from item (e), Plan Aid 27a: Example on page 256. Then, in box (b), enter your *Hypothetical Value of Roth IRA Contributions*, which comes from item (l), Plan Aid 29a: Example on page 263. Then, in box (c), enter your *Hypothetical Value of Annuity Contributions*, which comes from item (j), Plan Aid 31a: Example on page 271. Then, in box (d), enter your *Hypothetical Value of Tax Account Contributions*, which comes from item (l), Plan Aid 33a: Example on page 284. And finally, add boxes (a) through (d) to determine the *Hypothetical Value of* **All**

Monthly Contributions, which should be entered into box (e). This is the total hypothetical value of all the future contributions you plan to make into these accounts.

Plan Aid 35a: Example
Future Value of Monthly Contributions (Summary)

Hypothetical Value of IRA Contributions .... (a) $ **69,000**
  (From item (e), Plan Aid 27a: Example on page 256)

Hypothetical Value of Roth IRA Contributions ... . (b) $ **98,571**
  (From item (l), Plan Aid 29a: Example on page 263)

Hypothetical Value of Annuity Contributions .... (c) $ **75,210**
  (From item (j), Plan Aid 31a: Example on page 271)

Hypothetical Value of Tax Account Contributions ..... (d) $ **61,589**
  (From item (l), Plan Aid 33a: Example on page 284)

Hypothetical Value of **All Monthly Contributions** .... (e) $ **304,370**
  Future Value Dollars in Year 1 of Retirement   *Total of (a) through (d)*

For illustration purposes only. Not representative of an actual investment. An individual investor's results may vary. All assumptions and computational results are hypothetical in nature. There are no guarantees that you will achieve the results shown. You should consult with a financial professional.

Using Your Own Numbers

After reviewing the example, fill in Plan Aid 35b: Your Plan now to determine how much your own future contributions may be worth at retirement.

Setting Your Retirement Plan Accumulation Target

Now that you know the hypothetical value of your future contributions, you can calculate how much you may still need to save and invest in your retirement plans at work. To do this, turn to Plan Aid 36a: Example and enter your *Hypothetical "Missing Money" Target* into box (a). This is the amount you determined in item (c), Plan Aid 26a: Example on page 242.

Then, enter the *Hypothetical Value of* **All Monthly Contributions** into box (b), which is the amount you just determined in item (e) on Plan

Plan Aid 35b: Your Plan
Future Value of Monthly Contributions (Summary)

Hypothetical Value of IRA Contributions .... (a) $ [_____]
(From item (e), Plan Aid 27b: Your Plan on page 259)

Hypothetical Value of Roth IRA Contributions .... (b) $ [_____]
(From item (l), Plan Aid 29b: Your Plan on page 267)

Hypothetical Value of Annuity Contributions .... (c) $ [_____]
(From item (j), Plan Aid 31b: Your Plan on page 277)

Hypothetical Value of Tax Account Contributions ..... (d) $ [_____]
(From item (l), Plan Aid 33b: Your Plan on page 295)

Hypothetical Value of **All Monthly Contributions** .... (e) $ [_____]
Future Value Dollars in Year 1 of Retirement   *Total of (a) through (d)*

For illustration purposes only. Not representative of an actual investment. An individual investor's results may vary. All assumptions and computational results are hypothetical in nature. There are no guarantees that you will achieve the results shown. You should consult with a financial professional.

Aid 35a: Example on page 299. The final step is to subtract the hypothetical future value of your contributions in box (b) from your hypothetical "missing money" accumulation target in box (a) to determine your *Hypothetical Future Retirement Plan Target*, which should be

Plan Aid 36a: Example
Setting the Future Retirement Plan Target

Hypothetical "Missing Money" Target .... (a) $ **1,210,229**
(From item (c), Plan Aid 26a: Example on page 242)

Hypothetical Value of **All Monthly Contributions** ... (b) $ **304,370**
(From item (e), Plan Aid 35a: Example on page 299)

Hypothetical Future Retirement Plan Target .... (c) $ **905,859**
Future Value Dollars in Year 1 of Retirement   *(a) - (b)*

For illustration purposes only. Not representative of an actual investment. An individual investor's results may vary. All assumptions and computational results are hypothetical in nature. There are no guarantees that you will achieve the results shown. You should consult with a financial professional.

entered into box (c). This is the amount of money you may still need to accumulate in your retirement plans at work, and it consists of everything you contribute as well as everything that may be contributed by your employer.

Using Your Own Numbers

After reviewing the example, fill in Plan Aid 36b: Your Plan now to determine your own hypothetical retirement plan accumulation target.

If your *Hypothetical Future Retirement Plan Target* in box (c) is *equal to or less than zero*, it means that along with the assets you've already accumulated and the future contributions you intend to make into your various savings vehicles, you may already have enough to meet your retirement objectives—without putting anything into your retirement plans at work.

Obviously, you want to use your retirement plans at work to continue saving and investing for retirement. So at this point, if you came up with a negative number, you should go back to the beginning and change some of your planning variables to give yourself a higher goal to shoot

Plan Aid 36b: Your Plan
Setting the Future Retirement Plan Target

Hypothetical "Missing Money" Target .... (a) $ _____
(From item (c), Plan Aid 26b: Your Plan on page 243)

Hypothetical Value of **All Monthly Contributions** ... (b) $ _____
(From item (e), Plan Aid 35b: Your Plan on page 300)

Hypothetical Future Retirement Plan Target .... (c) $ _____
Future Value Dollars in Year 1 of Retirement   *(a) - (b)*

For illustration purposes only. Not representative of an actual investment. An individual investor's results may vary. All assumptions and computational results are hypothetical in nature. There are no guarantees that you will achieve the results shown. You should consult with a financial professional.

for. For example, you could plan to retire earlier, plan to maintain a higher percentage of your preretirement income during retirement, or reduce the rates of return you estimated for some of your existing assets or future contributions.

PART SIX

Taking Advantage of Employer-Sponsored Retirement Plans

In this section, we cover:

Step #22: Account for Employer Contributions;

Step #23: Formulate a "Fixed-Amount" Savings Plan;

Step #24: Prepare a "Percent-of-Salary" Savings Plan; and

Step #25: Get Started Now!

After completing this part of the book, you should have determined how much your employer is likely to put away for you, how much you may need to save for yourself, and how to use the worksheets and lookup tables to refine your plan.

Accounting for Employer Contributions

One of the reasons that your retirement plans at work will make up such an important part of your overall financial strategy is that many employers contribute money into these plans for you. As a result, you are often able to accumulate much larger balances for retirement. That's why you need to follow *Step #22: Account for Employer Contributions,* because they can make a really big difference.

Employers Generally Contribute in One of Two Ways, or Both

The contributions employers make for their employees generally come from one of two sources, or sometimes from both. They're either matching contributions into 401(k)-type plans, which are computed as a percentage of the amount you put in, or they're outright contributions that are calculated as a percent of your salary, and then deposited into your account without reference as to whether or not you contribute. These kinds of arrangements are often referred to as money purchase pension plans and/or profit sharing plans, and some employers have both, as well as 401(k)-type matching plans—so it's possible to have many different combinations.

Money Purchase Pension Plans and Profit Sharing Plans

Obviously, if an employer is willing to contribute money into your account without requiring you to do anything yourself, you want to make the most of it. In many instances, the money they put in can take care of a significant amount of the total you need to accumulate for retirement, so you'll want to manage it carefully and account for it properly in your plan. I refer to these kinds of accounts, which you don't have to contribute to, as *fixed-percentage pension plans*, and they can play an important role in your accumulation strategy if you're fortunate enough to have one or more of them.

Matching Contribution Plans

I refer to the other kind of accounts as *matching contribution plans*. One of the most important things to remember is that if you're lucky enough to have a matching contribution plan, you should always put in enough to get the full amount of any matching benefit—because it's like getting free money.

For example, let's say your employer offers a 50 percent matching contribution on the first 6 percent of salary that you contribute into a 401(k) plan. In other words, they deposit fifty cents for every dollar you put in, up to the first 6 percent of your salary.

Say you're making $60,000 a year, or $5,000 per month. You would be able to contribute up to 6 percent of your salary, or $300 per month, and then have your employer contribute another $150, or half as much. How can you beat that? It's like getting a guaranteed 50 percent rate of return as soon as you make your contribution.

Keep in mind that even though you would normally be allowed to put in more than $300 a month, and in many instances would, your employer would never put in more than $150, because in this case, they only match up to half of the first 6 percent of your salary. But no matter how you cut it, that's still a great deal, and you definitely want to put in at least enough to get the full match. For every dollar you don't contribute up to the matching limit of $300, you give up fifty cents—and those little amounts add up quickly over long investment periods.

The Financial Impact of Matching Contributions

If you have a plan that does *not* include a matching contribution, and you deposit $300 per month for thirty-five years and earn a hypothetical 11 percent rate of return, you may have about $1,291,000 by the time you get to retirement—which isn't bad. On the other hand, if your employer matches fifty cents for every dollar you contribute, they'll put in another $150 per month.

If you invest the entire $450 each month at the same hypothetical 11 percent rate of return for thirty-five years, you might end up with almost $1,936,000, or $645,000 more. So you don't want to leave any of the potential matching contributions on the table, because they obviously can make a big difference.

Consider Everything Your Employer Will Do for You

The combination of employer matching amounts and outright contributions can have a big impact on how much you may need to save in your retirement plans at work. Until you consider how much you're likely to get from your employer, you can't possibly determine how much you need to save for yourself—so the next step in the process is to quantify the amounts and percentages you might plan to get from them. But remember, every company is different, so if you change jobs, you will probably run into different benefits—and you'll have to take them into account as you move forward.

Create Your Own Plan

To evaluate the contributions you might plan to get from your employer, you need to follow a two-step process. You start by considering the value of any fixed-percentage pension plans you have, and then move on to matching contribution plans like 401(k) and 403(b) accounts.

Fixed-Percentage Pension Plans

These are the kinds of plans in which your employer specifies a percent of salary to contribute into your account without considering whether or not you contribute.

To get started, turn to Plan Aid 37a: Example. In box (a), enter your *Employer Pension Contribution Percentage*. This is the percent of salary that your employer will contribute into your account. Remember, with these kinds of plans, you shouldn't have to do anything special to get the contributions. They simply result from the fact that you're an employee.

If you have more than one plan, you'll need to total up the percentages in all of them. For example, if you have a profit sharing plan that contributes 2 percent of your salary, and a money purchase plan that contributes 3 percent, the total percentage contribution is 5 percent. You should be able to get this information from your human resource department if you don't already know it.

Plan Aid 37a: Example
Employer Contributions—Fixed Percentage Pension Plans

Employer Pension Contribution Percentage .... (a)   **2.0** %

Current Annual Salary .... (b) $ **75,000**
    (From item (d), Plan Aid 3a: Example on page 75)

Annual Employer Pension Contribution Amount ...... (c) $ **1,500**
                                  (a) x (b)

Monthly Employer Pension Contribution Amount ..... (d) $ **125**
                                  (c) ÷ 12

The next step is to enter your *Current Annual Salary* into box (b). This is the same amount you used in item (d), Plan Aid 3a: Example on page 75. Then, multiply the contribution percentage in box (a) by your current salary in box (b) to determine the *Annual Employer Pension Contribution Amount*, which should be entered into box (c). This is the actual dollar amount you might plan for your employer to contribute into your retirement account this year. Of course, the amount of the contribution may go up in subsequent years as your employer's contribution percentage is applied to an increasing annual salary.

Since you need to look at everything on a monthly basis, the final step is to divide the annual contribution amount in box (c) by twelve, to compute the *Monthly Employer Pension Contribution Amount*, which should be entered into box (d). This is the amount you might expect to get from your employer on a monthly basis during the current year.

Using Your Own Numbers

After reviewing the example, fill in Plan Aid 37b: Your Plan now, to determine how much your employer is likely to contribute to your fixed-percentage pension plans. If you don't have any of these kinds of plans you can leave this part blank.

Plan Aid 37b: Your Plan
Employer Contributions—Fixed Percentage Pension Plans

Employer Pension Contribution Percentage .... (a)   %

Current Annual Salary .... (b) $

   (From item (d), Plan Aid 3b: Your Plan on page 77)

Annual Employer Pension Contribution Amount ...... (c) $

                          (a) x (b)

Monthly Employer Pension Contribution Amount ..... (d) $

                      (c) ÷ 12

For illustration purposes only. All assumptions and computational results are hypothetical in nature. There are no guarantees that you will achieve the results shown. You should consult with a financial professional.

Retirement Plan Matching Contributions

The next step is to consider the kinds of plans into which your employer contributes a percentage of the amount you put in—generally up to a certain limit. To do this, turn to Plan Aid 38a: Example, and start by entering your *Employer Contribution Match Percentage* in box (e). This is the percentage of your contribution that the company will match. In other words, if the match percentage is 25 percent, the company will put in twenty-five cents for every dollar you put in. If the match percentage is 50 percent, the company will contribute fifty cents for every dollar you deposit, and so on. Information about your plans should be available through your human resource department.

Then, enter your company's *Salary Limitation Percentage* in box (f). This is the maximum percent of your salary that will be considered in determining how much of a matching contribution your employer will make into your account. In the example we went through a moment ago, your company's contribution was limited to $150, or 50 percent of $300. The limitation came into play because $300 is 6 percent of your $5,000 monthly salary, which is the most the company was willing to consider when calculating their matching contribution.

Remember too that even if your contributions exceed $300, the company will still only put in $150, because again, they only consider the first 6 percent of your salary when calculating their match. Most companies have this kind of limitation, so you should talk to your human resource department if you don't know the specifics about your own plan.

Once you know the contribution match percentage in box (e) and the salary limitation percentage in box (f), you can multiply them together to come up with a *Maximum Salary Match Percentage*, which should be entered into box (g). This is the maximum percent of your salary that your employer will be willing to put into your account as a matching contribution. In this case, they will contribute up to 50 percent, or half, of the first 6 percent of your salary, which is 3 percent of your total compensation. Remember, however, they're only going to put this much into your account if you contribute a full 6 percent yourself. If you put in less, they will too.

The next step is to translate the maximum match *percentage* into a maximum *dollar* match. You do this by entering your *Current Monthly Salary* into box (h), which is the same as the amount you used in item (e), Plan Aid 3a: Example on page 75. Then, multiply your current monthly salary in box (h) by the maximum salary match percentage in box (g) to

Plan Aid 38a: Example
Employer Contributions—
Retirement Plan Matching Contributions

Employer Contribution Match Percentage	(e)	**50.0** %
Salary Limitation Percentage	(f)	**6.0** %
Maximum Salary Match Percentage	(g)	**3.0** %

(e) x (f)

Current Monthly Salary	(h) $	**6,250**

(From item (e), Plan Aid 3a: Example, on page 75)

Max. Monthly Employer Matching Contribution	(i) $	**188**

(g) x (h)

Employer Matching Contribution Factor	(j)	**.33**

Select factor for appropriate Match Percent below   *From Match Table below*

CONTRIBUTION MATCH PERCENTAGE TABLE

Use Match Percent in item (e) above to select appropriate factor below

Match Percent is	10%	0.09
Match Percent is	20%	0.17
Match Percent is	25%	0.20
Match Percent is	30%	0.23
Match Percent is	40%	0.29
Match Percent is	50%	0.33
Match Percent is	60%	0.38
Match Percent is	70%	0.41
Match Percent is	75%	0.43
Match Percent is	80%	0.44
Match Percent is	90%	0.47
Match Percent is	100%	0.50

determine your *Max. Monthly Employer Matching Contribution*, which should be entered into box (i). This is the maximum monthly *dollar* amount your employer will be willing to put into your account as a matching contribution in the current year. Remember, this amount may go up in the future as your employer's matching percentage is applied to an increasing monthly salary.

The final step is to determine an *Employer Matching Contribution Factor*, which will be entered into box (j). This is a multiplication factor that is selected from the *Contribution Match Percentage Table* at the bottom of the page. Based upon the employer contribution match percentage in box (e), this factor will be used to determine how much of your total retirement plan contributions may have to come from you, and how much you may be able to get from your employer.

Using Your Own Numbers

After reviewing the example, fill in Plan Aid 38b: Your Plan now to calculate how much you might plan to get as a matching contribution from your employer. If your employer does not provide matching contributions you can leave this part blank.

Plan Aid 38b: Your Plan
Employer Contributions—
Retirement Plan Matching Contributions

Employer Contribution Match Percentage .... (e)   %

Salary Limitation Percentage .... (f)   %

Maximum Salary Match Percentage .... (g)   %

(e) x (f)

Current Monthly Salary .... (h) $

(From item (e), Plan Aid 3b: Your Plan on page 77)

Max. Monthly Employer Matching Contribution .... (i) $

(g) x (h)

Employer Matching Contribution Factor .... (j)

Select factor for appropriate Match Percent below   *From Match Table below*

CONTRIBUTION MATCH PERCENTAGE TABLE

Use Match Percent in item (e) above to select appropriate factor below

Match Percent is	10%	0.09
Match Percent is	20%	0.17
Match Percent is	25%	0.20
Match Percent is	30%	0.23
Match Percent is	40%	0.29
Match Percent is	50%	0.33
Match Percent is	60%	0.38
Match Percent is	70%	0.41
Match Percent is	75%	0.43
Match Percent is	80%	0.44
Match Percent is	90%	0.47
Match Percent is	100%	0.50

28

Saving a Fixed Monthly Dollar Amount

The next part of the planning process is to follow *Step #23: Formulate a "Fixed-Amount" Savings Plan*, because you have to figure out how much you may need to contribute to your retirement plans at work every month to accumulate the rest of the money you need to retire.

Employer-Sponsored Retirement Plans

There are many types of employer-sponsored retirement plans—401(k) and 403(b) plans, SEP plans, SIMPLE plans, Keogh plans, and others. They each have different rules, regulations and limitations, so you need to understand what kind of plan you have and how it works. You should be able to get this information from your human resource department.

How They Work

Employer-sponsored retirement plans are accounts at work that allow you to grow your money tax-free until you take it out during retirement. The other important benefit is that your contributions are normally tax-deductible, so you can typically save more up front because you don't have to pay taxes on the money you put in.

Employer-Sponsored Retirement Plans and Financial Planning

Tax-deductible contributions, tax-free growth rates, the potential for employer matching contributions, the ease of saving through payroll deduction, and higher overall contribution limits make retirement plans at work the backbone of most retirement plans. In fact, many people do most, if not all, of their retirement investing in their retirement accounts at work—so no matter how you cut it, they're likely to be an important part of your financial plan.

Saving a Fixed Amount *Versus Saving a* Percent *of Salary*

In this chapter we are going to assume that you want to save the same amount each month for the rest of your working career. In the next chapter we will look at saving a percentage of your salary each month. The two approaches lead to very different outcomes.

Saving a fixed amount each month forces you to save more in the early years than if you were saving a percent of your salary, but should help you get off to a quicker start. On the other hand, saving a percentage of your salary each month lets you get by with lower contributions in the early years—when it may be more difficult to save, as long as you're willing to increase your contributions later when your salary goes up.

Planning to save a fixed amount each month is the most conservative way to plan, because making the same monthly contributions for the rest of your life requires you to set aside a larger portion of your salary in the early years, and a smaller portion later on. As a result, you give up more lifestyle now and less in the future. If you can afford to do it this way, you should, because it may help you get ahead of the game. Then, if circumstances change, it might not be so terrible if you have to cut back on your savings for a while.

Unfortunately, most people don't have the luxury of doing it this way, because they don't make enough to be able to afford a fixed-amount savings strategy—so they have to use a *percent-of-salary* method instead. Under a percent-of-salary approach, you save a percentage of your income each month rather than a fixed dollar amount—so as your salary goes up, your contributions do too. This tends to level out the economic impact of saving for retirement, and it's the way many younger people end up doing it.

There Are Limits on How Much You Can Put into Your Accounts at Work

You are not allowed to contribute as much as you want into your retirement plans at work. There are contribution limits imposed on all employer-sponsored plans, and they vary considerably from one type of plan to another. You need to talk with your advisors and your human resource department about the rules and contribution limits related to your own plans.

How Much You Need to Save Versus How Much You Are Saving

So far, you projected the hypothetical future value of existing accounts and the contributions you intend to make, and subtracted them from the total amount you need to accumulate for retirement. That helped you to determine how much more you may need to amass in your savings plans at work. In other words, you started with the balances you already have and the future contributions you plan to make, projected them forward to see what they may be worth when you retire, and then used them to determine how much more you may still need to accumulate.

We're going to take a much different approach with your retirement plans at work. Since at this point you know what you may have left to accumulate, and because your plans at work are the last accounts you're going to consider, you can simply go ahead and finish the job by calculating how much you may have to save each month to accumulate the rest of what you should need in your retirement accounts at work.

In other words, rather than projecting the future value of the monthly contributions you're currently making, you're just going to figure out exactly how much you need to save each month and then adjust what you're currently doing to that amount. You're not going to explicitly account for the future value of the monthly contributions you're making now. You're just going to compute a required monthly savings amount and then modify your current savings activities either up or down to that amount to reach your accumulation target.

Some Plans May Require You to Save a Certain Amount

Some retirement plans actually require participants to save a certain percentage of their salary each month. If you have this kind of participation requirement, you still need to determine how much you have to save each month, like we just discussed, but then simply remember that you are already taking care of at least as much as you are required to contribute. Then, you can figure out how much more or less you need to save to get to the required monthly amount.

Create Your Own Plan

Follow the steps outlined in Plan Aid 39a: Example to determine how much you may need to save each month on a fixed-amount basis. Start with your *Hypothetical Future Retirement Plan Target* in box (a), which is the same amount you calculated in item (c), Plan Aid 36a: Example on page 300. Then, enter the *Number of Years Until Retirement* in box (b), which is the same amount you calculated in item (c), Plan Aid 1a: Example on page 13.

Computing Your Weighted Average Rate of Return

Then, using Plan Aid 40a: Example, calculate a hypothetical weighted average rate of return for the contributions you and your employer will ultimately make into your retirement plans at work. This is the average annual rate of return you might plan to earn on all of your future retirement plan contributions until the day you quit working. Since your investments are probably going to be spread across a variety of different assets and mutual funds, you need to compute a hypothetical weighted average rate of return for all of your accounts.

Next, round the hypothetical weighted average rate of return either up or down to the nearest whole percentage, and enter it as your *Asset*

Plan Aid 39a: Example
Fixed Monthly Retirement Plan Contributions

TOTAL FIXED MONTHLY SAVINGS AMOUNTS

Hypothetical Future Retirement Plan Target .... (a) $ **905,859**
   (From item (c), Plan Aid 36a: Example on page 300)

Number of Years Until Retirement .... (b) **22**
   (From item (c), Plan Aid 1a: Example on page 13)

Asset Growth Rate Assumption .... (c) **10.0** %
   (Use Plan Aid 40a: Example on page 319 to estimate rate of return)
   (Select 5%, 6%, 7%, 8%, 9%, 10%, 11%, or 12%)

Retirement Plan Monthly Fixed Savings Factor .... (d) **895**
   Look Up on Plan Aid Table 40, Using Items (b) and (c) above

Hypothetical Total Monthly Savings Amount .... (e) $ **1,012**
   (a) ÷ (d)

MONTHLY EMPLOYER CONTRIBUTION AMOUNTS

Monthly Employer Pension Contribution Amount ..... (f) $ **125**
   (From item (d), Plan Aid 37a: Example on page 308)

Hypothetical Net Monthly Savings Amount .... (g) $ **887**
   (e) - (f)

Employer Matching Contribution Factor .... (h) **.33**
   (From item (j), Plan Aid 38a: Example on page 311)

Preliminary Matching Contribution Amount .... (i) $ **293**
   (g) x (h)

Max. Monthly Employer Matching Contribution .... (j) $ **188**
   (From item (i), Plan Aid 38a: Example on page 311)

Hypothetical Employer Matching Contribution .... (k) $ **188**
   Smaller of (i) or (j) above

FINAL MONTHLY FIXED CONTRIBUTION AMOUNTS

Hypothetical Employee Monthly Contribution .... (l) $ **699**
   (g) - (k)

Hypothetical Employer Monthly Contribution .... (m) $ **313**
   (f) + (k)

Plan Aid 40a: Example
Weighted Average Rate of Return
Monthly Retirement Plan Contributions

Type of Asset	Asset Value	% of Assets	Expect. Ret.	Wtd. Ret.
Treasury Bonds	na	10.0%	5.0%	0.5%
Large Company Growth Stocks	na	25.0%	10.0%	2.5%
Small Company Growth Stocks	na	30.0%	11.5%	3.5%
International Stocks	na	15.0%	9.5%	1.4%
Mid-Cap Stocks	na	20.0%	11.0%	2.2%
Tot. Assets & Wtd. Ave. Return	na	100.0%		10.1%

For illustration purposes only. Not representative of an actual investment. An individual investors results may vary. All assumptions and computational results are hypothetical in nature. There are no guarantees that you will achieve the results shown. Higher volatility has historically been associated with higher rates of return, and average returns have had a tendency to fluctuate from year to year. The prices of large company, small company, international, and mid-cap stocks will fluctuate. Investing in international stocks may carry additional risks such as differing securities regulations and more volatile political and economic environments. Treasury Bonds are guaranteed by the U.S. government and, if held to maturity, offer a fixed rate of return and principal value. You should consult with a financial professional.

Growth Rate Assumption in box (c) on Plan Aid 39a: Example. If you want to be on the conservative side, round it down, and if you want to be a little more aggressive, round it up.

After estimating your hypothetical weighted average rate of return, turn to Plan Aid Table 40, and find the column related to your asset growth rate assumption and the row related to the number of years until retirement. Where they intersect in the table, you will find your *Retirement Plan Monthly Fixed Savings Factor*, which should be entered into box (d). This factor is used to help determine the *total* amount of monthly savings required to reach your retirement plan accumulation objectives.

The next step is to calculate your *Hypothetical Total Monthly Savings Amount* in box (e), which is determined by dividing your *Hypothetical Future Retirement Plan Target* in box (a) by the *Retirement Plan Monthly Fixed Savings Factor* in box (d). This is the total hypothetical monthly amount (coming from both you and your employer) that would have to be contributed into your retirement plans at work if you want to save a fixed dollar amount each month and be able to accumulate the balance of what you should need to meet your overall retirement objectives. Since this is the total amount required, and because your employer will probably make some of the contributions, you will probably not be responsible for all of it.

How Much Will Your Employer Kick In?

The next thing you have to figure out is how much your employer is likely to contribute to your plans for you. The first step is to enter the *Monthly Employer Pension Contribution Amount* in box (f). This is the same amount you computed in item (d) on Plan Aid 37a: Example on page 308, and it's what you might plan to get from your employer's fixed-percentage pension plans if they have any. Then, subtract the *Monthly Employer Pension Contribution Amount* in box (f) from the *Hypothetical Total Monthly Savings Amount* in box (e) to see how much you may still need to save after taking your employer's fixed-percentage pension plan contributions into account, and enter it into box (g), *Hypothetical Net Monthly Savings Amount*.

Plan Aid Table 40: Retirement Plan Savings Factors Table for Monthly Contributions—Fixed Savings Amount

Years to Retire	Asset Growth Rate Assumption							
	5.0%	6.0%	7.0%	8.0%	9.0%	10.0%	11.0%	12.0%
1	12	12	12	12	12	13	13	13
2	25	25	26	26	26	26	27	27
3	39	39	40	40	41	42	42	43
4	53	54	55	56	57	58	59	60
5	68	69	71	73	75	77	78	80
6	83	86	89	91	94	97	100	103
7	100	103	107	111	115	119	123	128
8	117	122	127	132	138	143	149	156
9	135	142	148	155	163	170	178	187
10	154	162	171	180	190	200	211	222
11	174	185	195	207	219	232	246	261
12	195	208	221	236	252	268	286	305
13	217	233	249	267	287	308	330	354
14	241	259	279	301	325	351	379	410
15	265	287	311	338	367	398	433	471
16	290	316	345	377	412	451	494	541
17	317	348	382	420	462	508	560	618
18	345	381	421	466	516	572	635	705
19	375	416	463	515	575	642	717	802
20	406	453	508	569	639	718	809	911
21	438	493	555	627	709	803	910	1,033
22	473	535	607	690	785	895	1,023	1,170
23	508	579	662	757	868	998	1,148	1,323
24	546	626	720	830	959	1,110	1,287	1,494
25	586	676	783	909	1,058	1,233	1,441	1,686
26	627	729	850	994	1,165	1,369	1,612	1,901
27	671	785	922	1,086	1,283	1,519	1,802	2,142
28	717	845	999	1,185	1,411	1,683	2,013	2,412
29	765	908	1,081	1,293	1,550	1,864	2,247	2,714
30	815	975	1,169	1,409	1,702	2,063	2,506	3,052
31	868	1,045	1,264	1,534	1,868	2,282	2,795	3,431
32	924	1,120	1,365	1,669	2,048	2,522	3,115	3,855
33	983	1,200	1,472	1,815	2,245	2,787	3,470	4,331
34	1,044	1,284	1,588	1,972	2,460	3,078	3,864	4,863
35	1,108	1,374	1,711	2,143	2,694	3,399	4,302	5,459
36	1,176	1,468	1,844	2,326	2,949	3,751	4,788	6,127
37	1,247	1,569	1,985	2,525	3,226	4,139	5,327	6,875
38	1,322	1,675	2,136	2,739	3,529	4,565	5,925	7,712
39	1,400	1,788	2,298	2,971	3,859	5,034	6,590	8,650
40	1,483	1,908	2,472	3,221	4,219	5,550	7,327	9,701
41	1,569	2,034	2,657	3,491	4,611	6,118	8,146	10,878
42	1,660	2,169	2,855	3,783	5,039	6,742	9,055	12,196
43	1,755	2,311	3,068	4,098	5,505	7,429	10,063	13,672
44	1,855	2,462	3,295	4,438	6,013	8,184	11,183	15,325
45	1,960	2,622	3,538	4,806	6,567	9,015	12,425	17,177
46	2,070	2,792	3,798	5,203	7,170	9,930	13,805	19,251
47	2,186	2,972	4,076	5,631	7,828	10,935	15,336	21,573
48	2,308	3,163	4,374	6,094	8,545	12,041	17,035	24,175
49	2,435	3,365	4,692	6,594	9,326	13,258	18,922	27,089
50	2,569	3,579	5,033	7,134	10,178	14,596	21,016	30,352

If your *Hypothetical Net Monthly Savings Amount* in item (g) is equal to or less than zero, it means that the amounts you have already saved in your other retirement accounts, along with the future contributions you plan to make into these accounts and the contributions you might plan to get from your employer, may be sufficient to meet your overall retirement objectives—given all the assumptions you've made so far.

However, this doesn't mean that you should stop saving and investing for retirement, especially in your retirement plans at work. At this point, if you came up with a negative number, you should go back to the beginning and change some planning variables to give yourself a higher goal to shoot for.

For example, you could plan to retire earlier, plan to maintain a higher percentage of your preretirement income during retirement, or reduce the rates of return you estimated for your retirement plan contributions or some of your other investment accounts. The important thing is to keep building on what you've done so far. Don't stop because it looks like you're in good shape. You never know what may happen in the future.

Taking Matching Contributions into Account

Next, you need to consider the matching contributions you may be expecting to get from your employer. Start with the *Employer Matching Contribution Factor* in box (h), which is the same as in item (j) on Plan Aid 38a: Example on page 311. Then, multiply the *Hypothetical Net Monthly Savings Amount* in box (g) by the *Employer Matching Contribution Factor* in box (h) to determine the *Preliminary Matching Contribution Amount,* which should be entered into box (i).

This is the amount of your employer's matching contribution prior to applying the matching contribution limit. In other words, this should be the amount of your employer's match if there was no limitation. As long as this amount is less than the previously determined maximum, it should in fact be the matching contribution. However, if it's larger than the maximum amount allowed, the maximum amount will be used as the matching contribution.

To determine how big your company's matching contribution may be, start by entering the *Max. Monthly Employer Matching Contribution* in box (j), which is the same amount as item (i) on Plan Aid 38a: Example on page 311. Then, you can determine the actual amount of the matching contribution by selecting the smaller of the *Preliminary Matching Contribution Amount* in box (i) or the *Max. Monthly Employer Matching Contribution* in box (j), and entering it as your *Hypothetical Employer Matching Contribution* in box (k).

How Much Will You Have to Contribute Each Month?

Now that you know how much you may get from your employer's fixed-percentage pension plans and matching contributions each month, you can determine how much you may need to put away yourself. Simply subtract the *Hypothetical Employer Matching Contribution* in box (k) from the *Hypothetical Net Monthly Savings Amount* in box (g), and put the answer in box (l), *Hypothetical Employee Monthly Contribution*. This is the hypothetical monthly amount that you may need to contribute to your retirement plans at work after taking into account all of your employer's contributions.

This is the bottom line. This is the amount that you would instruct your human resource department to withhold from your wages if you wanted to save a *fixed monthly amount in your retirement plans for the rest of your working career.*

Ultimately, you probably also want to know how much your employer may be putting away for you each month. Simply add the *Monthly Employer Pension Contribution Amount* in box (f) to the *Hypothetical Employer Matching Contribution* in box (k) to determine the *Hypothetical Employer Monthly Contribution* in box (m). This is the hypothetical monthly amount your employer may contribute to your retirement plans this year on your behalf.

After reviewing the example, use Plan Aid 39b: Your Plan now to figure out how much you and your employer may need to put away on a fixed monthly basis to meet your own retirement objectives. Use Plan Aid 40b: Your Plan to estimate your own hypothetical weighted average rate of return.

Plan Aid 39b: Your Plan
Fixed Monthly Retirement Plan Contributions

TOTAL FIXED MONTHLY SAVINGS AMOUNTS

Hypothetical Future Retirement Plan Target .... (a) $
(From item (c), Plan Aid 36b: Your Plan on page 301)

Number of Years Until Retirement .... (b)
(From item (c), Plan Aid 1b: Your Plan on page 13)

Asset Growth Rate Assumption .... (c)   %
(Use Plan Aid 40b: Your Plan on page 325 to estimate rate of return)
(Select 5%, 6%, 7%, 8%, 9%, 10%, 11%, or 12%)

Retirement Plan Monthly Fixed Savings Factor .... (d)
Look Up on Plan Aid Table 40, Using Items (b) and (c) above

Hypothetical Total Monthly Savings Amount .... (e) $
(a) ÷ (d)

MONTHLY EMPLOYER CONTRIBUTION AMOUNTS

Monthly Employer Pension Contribution Amount ..... (f) $
(From item (d), Plan Aid 37b: Your Plan on page 309)

Hypothetical Net Monthly Savings Amount .... (g) $
(e) - (f)

Employer Matching Contribution Factor .... (h)
(From item (j), Plan Aid 38b: Your Plan on page 313)

Preliminary Matching Contribution Amount .... (i) $
(g) x (h)

Max. Monthly Employer Matching Contribution .... (j) $
(From item (i), Plan Aid 38b: Your Plan on page 313)

Hypothetical Employer Matching Contribution .... (k) $
Smaller of (i) or (j) above

FINAL MONTHLY FIXED CONTRIBUTION AMOUNTS

Hypothetical <u>Employee</u> Monthly Contribution .... (l) $
(g) - (k)

Hypothetical <u>Employer</u> Monthly Contribution .... (m) $
(f) + (k)

Plan Aid 40b: Your Plan
Weighted Average Rate of Return
Monthly Retirement Plan Contributions

Type of Asset	Asset Value	% of Assets	Expect. Ret.	Wtd. Ret.
	na	%	%	%
	na	%	%	%
	na	%	%	%
	na	%	%	%
	na	%	%	%
	na	%	%	%
	na	%	%	%
	na	%	%	%
	na	%	%	%
	na	%	%	%
Tot. Assets & Wtd. Ave. Return	na	%		%

For illustration purposes only. Not representative of an actual investment. An individual investors results may vary. All assumptions and computational results are hypothetical in nature. There are no guarantees that you will achieve the results shown. Higher volatility has historically been associated with higher rates of return, and average returns have had a tendency to fluctuate from year to year. You should consult with a financial professional.

Don't Save Less Than You Are Able to Save

You now know, perhaps for the first time in your life, how much you may need to save in your retirement plans at work each month—and it's very possible that the amount you came up with is less than you are already saving. **Don't stop doing what you're doing!** Just because under this one planning scenario it looks like you could get by saving less, doesn't mean that you should. Instead, you need to go back and make some adjustments in your plan to go after a better retirement scenario or perhaps build a little more conservatism into the plan you already have.

For example, you could plan to retire earlier or try to maintain a higher percentage of your preretirement income. Or, if you want to be a little more conservative, you could reduce some of your rates of return or increase your inflation rate assumption.

What If You Can't Put Enough into Your Plans at Work?

It may turn out that the amount you need to contribute each month is more than you're allowed to put into your plans at work. In that case, you may have to go back to some of your other tax-deferred savings vehicles—like annuities and/or regular and Roth IRAs, to increase the amounts you plan to invest in them. Because of the limitations on how much you can put into IRAs, it may really boil down to putting more into your annuities. It will be different for everyone, but you need to find a way to save as much as you have to—whether it's in your plans at work or in some of the other saving vehicles we have been talking about.

What If You Just Can't Save Enough?

You may also come up with a monthly savings amount that is just too big for you to afford, no matter what accounts you plan to use. In that case, you may simply need to start over—by scaling back your plans, reconsidering your overall expectations, and thereby reducing the amounts you need to save and accumulate. As you will come to understand by working through a few different scenarios, in many cases things may not be nearly as bad as they might at first appear. You often just have to take a fresh look at the options to come up with a workable plan.

For example, you could retire a few years later or perhaps reduce the percentage of preretirement income you're planning to maintain during retirement. Or, you could increase the hypothetical rates of return you're planning to earn on some of your retirement assets. By changing the mix of investments from potentially lower-return, lower-risk assets like bonds and money market accounts, to potentially higher-return, higher-risk stock market accounts, you may be able to pick up some of the additional accumulation you need. It doesn't take that much of a change in rates of return to have a significant impact on the overall amount you might accumulate over longer investment periods.

Another adjustment you might want to consider is using a more aggressive retirement asset management strategy, as discussed in Chapter 12. Changing your retirement factor may have more impact on your plan than almost anything else you can do, and combined with some of the other changes mentioned above, it may help give you more flexibility in putting together a plan to help you meet your overall objectives.

Of course, you always have to stay within your comfort zone for investment risk when making these kinds of adjustments. You can't just make changes on paper and then not follow through.

29

Saving a Percent of Your Salary

In this chapter we are going to investigate *Step #24: Prepare a "Percent-of-Salary" Savings Plan*. In other words, you are going to learn about another way to figure out how much you might need to contribute to your retirement plans at work.

Saving a *Percent* of Your Salary

In this chapter we are going to assume that you want to save a percentage of your salary each month, rather than a fixed amount. This approach will normally lead to very different outcomes than if you use a fixed approach, because saving a percentage of your salary each month allows you to contribute less in the early years as long as you're willing to make it up over time as your salary increases.

A Brief Example

Let's say you're thirty years old and plan to retire when you're sixty-five—so you have a thirty-five-year accumulation period. If your current salary is $40,000, and you plan for total salary growth, including inflation, of 5 percent per year, your salary in the year prior to retirement should be around $220,000.

Now, let's say that you have a retirement plan accumulation target of $1,500,000. In other words, that's the amount you need to accumulate in your retirement plans at work. If you earn a hypothetical 10 percent rate of return on your retirement plan assets, you and your employer would need to contribute about $440 per month if you want to save a *fixed amount* for the rest of your working career.

On the other hand, you may only have to save a combined $265 per month, or about 40 percent less in the first year, if you decided to save a *percent* of your salary each month rather than a fixed amount. Of course, the amount you need to save will likely go up each year under a percent-of-salary method—so after fifteen years you may be saving about $550 per month, and by the time you get to retirement you may be saving over $1,450 per month. But in all three cases, you would be saving about 8 percent of your salary. In other words, you will be giving up the same relative percentage of your lifestyle each and every year under this approach.

In contrast, under a *fixed-amount* approach, the $440 you have to save each month represents over 13 percent of your current salary, and only 2.5 percent of your final salary. So you have to save a much larger percentage of your current income and a much smaller percentage later on. Compare that with saving the same 8 percent each and every year, and you'll understand why so many younger people choose a percent-of-salary approach.

Please remember that these are only hypothetical examples to help you understand the impact of these two approaches, and shouldn't be considered a guarantee of future results or representative of any particular investment. Your individual circumstances and results will vary from the examples shown.

Accounting for Your Current Retirement Plan Contributions

Just like when you figured out how much you might need to save on a fixed-amount basis, in this chapter we're not going to explicitly account for the monthly contributions you're currently making into your plans.

You're just going to compute a total required monthly savings amount and adjust your current savings either up or down to that amount.

Also, if you have the kind of retirement plans that require you to save a percentage of your salary each month, you have to remember that you will already be taking care of at least that much through your mandatory contributions.

Create Your Own Plan

Follow the steps outlined in Plan Aid 41a: Example to determine how much you may need to save each month on a percent-of-salary basis. Start with your *Hypothetical Future Retirement Plan Target* in box (a), which is the same amount you calculated in item (c), Plan Aid 36a: Example on page 300. Then, enter the *Number of Years Until Retirement* in box (b), which is the same amount you calculated in item (c), Plan Aid 1a: Example on page 13.

Next, enter your *Total Salary Growth Rate Assumption* in box (c), which is the same percentage as in item (k) on Plan Aid 4a: Example on page 84. Then, enter your *Asset Growth Rate Assumption* in box (d), which is the same as item (c) on Plan Aid 39a: Example on page 318. And finally, based upon the *Asset Growth Rate Assumption* in box (d), select a table at the bottom of the page to use in computing the amount you may need to save under a percent-of-salary method, and make note of it in box (e), *Lookup Table for Appropriate Asset Growth Rate*.

Next, turn to Plan Aid Table 41(a, b, c, d, e, f, g, or h) and find the column related to your total salary growth rate assumption in box (c) and the row related to the number of years until retirement. Where they intersect in the table, you will find your *Retirement Plan Monthly Percent Savings Factor*, which should be entered into box (f). This factor is used to determine the total hypothetical amount of monthly savings which may be required to reach your retirement plan accumulation objectives under a percent-of-salary approach.

Next, compute your *Hypothetical Total Monthly Savings Amount* in box (g) by dividing your *Hypothetical Future Retirement Plan Target* in box (a) by the *Retirement Plan Monthly Percent Savings Factor* in box (f). This should be the total hypothetical monthly amount (coming from

Plan Aid 41a: Example
Percent of Salary Monthly Retirement Plan Contributions

TOTAL PERCENTAGE MONTHLY SAVINGS AMOUNT

Hypothetical Future Retirement Plan Target .... | (a) $ **905,859**
(From item (c), Plan Aid 36a: Example, on page 300)

Number of Years Until Retirement .... | (b) **22**
(From item (c), Plan Aid 1a: Example, on page 13)

Total Salary Growth Rate Assumption .... | (c) **4.5** %
(From item (k), Plan Aid 4a: Example, on page 84)

Asset Growth Rate Assumption .... | (d) **10.0** %
(From item (c), Plan Aid 39a: Example, on page 318)

Lookup Table for Appropriate Asset Growth Rate .... | (e) **Table 41f**
Select lookup table for appropriate growth rate below | *From Index Table below*

Retirement Plan Monthly Percent Savings Factor .... | (f) **1,256**
Look Up on Table Noted in Item (e) above, Using Items (b) and (c) above

Hypothetical Total Monthly Savings Amount .... | (g) $ **721**
(a) ÷ (f)

Current Monthly Salary .... | (h) $ **6,250**
(From item (e), Plan Aid 3a: Example, on page 75)

Hypothetical Total Monthly Savings Percent .... | (i) **11.5** %
(g) ÷ (h)

INDEX FOR ASSET GROWTH RATE TABLES
Use Asset Growth Rate in item (d) above to select appropriate lookup table below

Asset Growth Rate	5%	Table 41a
Asset Growth Rate	6%	Table 41b
Asset Growth Rate	7%	Table 41c
Asset Growth Rate	8%	Table 41d
Asset Growth Rate	9%	Table 41e
Asset Growth Rate	10%	Table 41f
Asset Growth Rate	11%	Table 41g
Asset Growth Rate	12%	Table 41h

Plan Aid Table 41a: Retirement Plan Savings Factors Table for Monthly Contributions—Percentage Savings Amount (5% Asset Growth Rate Assumption)

Years to Retire	Total Salary Growth Rate Assumption									
	2.0%	2.5%	3.0%	3.5%	4.0%	4.5%	5.0%	5.5%	6.0%	6.5%
1	12	12	12	12	12	12	12	12	12	12
2	25	25	26	26	26	26	26	26	26	26
3	39	40	40	40	40	40	41	41	41	41
4	54	55	55	56	56	56	57	57	58	58
5	70	71	72	72	73	74	75	75	76	77
6	88	89	90	91	92	93	94	95	96	97
7	106	107	109	110	112	113	115	117	118	120
8	125	127	129	131	134	136	138	140	143	145
9	146	148	151	154	157	160	163	166	170	173
10	168	171	175	179	182	186	190	195	199	203
11	191	196	200	205	210	215	220	225	231	236
12	216	221	227	233	239	245	252	259	266	273
13	242	249	256	263	271	278	287	295	303	312
14	270	278	287	296	305	314	324	334	345	356
15	300	310	320	330	341	353	364	377	390	403
16	331	343	355	367	380	394	408	423	439	455
17	365	378	392	407	422	438	455	473	492	511
18	400	416	432	449	467	486	506	527	549	573
19	438	456	475	495	516	538	561	586	612	640
20	478	498	520	543	567	593	620	649	680	712
21	520	543	568	594	622	652	684	717	753	791
22	564	591	619	649	682	716	752	791	832	877
23	611	642	674	708	745	784	826	870	918	969
24	661	695	732	771	812	857	905	956	1,011	1,070
25	714	752	793	837	884	935	990	1,048	1,111	1,179
26	770	813	859	908	961	1,019	1,081	1,147	1,220	1,297
27	829	877	928	983	1,043	1,108	1,178	1,254	1,336	1,425
28	891	944	1,002	1,064	1,131	1,204	1,283	1,369	1,462	1,564
29	957	1,016	1,080	1,149	1,224	1,306	1,395	1,492	1,598	1,714
30	1,027	1,092	1,163	1,240	1,324	1,415	1,515	1,625	1,745	1,876
31	1,101	1,172	1,251	1,336	1,430	1,532	1,644	1,767	1,902	2,051
32	1,178	1,257	1,344	1,439	1,543	1,657	1,782	1,920	2,072	2,240
33	1,260	1,347	1,443	1,547	1,663	1,790	1,930	2,084	2,255	2,444
34	1,347	1,442	1,547	1,663	1,791	1,932	2,088	2,260	2,452	2,664
35	1,438	1,543	1,658	1,786	1,927	2,083	2,257	2,449	2,663	2,901
36	1,535	1,649	1,776	1,916	2,071	2,245	2,437	2,652	2,891	3,158
37	1,637	1,761	1,900	2,054	2,225	2,417	2,630	2,868	3,135	3,434
38	1,744	1,880	2,032	2,200	2,389	2,600	2,836	3,101	3,398	3,732
39	1,857	2,005	2,171	2,356	2,563	2,795	3,056	3,350	3,680	4,053
40	1,977	2,138	2,318	2,521	2,748	3,003	3,291	3,616	3,983	4,399
41	2,103	2,278	2,474	2,695	2,944	3,225	3,542	3,902	4,309	4,771
42	2,235	2,425	2,639	2,880	3,153	3,461	3,810	4,207	4,658	5,172
43	2,375	2,581	2,814	3,076	3,374	3,712	4,096	4,534	5,033	5,603
44	2,523	2,746	2,998	3,284	3,609	3,979	4,401	4,883	5,435	6,067
45	2,678	2,919	3,193	3,504	3,858	4,263	4,726	5,256	5,866	6,567
46	2,842	3,103	3,399	3,737	4,123	4,565	5,072	5,656	6,328	7,104
47	3,015	3,296	3,617	3,983	4,404	4,886	5,442	6,083	6,823	7,681
48	3,197	3,500	3,847	4,244	4,701	5,228	5,835	6,539	7,354	8,302
49	3,388	3,715	4,090	4,521	5,017	5,591	6,255	7,026	7,923	8,970
50	3,590	3,942	4,347	4,813	5,352	5,976	6,702	7,547	8,533	9,687

For illustration purposes only. Not representative of an actual investment. All assumptions and computational results are hypothetical in nature. Higher volatility has historically been associated with higher rates of return, and average returns have had a tendency to fluctuate from year to year.

Plan Aid Table 41b: Retirement Plan Savings Factors Table for Monthly Contributions—Percentage Savings Amount (6% Asset Growth Rate Assumption)

Years to Retire	Total Salary Growth Rate Assumption									
	2.0%	2.5%	3.0%	3.5%	4.0%	4.5%	5.0%	5.5%	6.0%	6.5%
1	12	12	12	12	12	12	12	12	12	12
2	26	26	26	26	26	26	26	26	26	26
3	40	40	40	41	41	41	41	41	42	42
4	55	56	56	57	57	57	58	58	59	59
5	72	73	74	74	75	76	76	77	78	79
6	90	91	92	93	94	96	97	98	99	100
7	109	111	112	114	116	117	119	121	122	124
8	130	132	134	137	139	141	143	146	148	151
9	152	155	158	161	164	167	170	174	177	180
10	176	180	184	187	191	195	200	204	208	213
11	202	206	211	216	221	226	232	237	243	249
12	229	235	241	247	253	260	267	274	281	288
13	259	266	273	281	288	296	305	313	322	332
14	290	299	307	317	326	336	346	357	368	380
15	324	334	345	356	367	379	392	405	418	432
16	360	372	384	398	411	426	441	456	473	490
17	398	412	427	443	459	476	494	513	532	553
18	439	456	473	492	511	531	552	574	597	622
19	483	503	523	544	566	590	615	641	668	698
20	530	552	576	600	626	654	683	713	746	780
21	581	606	632	661	691	723	756	792	830	871
22	634	663	693	726	760	797	836	878	922	969
23	691	724	759	796	835	877	922	970	1,022	1,076
24	752	789	828	871	916	964	1,016	1,071	1,130	1,193
25	817	859	903	951	1,002	1,057	1,116	1,180	1,248	1,321
26	886	933	983	1,037	1,095	1,158	1,225	1,297	1,376	1,460
27	960	1,012	1,069	1,129	1,195	1,266	1,342	1,425	1,514	1,611
28	1,039	1,097	1,160	1,228	1,302	1,382	1,469	1,563	1,664	1,775
29	1,122	1,188	1,258	1,334	1,417	1,507	1,605	1,712	1,827	1,953
30	1,212	1,284	1,363	1,448	1,541	1,642	1,752	1,872	2,004	2,147
31	1,307	1,387	1,474	1,569	1,673	1,787	1,911	2,046	2,195	2,357
32	1,408	1,497	1,594	1,699	1,815	1,942	2,081	2,234	2,401	2,586
33	1,516	1,614	1,721	1,838	1,967	2,109	2,265	2,436	2,625	2,833
34	1,630	1,738	1,857	1,987	2,130	2,288	2,462	2,655	2,867	3,102
35	1,752	1,871	2,002	2,146	2,305	2,481	2,675	2,890	3,128	3,393
36	1,882	2,013	2,157	2,316	2,492	2,687	2,903	3,144	3,411	3,708
37	2,020	2,163	2,322	2,497	2,692	2,908	3,149	3,417	3,716	4,049
38	2,167	2,324	2,498	2,691	2,906	3,146	3,413	3,711	4,045	4,419
39	2,323	2,495	2,686	2,898	3,135	3,400	3,696	4,028	4,401	4,819
40	2,489	2,677	2,886	3,119	3,380	3,673	4,001	4,370	4,784	5,252
41	2,666	2,871	3,099	3,355	3,642	3,965	4,328	4,737	5,198	5,720
42	2,854	3,077	3,327	3,607	3,922	4,278	4,678	5,132	5,645	6,226
43	3,053	3,296	3,569	3,876	4,222	4,613	5,055	5,556	6,126	6,774
44	3,265	3,529	3,827	4,162	4,542	4,971	5,459	6,013	6,644	7,365
45	3,490	3,778	4,102	4,468	4,883	5,355	5,892	6,504	7,203	8,004
46	3,730	4,042	4,395	4,794	5,248	5,766	6,356	7,031	7,805	8,693
47	3,984	4,323	4,706	5,142	5,638	6,205	6,853	7,598	8,453	9,438
48	4,255	4,622	5,038	5,513	6,054	6,675	7,387	8,206	9,151	10,243
49	4,542	4,939	5,391	5,908	6,499	7,177	7,958	8,859	9,902	11,110
50	4,847	5,277	5,767	6,329	6,973	7,714	8,570	9,561	10,710	12,047

For illustration purposes only. Not representative of an actual investment. All assumptions and computational results are hypothetical in nature. Higher volatility has historically been associated with higher rates of return, and average returns have had a tendency to fluctuate from year to year.

Plan Aid Table 41c: Retirement Plan Savings Factors Table for Monthly Contributions—Percentage Savings Amount (7% Asset Growth Rate Assumption)

Years to Retire	Total Salary Growth Rate Assumption									
	2.0%	2.5%	3.0%	3.5%	4.0%	4.5%	5.0%	5.5%	6.0%	6.5%
1	12	12	12	12	12	12	12	12	12	12
2	26	26	26	26	26	26	26	26	26	26
3	41	41	41	41	41	42	42	42	42	42
4	57	57	57	58	58	59	59	59	60	60
5	74	75	75	76	77	77	78	79	80	80
6	93	94	95	96	97	98	99	101	102	103
7	113	115	116	118	120	121	123	125	126	128
8	135	137	140	142	144	147	149	151	154	156
9	159	162	165	168	171	174	178	181	184	188
10	185	189	193	197	201	205	209	214	218	223
11	213	218	223	228	233	239	244	250	256	262
12	244	250	256	262	269	275	282	290	297	305
13	276	284	291	299	307	316	324	334	343	352
14	312	321	330	340	349	360	371	382	393	405
15	350	361	372	383	395	408	421	435	449	463
16	391	404	417	431	445	460	476	493	510	528
17	435	450	466	483	500	518	537	556	577	599
18	483	501	519	539	559	580	602	626	651	677
19	535	555	577	599	623	648	674	702	732	762
20	590	614	639	665	693	722	753	786	820	857
21	650	677	706	736	768	802	839	877	917	960
22	714	745	778	813	850	890	932	976	1,024	1,074
23	783	819	856	896	939	985	1,033	1,085	1,140	1,199
24	858	898	941	987	1,035	1,088	1,143	1,203	1,267	1,335
25	938	983	1,032	1,084	1,140	1,199	1,263	1,332	1,406	1,485
26	1,024	1,075	1,130	1,189	1,252	1,321	1,394	1,473	1,557	1,649
27	1,116	1,174	1,236	1,303	1,374	1,452	1,535	1,626	1,723	1,828
28	1,215	1,280	1,350	1,425	1,506	1,594	1,689	1,792	1,903	2,023
29	1,322	1,394	1,473	1,557	1,649	1,748	1,856	1,973	2,100	2,237
30	1,436	1,517	1,605	1,700	1,803	1,915	2,037	2,169	2,314	2,471
31	1,559	1,649	1,747	1,854	1,969	2,095	2,233	2,383	2,547	2,726
32	1,691	1,791	1,900	2,019	2,149	2,290	2,445	2,615	2,800	3,004
33	1,833	1,944	2,065	2,198	2,343	2,501	2,675	2,866	3,076	3,307
34	1,985	2,108	2,243	2,390	2,552	2,729	2,925	3,140	3,376	3,637
35	2,148	2,284	2,434	2,597	2,778	2,976	3,194	3,436	3,702	3,997
36	2,324	2,474	2,639	2,820	3,021	3,242	3,486	3,757	4,057	4,389
37	2,511	2,677	2,859	3,061	3,283	3,529	3,802	4,105	4,441	4,816
38	2,713	2,895	3,096	3,319	3,566	3,839	4,144	4,482	4,859	5,280
39	2,929	3,130	3,351	3,597	3,870	4,174	4,513	4,890	5,313	5,785
40	3,161	3,381	3,625	3,896	4,198	4,535	4,912	5,333	5,805	6,335
41	3,410	3,651	3,919	4,218	4,552	4,925	5,343	5,811	6,338	6,932
42	3,676	3,941	4,235	4,564	4,932	5,345	5,808	6,329	6,917	7,581
43	3,962	4,251	4,574	4,936	5,342	5,797	6,311	6,890	7,544	8,286
44	4,268	4,585	4,939	5,336	5,782	6,285	6,853	7,496	8,224	9,051
45	4,597	4,942	5,330	5,766	6,257	6,811	7,439	8,151	8,961	9,883
46	4,949	5,326	5,750	6,228	6,767	7,378	8,071	8,859	9,758	10,785
47	5,326	5,737	6,201	6,724	7,316	7,988	8,753	9,625	10,622	11,764
48	5,730	6,178	6,684	7,257	7,906	8,645	9,488	10,452	11,557	12,827
49	6,163	6,651	7,203	7,829	8,541	9,353	10,281	11,345	12,569	13,979
50	6,627	7,159	7,760	8,444	9,223	10,114	11,136	12,310	13,664	15,229

Plan Aid Table 41d: Retirement Plan Savings Factors Table for Monthly Contributions—Percentage Savings Amount (8% Asset Growth Rate Assumption)

Years to Retire	Total Salary Growth Rate Assumption									
	2.0%	2.5%	3.0%	3.5%	4.0%	4.5%	5.0%	5.5%	6.0%	6.5%
1	12	12	12	12	12	12	12	12	12	12
2	26	26	26	26	26	26	26	27	27	27
3	41	41	42	42	42	42	42	43	43	43
4	58	58	58	59	59	60	60	61	61	61
5	76	76	77	78	79	79	80	81	82	82
6	95	97	98	99	100	101	102	103	105	106
7	117	119	120	122	124	125	127	129	131	132
8	141	143	145	148	150	152	155	157	160	162
9	167	170	173	176	179	182	186	189	192	196
10	195	199	203	207	211	215	220	224	229	234
11	226	230	236	241	246	252	258	263	269	276
12	259	265	272	278	285	292	299	307	315	323
13	296	303	311	319	328	337	346	355	365	375
14	335	345	354	364	375	386	397	408	420	433
15	378	390	401	414	426	439	453	467	482	498
16	425	439	453	468	483	499	515	533	551	569
17	477	492	509	526	545	564	584	604	626	649
18	532	551	570	591	612	635	659	684	710	737
19	592	614	637	661	687	713	741	771	802	835
20	658	683	710	738	768	799	832	867	904	943
21	729	758	789	822	856	893	932	973	1,016	1,062
22	806	840	875	913	953	996	1,041	1,089	1,140	1,194
23	890	928	969	1,013	1,059	1,108	1,160	1,216	1,276	1,339
24	981	1,025	1,071	1,121	1,174	1,231	1,291	1,356	1,425	1,499
25	1,079	1,129	1,182	1,239	1,300	1,365	1,435	1,510	1,589	1,675
26	1,186	1,242	1,303	1,368	1,437	1,512	1,592	1,678	1,770	1,869
27	1,302	1,366	1,434	1,508	1,587	1,672	1,763	1,862	1,968	2,083
28	1,427	1,499	1,576	1,660	1,750	1,846	1,951	2,064	2,186	2,317
29	1,563	1,644	1,731	1,825	1,927	2,037	2,156	2,284	2,424	2,575
30	1,710	1,801	1,899	2,005	2,120	2,244	2,379	2,526	2,685	2,858
31	1,869	1,971	2,081	2,200	2,330	2,470	2,623	2,790	2,971	3,169
32	2,042	2,155	2,278	2,412	2,558	2,717	2,890	3,079	3,285	3,510
33	2,229	2,355	2,493	2,643	2,806	2,985	3,180	3,394	3,628	3,885
34	2,431	2,572	2,725	2,893	3,076	3,277	3,497	3,738	4,003	4,295
35	2,650	2,806	2,977	3,164	3,369	3,594	3,842	4,114	4,414	4,744
36	2,886	3,060	3,250	3,459	3,688	3,940	4,218	4,524	4,862	5,236
37	3,143	3,335	3,546	3,778	4,034	4,316	4,627	4,971	5,353	5,775
38	3,420	3,633	3,867	4,125	4,410	4,725	5,073	5,459	5,888	6,365
39	3,720	3,955	4,215	4,501	4,818	5,169	5,558	5,991	6,473	7,010
40	4,044	4,304	4,591	4,909	5,261	5,651	6,086	6,571	7,111	7,716
41	4,395	4,682	4,999	5,351	5,741	6,176	6,661	7,202	7,808	8,488
42	4,775	5,091	5,441	5,830	6,263	6,746	7,285	7,890	8,568	9,331
43	5,186	5,533	5,919	6,349	6,828	7,364	7,965	8,639	9,398	10,253
44	5,630	6,012	6,437	6,911	7,442	8,036	8,703	9,454	10,302	11,259
45	6,110	6,529	6,998	7,521	8,107	8,765	9,506	10,342	11,287	12,359
46	6,629	7,090	7,604	8,181	8,828	9,556	10,378	11,308	12,362	13,559
47	7,190	7,696	8,261	8,896	9,610	10,415	11,326	12,358	13,532	14,869
48	7,797	8,351	8,972	9,670	10,457	11,346	12,355	13,501	14,807	16,298
49	8,453	9,060	9,741	10,508	11,375	12,357	13,473	14,743	16,195	17,858
50	9,162	9,826	10,573	11,416	12,370	13,453	14,686	16,094	17,707	19,558

For illustration purposes only. Not representative of an actual investment. All assumptions and computational results are hypothetical in nature. Higher volatility has historically been associated with higher rates of return, and average returns have had a tendency to fluctuate from year to year.

Plan Aid Table 41e: Retirement Plan Savings Factors Table for Monthly Contributions—Percentage Savings Amount (9% Asset Growth Rate Assumption)

Years to Retire	Total Salary Growth Rate Assumption									
	2.0%	2.5%	3.0%	3.5%	4.0%	4.5%	5.0%	5.5%	6.0%	6.5%
1	12	12	12	12	12	12	12	12	12	12
2	26	26	26	27	27	27	27	27	27	27
3	42	42	42	42	42	43	43	43	43	43
4	59	59	60	60	60	61	61	62	62	62
5	78	78	79	80	80	81	82	83	83	84
6	98	99	101	102	103	104	105	106	108	109
7	121	123	124	126	128	130	131	133	135	137
8	146	149	151	153	156	158	161	163	166	169
9	174	177	180	184	187	190	194	197	201	204
10	205	209	213	217	222	226	231	235	240	245
11	239	244	249	254	260	266	272	278	284	290
12	276	282	289	296	303	310	317	325	333	341
13	316	324	332	341	350	359	368	378	388	399
14	361	371	381	391	402	413	425	437	450	463
15	410	422	434	447	460	474	488	503	519	535
16	463	478	492	508	524	541	558	576	595	615
17	522	539	557	575	594	614	635	657	680	705
18	587	607	627	649	672	696	721	748	775	804
19	657	681	705	731	758	786	816	848	881	916
20	735	762	791	821	852	886	921	959	998	1,039
21	819	851	884	919	957	996	1,037	1,081	1,128	1,177
22	912	948	987	1,028	1,071	1,117	1,165	1,217	1,272	1,330
23	1,013	1,055	1,100	1,147	1,197	1,250	1,307	1,367	1,431	1,499
24	1,124	1,172	1,223	1,278	1,336	1,397	1,463	1,533	1,608	1,687
25	1,246	1,300	1,359	1,421	1,488	1,559	1,635	1,716	1,803	1,896
26	1,378	1,441	1,507	1,579	1,655	1,737	1,824	1,918	2,019	2,127
27	1,523	1,594	1,670	1,751	1,839	1,932	2,033	2,141	2,257	2,382
28	1,682	1,762	1,848	1,941	2,040	2,147	2,262	2,387	2,521	2,665
29	1,855	1,945	2,043	2,148	2,261	2,383	2,515	2,657	2,811	2,978
30	2,044	2,146	2,256	2,375	2,504	2,642	2,793	2,955	3,132	3,323
31	2,250	2,365	2,489	2,624	2,769	2,927	3,098	3,284	3,485	3,705
32	2,476	2,605	2,745	2,896	3,061	3,239	3,434	3,645	3,875	4,126
33	2,722	2,867	3,024	3,194	3,380	3,582	3,802	4,042	4,305	4,591
34	2,991	3,153	3,329	3,521	3,730	3,958	4,207	4,479	4,777	5,104
35	3,285	3,466	3,663	3,878	4,113	4,370	4,651	4,959	5,298	5,670
36	3,606	3,807	4,028	4,269	4,532	4,821	5,138	5,487	5,871	6,294
37	3,955	4,180	4,426	4,696	4,991	5,316	5,673	6,067	6,501	6,980
38	4,337	4,588	4,862	5,163	5,494	5,858	6,260	6,703	7,194	7,737
39	4,754	5,033	5,338	5,674	6,044	6,452	6,903	7,402	7,955	8,570
40	5,209	5,518	5,858	6,232	6,645	7,102	7,608	8,169	8,793	9,487
41	5,706	6,048	6,426	6,843	7,303	7,814	8,380	9,010	9,712	10,496
42	6,247	6,627	7,046	7,510	8,023	8,593	9,227	9,933	10,723	11,606
43	6,838	7,259	7,724	8,239	8,810	9,446	10,154	10,946	11,832	12,826
44	7,483	7,948	8,463	9,035	9,670	10,379	11,170	12,056	13,050	14,168
45	8,186	8,701	9,271	9,905	10,611	11,399	12,282	13,272	14,386	15,642
46	8,953	9,522	10,153	10,855	11,639	12,516	13,500	14,606	15,853	17,262
47	9,790	10,417	11,115	11,893	12,762	13,737	14,832	16,067	17,462	19,042
48	10,703	11,395	12,165	13,026	13,989	15,072	16,291	17,668	19,227	20,997
49	11,699	12,461	13,312	14,263	15,331	16,532	17,887	19,421	21,162	23,143
50	12,784	13,625	14,563	15,614	16,796	18,127	19,633	21,341	23,284	25,499

For illustration purposes only. Not representative of an actual investment. All assumptions and computational results are hypothetical in nature. Higher volatility has historically been associated with higher rates of return, and average returns have had a tendency to fluctuate from year to year.

Plan Aid Table 41f: Retirement Plan Savings Factors Table for Monthly Contributions—Percentage Savings Amount (10% Asset Growth Rate Assumption)

Years to Retire	Total Salary Growth Rate Assumption									
	2.0%	2.5%	3.0%	3.5%	4.0%	4.5%	5.0%	5.5%	6.0%	6.5%
1	13	13	13	13	13	13	13	13	13	13
2	27	27	27	27	27	27	27	27	27	27
3	42	42	43	43	43	43	43	44	44	44
4	60	60	61	61	61	62	62	63	63	64
5	79	80	81	82	82	83	84	85	85	86
6	101	102	103	105	106	107	108	109	111	112
7	125	127	129	131	132	134	136	138	140	141
8	152	155	157	160	162	165	167	170	172	175
9	182	185	189	192	195	199	202	206	210	213
10	216	220	224	228	233	237	242	247	252	257
11	252	258	263	269	275	281	287	293	299	306
12	293	300	307	314	321	329	337	345	353	362
13	338	347	355	364	374	383	393	403	414	425
14	388	399	409	420	432	444	456	469	482	495
15	444	456	469	483	497	511	526	542	558	575
16	505	520	536	552	569	587	605	624	644	665
17	573	591	609	629	649	671	693	716	740	766
18	648	669	691	714	739	764	791	819	848	879
19	730	755	782	809	838	868	900	934	969	1,006
20	822	851	882	914	948	984	1,022	1,062	1,104	1,148
21	922	957	992	1,030	1,070	1,113	1,157	1,204	1,254	1,307
22	1,034	1,073	1,115	1,159	1,206	1,256	1,308	1,364	1,422	1,485
23	1,156	1,202	1,251	1,302	1,356	1,414	1,475	1,541	1,610	1,683
24	1,292	1,345	1,400	1,460	1,523	1,590	1,662	1,738	1,819	1,905
25	1,441	1,502	1,566	1,634	1,707	1,785	1,868	1,957	2,051	2,152
26	1,606	1,675	1,749	1,827	1,912	2,001	2,097	2,200	2,310	2,428
27	1,788	1,866	1,951	2,041	2,137	2,241	2,352	2,471	2,598	2,735
28	1,988	2,077	2,174	2,277	2,387	2,506	2,634	2,771	2,919	3,078
29	2,208	2,310	2,420	2,537	2,664	2,800	2,946	3,104	3,275	3,458
30	2,451	2,567	2,691	2,825	2,969	3,125	3,293	3,474	3,670	3,882
31	2,719	2,850	2,991	3,143	3,307	3,484	3,676	3,884	4,109	4,353
32	3,014	3,162	3,321	3,493	3,680	3,882	4,100	4,338	4,596	4,877
33	3,339	3,506	3,686	3,880	4,092	4,321	4,570	4,841	5,137	5,459
34	3,697	3,885	4,087	4,308	4,547	4,807	5,090	5,399	5,736	6,105
35	4,092	4,302	4,530	4,779	5,049	5,343	5,665	6,016	6,401	6,822
36	4,526	4,762	5,019	5,298	5,603	5,936	6,301	6,700	7,137	7,618
37	5,004	5,269	5,557	5,871	6,215	6,591	7,003	7,456	7,953	8,501
38	5,531	5,827	6,150	6,503	6,890	7,314	7,780	8,292	8,857	9,480
39	6,110	6,442	6,804	7,200	7,635	8,112	8,638	9,217	9,857	10,565
40	6,749	7,119	7,524	7,968	8,456	8,993	9,586	10,240	10,965	11,768
41	7,451	7,864	8,317	8,815	9,362	9,966	10,633	11,371	12,190	13,100
42	8,224	8,685	9,191	9,747	10,361	11,038	11,789	12,621	13,546	14,576
43	9,076	9,589	10,153	10,775	11,462	12,222	13,065	14,002	15,045	16,210
44	10,013	10,584	11,214	11,908	12,676	13,527	14,474	15,527	16,704	18,019
45	11,044	11,680	12,381	13,156	14,014	14,967	16,028	17,212	18,537	20,022
46	12,179	12,886	13,666	14,530	15,489	16,555	17,744	19,073	20,563	22,237
47	13,428	14,214	15,082	16,044	17,114	18,305	19,636	21,128	22,802	24,688
48	14,803	15,675	16,640	17,712	18,904	20,235	21,724	23,396	25,277	27,399
49	16,315	17,283	18,356	19,548	20,877	22,362	24,027	25,899	28,010	30,396
50	17,980	19,054	20,245	21,571	23,050	24,707	26,567	28,662	31,029	33,710

For illustration purposes only. Not representative of an actual investment. All assumptions and computational results are hypothetical in nature. Higher volatility has historically been associated with higher rates of return, and average returns have had a tendency to fluctuate from year to year.

Plan Aid Table 41g: Retirement Plan Savings Factors Table for Monthly Contributions—Percentage Savings Amount (11% Asset Growth Rate Assumption)

Years to Retire	Total Salary Growth Rate Assumption									
	2.0%	2.5%	3.0%	3.5%	4.0%	4.5%	5.0%	5.5%	6.0%	6.5%
1	13	13	13	13	13	13	13	13	13	13
2	27	27	27	27	27	27	27	27	27	27
3	43	43	43	43	44	44	44	44	44	45
4	61	61	62	62	63	63	64	64	64	65
5	81	82	83	84	84	85	86	87	87	88
6	104	105	106	108	109	110	111	113	114	115
7	130	131	133	135	137	139	140	142	144	146
8	159	161	163	166	168	171	174	176	179	182
9	191	194	197	201	204	208	211	215	219	223
10	227	231	235	240	245	249	254	259	264	269
11	267	273	278	284	290	296	303	309	316	323
12	312	319	326	334	341	349	357	366	374	383
13	362	371	380	389	399	409	419	430	441	452
14	419	429	440	452	464	476	489	502	516	530
15	481	494	508	522	537	552	568	584	601	619
16	551	567	583	601	619	637	657	677	698	720
17	629	648	668	689	710	733	756	781	807	833
18	716	738	762	787	813	840	868	898	929	962
19	813	839	867	897	928	960	994	1,030	1,067	1,107
20	920	952	985	1,020	1,056	1,095	1,135	1,178	1,223	1,270
21	1,040	1,077	1,116	1,157	1,200	1,246	1,294	1,344	1,398	1,454
22	1,174	1,217	1,262	1,310	1,361	1,414	1,471	1,531	1,594	1,662
23	1,322	1,372	1,425	1,481	1,540	1,603	1,670	1,740	1,815	1,895
24	1,488	1,545	1,607	1,672	1,741	1,814	1,892	1,975	2,063	2,157
25	1,671	1,738	1,809	1,884	1,965	2,050	2,141	2,238	2,341	2,451
26	1,876	1,953	2,034	2,121	2,214	2,313	2,419	2,532	2,652	2,781
27	2,103	2,191	2,285	2,386	2,493	2,607	2,730	2,861	3,001	3,152
28	2,356	2,457	2,565	2,680	2,803	2,935	3,077	3,229	3,392	3,568
29	2,637	2,752	2,876	3,008	3,149	3,301	3,465	3,641	3,830	4,034
30	2,950	3,081	3,222	3,373	3,535	3,710	3,898	4,101	4,319	4,556
31	3,297	3,446	3,607	3,779	3,965	4,165	4,381	4,614	4,867	5,140
32	3,683	3,852	4,035	4,231	4,443	4,672	4,920	5,188	5,479	5,794
33	4,112	4,304	4,511	4,735	4,976	5,238	5,521	5,829	6,163	6,526
34	4,588	4,806	5,041	5,295	5,570	5,868	6,192	6,544	6,927	7,344
35	5,118	5,364	5,629	5,918	6,230	6,570	6,939	7,341	7,780	8,259
36	5,706	5,984	6,284	6,610	6,965	7,351	7,772	8,231	8,733	9,282
37	6,359	6,672	7,012	7,381	7,783	8,221	8,699	9,223	9,796	10,425
38	7,085	7,438	7,821	8,238	8,693	9,189	9,733	10,328	10,982	11,701
39	7,891	8,288	8,720	9,191	9,705	10,267	10,884	11,561	12,305	13,126
40	8,787	9,233	9,719	10,250	10,830	11,467	12,166	12,934	13,781	14,716
41	9,781	10,282	10,829	11,427	12,082	12,801	13,592	14,464	15,427	16,491
42	10,885	11,448	12,063	12,736	13,474	14,286	15,181	16,168	17,261	18,472
43	12,111	12,743	13,433	14,190	15,022	15,938	16,948	18,066	19,305	20,681
44	13,473	14,181	14,956	15,806	16,742	17,774	18,915	20,179	21,583	23,145
45	14,985	15,778	16,647	17,602	18,655	19,817	21,104	22,532	24,121	25,892
46	16,664	17,552	18,526	19,598	20,780	22,088	23,538	25,151	26,947	28,955
47	18,529	19,522	20,613	21,815	23,142	24,613	26,246	28,065	30,095	32,368
48	20,599	21,709	22,931	24,278	25,768	27,420	29,258	31,308	33,601	36,171
49	22,897	24,138	25,505	27,014	28,685	30,541	32,608	34,917	37,503	40,409
50	25,449	26,836	28,364	30,053	31,926	34,009	36,332	38,931	41,847	45,129

For illustration purposes only. Not representative of an actual investment. All assumptions and computational results are hypothetical in nature. Higher volatility has historically been associated with higher rates of return, and average returns have had a tendency to fluctuate from year to year.

Plan Aid Table 41h: Retirement Plan Savings Factors Table for Monthly Contributions—Percentage Savings Amount (12% Asset Growth Rate Assumption)

Years to Retire	Total Salary Growth Rate Assumption									
	2.0%	2.5%	3.0%	3.5%	4.0%	4.5%	5.0%	5.5%	6.0%	6.5%
1	13	13	13	13	13	13	13	13	13	13
2	27	27	27	27	27	27	27	28	28	28
3	43	44	44	44	44	44	45	45	45	45
4	62	63	63	63	64	64	65	65	66	66
5	83	84	85	85	86	87	88	89	89	90
6	107	108	110	111	112	113	114	116	117	118
7	134	136	138	140	141	143	145	147	149	151
8	165	167	170	172	175	178	180	183	186	189
9	200	203	206	210	213	217	221	225	228	232
10	239	243	248	252	257	262	267	272	277	283
11	283	288	294	300	307	313	319	326	333	340
12	332	340	347	355	363	371	379	388	397	406
13	388	397	407	417	427	437	448	459	470	482
14	451	462	474	486	499	512	525	539	554	568
15	522	536	550	565	581	597	613	631	649	667
16	602	618	636	654	673	693	713	734	757	780
17	691	711	733	755	777	801	826	852	880	908
18	792	816	841	868	895	924	955	986	1,019	1,054
19	905	934	964	995	1,028	1,063	1,099	1,138	1,178	1,220
20	1,032	1,066	1,102	1,139	1,179	1,220	1,263	1,309	1,357	1,408
21	1,175	1,215	1,257	1,301	1,348	1,397	1,449	1,503	1,561	1,621
22	1,335	1,382	1,431	1,483	1,538	1,596	1,658	1,722	1,791	1,863
23	1,514	1,569	1,627	1,688	1,753	1,821	1,894	1,970	2,051	2,137
24	1,716	1,780	1,847	1,919	1,994	2,074	2,160	2,250	2,346	2,448
25	1,942	2,016	2,095	2,178	2,266	2,360	2,460	2,566	2,679	2,799
26	2,196	2,282	2,372	2,469	2,572	2,681	2,797	2,922	3,054	3,196
27	2,481	2,579	2,684	2,796	2,915	3,042	3,178	3,323	3,478	3,644
28	2,800	2,914	3,035	3,164	3,302	3,449	3,607	3,776	3,957	4,151
29	3,158	3,289	3,428	3,576	3,736	3,906	4,089	4,285	4,496	4,723
30	3,560	3,709	3,869	4,040	4,223	4,420	4,632	4,859	5,104	5,368
31	4,010	4,181	4,364	4,560	4,771	4,998	5,242	5,506	5,789	6,096
32	4,514	4,710	4,919	5,144	5,386	5,647	5,929	6,233	6,561	6,916
33	5,080	5,303	5,542	5,799	6,077	6,377	6,701	7,051	7,430	7,841
34	5,714	5,967	6,240	6,535	6,853	7,196	7,568	7,971	8,408	8,883
35	6,424	6,713	7,024	7,360	7,723	8,116	8,542	9,005	9,509	10,057
36	7,221	7,548	7,902	8,285	8,699	9,149	9,637	10,168	10,747	11,378
37	8,113	8,485	8,887	9,323	9,795	10,309	10,867	11,476	12,140	12,866
38	9,113	9,535	9,991	10,487	11,025	11,610	12,248	12,944	13,706	14,540
39	10,233	10,711	11,229	11,792	12,404	13,071	13,798	14,594	15,466	16,423
40	11,488	12,030	12,617	13,255	13,951	14,709	15,539	16,448	17,445	18,541
41	12,895	13,507	14,172	14,896	15,685	16,548	17,493	18,529	19,668	20,923
42	14,471	15,163	15,915	16,735	17,631	18,611	19,685	20,866	22,166	23,601
43	16,236	17,018	17,869	18,797	19,812	20,924	22,146	23,490	24,973	26,611
44	18,214	19,097	20,058	21,108	22,258	23,519	24,906	26,435	28,124	29,994
45	20,430	21,426	22,512	23,699	25,000	26,429	28,003	29,741	31,663	33,795
46	22,913	24,035	25,261	26,602	28,074	29,693	31,477	33,450	35,637	38,066
47	25,694	26,959	28,341	29,856	31,520	33,351	35,374	37,613	40,098	42,863
48	28,809	30,234	31,793	33,502	35,382	37,454	39,744	42,283	45,105	48,250
49	32,299	33,904	35,661	37,589	39,711	42,053	44,645	47,522	50,725	54,300
50	36,208	38,015	39,994	42,167	44,562	47,208	50,141	53,399	57,032	61,093

For illustration purposes only. Not representative of an actual investment. All assumptions and computational results are hypothetical in nature. Higher volatility has historically been associated with higher rates of return, and average returns have had a tendency to fluctuate from year to year.

both *you* and your *employer*) that would have to be contributed into your retirement plans at work during the current year, if you want to save a percentage of your salary each month and be able to accumulate enough to meet your overall retirement objectives.

Over the years, although the savings percentage will not change, this amount may likely increase, because you will be applying the same percentage to a growing annual salary. Since this is the total amount required, and because your employer will probably make some of the contributions, you will most likely not be responsible for all of it.

Calculating the Actual Percent of Salary

You ultimately want to know what percent of salary you need to save— that's what this chapter is all about. To do that, enter your *Current Monthly Salary* in box (h), which is the same as item (e) on Plan Aid 3a: Example on page 75. Then, you can determine your *Hypothetical Total Monthly Savings Percent*, which should be entered into box (i), by dividing your *Hypothetical Total Monthly Savings Amount* in box (g) by your *Current Monthly Salary* in box (h).

This is the total percent of your salary (coming from both you and your employer) that would have to be contributed into your retirement plans at work if you want to be able to accumulate enough to meet your overall objectives.

After reviewing the example, use Plan Aid 41b: Your Plan now, to figure out the total amount and percent that will have to be contributed into your retirement plans at work if you want to save on a percent-of-salary basis.

How Much Will Your Employer Kick In?

The next thing to do is turn to Plan Aid 42a: Example to figure out how much your employer may contribute into your plans under this approach. The first step is to enter your *Hypothetical Total Monthly Savings Amount* into box (a), which is the same as item (g) on Plan Aid 41a: Example on page 331. Then, enter the *Monthly Employer Pension Contribution Amount* in box (b), which is the same as item (d) on Plan Aid 37a: Exam-

Plan Aid 41b: Your Plan
Percent of Salary Monthly Retirement Plan Contributions

TOTAL PERCENTAGE MONTHLY SAVINGS AMOUNT

Hypothetical Future Retirement Plan Target .... | (a) $
(From item (c), Plan Aid 36b: Your Plan on page 301)

Number of Years Until Retirement .... | (b)
(From item (c), Plan Aid 1b: Your Plan on page 13)

Total Salary Growth Rate Assumption .... | (c)   %
(From item (k), Plan Aid 4b: Your Plan on page 86)

Asset Growth Rate Assumption .... | (d)   %
(From item (c), Plan Aid 39b: Your Plan on page 324)

Lookup Table for Appropriate Asset Growth Rate .... | (e)
Select lookup table for appropriate growth rate below   *From Index Table below*

Retirement Plan Monthly Percent Savings Factor .... | (f)
Look Up on Table Noted in Item (e) above, Using Items (b) and (c) above

Hypothetical Total Monthly Savings Amount .... | (g) $
$(a) \div (f)$

Current Monthly Salary .... | (h) $
(From item (e), Plan Aid 3b: Your Plan on page 77)

Hypothetical Total Monthly Savings Percent .... | (i)   %
$(g) \div (h)$

INDEX FOR ASSET GROWTH RATE TABLES

Use Asset Growth Rate in item (d) above to select appropriate lookup table below

Asset Growth Rate	5%	Table 41a
Asset Growth Rate	6%	Table 41b
Asset Growth Rate	7%	Table 41c
Asset Growth Rate	8%	Table 41d
Asset Growth Rate	9%	Table 41e
Asset Growth Rate	10%	Table 41f
Asset Growth Rate	11%	Table 41g
Asset Growth Rate	12%	Table 41h

ple on page 308. Next, compute the *Hypothetical Net Monthly Savings Amount* in box (c), by subtracting the *Monthly Employer Pension Contribution Amount* in box (b) from the *Hypothetical Total Monthly Savings Amount* in box (a). This is the total amount that you may still need to save after taking into account potential contributions from your employer's fixed percentage pension plans.

Just like in the last chapter, if your *Hypothetical Net Monthly Savings Amount* in box (c) is *equal to or less than zero*, it means that the amounts you may have already saved, along with your future contributions into various retirement vehicles and the contributions you are hoping to get from your employer may be sufficient to meet your retirement objectives—given all of the assumptions you have made so far.

Obviously, you don't want to stop saving and investing for retirement, especially in your plans at work, so at this point, if you came up with a negative number, you should go back and change some of your planning variables to give yourself a higher goal to shoot for or adjust your hypothetical rates of return.

Accounting for Matching Contributions

Next, you need to consider the matching contributions you may be expecting from your employer. Start with the *Employer Matching Contribution Factor* in box (d), which is the same as in item (j) on Plan Aid 38a: Example on page 311. Then, multiply the *Hypothetical Net Monthly Savings Amount* in box (c) by the *Employer Matching Contribution Factor* in box (d) to determine the *Preliminary Matching Contribution Amount*, which should be entered into box (e).

This is the amount of your employer's matching contribution prior to applying the matching contribution limit. In other words, this would be the amount of your employer's match if there was no limitation. As long as this amount is less than the previously determined maximum, it should be the matching contribution. However, if it's larger than the maximum amount allowed, the maximum amount will be used as the matching contribution.

To determine how big your company's matching contribution might be, start by entering the *Max. Monthly Employer Matching Contribution*

Plan Aid 42a: Example
Percent of Salary Monthly Retirement Plan Contributions

MONTHLY EMPLOYER CONTRIBUTION AMOUNTS

Hypothetical Total Monthly Savings Amount .... (a) $ **721**
  (From item (g), Plan Aid 41a: Example on page 331)

Monthly Employer Pension Contribution Amount ..... (b) $ **125**
  (From item (d), Plan Aid 37a: Example on page 308)

Hypothetical Net Monthly Savings Amount .... (c) $ **596**
  (a) - (b)

Employer Matching Contribution Factor .... (d) **.33**
  (From item (j), Plan Aid 38a: Example on page 311)

Preliminary Matching Contribution Amount .... (e) $ **197**
  (c) x (d)

Max. Monthly Employer Matching Contribution .... (f) $ **188**
  (From item (i), Plan Aid 38a: Example on page 311)

Hypothetical Employer Matching Contribution .... (g) $ **188**
  Smaller of (e) or (f) above

FINAL MONTHLY PERCENT CONTRIBUTION AMOUNTS

Hypothetical <u>Employee</u> Monthly Contribution .... (h) $ **408**
  (c) - (g)

Current Monthly Salary .... (i) $ **6,250**
  (From item (e), Plan Aid 3a: Example on page 75)

Hypothetical <u>Employee</u> Contribution % of Salary ..... (j) **6.5** %
  (h) ÷ (i)

Hypothetical <u>Employer</u> Monthly Contribution .... (k) $ **313**
  (b) + (g)

Hypothetical <u>Employer</u> Contribution % of Salary ...... (l) **5.0** %
  (k) ÷ (i)

in box (f), which is the same amount as item (i) on Plan Aid 38a: Example on page 311. Then, you can determine the amount of the matching contribution by selecting the smaller of the *Preliminary Matching Contribution Amount* in box (e) or the *Max. Monthly Employer Matching Contribution* in box (f), and entering it as your *Hypothetical Employer Matching Contribution* in box (g).

How Much Will You Have to Contribute Each Month?

Now that you know how much you may get from your employer's fixed-percentage pension plans and matching contributions each month, you can determine how much *you* may need to put away for yourself. Simply subtract the *Hypothetical Employer Matching Contribution* in box (g) from the *Hypothetical Net Monthly Savings Amount* in box (c), and put the answer in box (h), *Hypothetical Employee Monthly Contribution*. This is the monthly amount that you may need to contribute to your retirement plans at work after taking into account all employer contributions.

This is the bottom line: This is the *amount* your human resource department would withhold from your wages each month during the current year, if you wanted to put a percentage of your salary into your retirement plans for the rest of your working career. Over the years, although the savings percentage will not change, this amount should increase, because you will apply the same percentage to a growing annual salary.

What Is the Actual Percentage of Salary?

Of course, you ultimately want to know what percent of salary you might need to put away. To figure it out, enter your *Current Monthly Salary* into box (i), which is the same as item (e) on Plan Aid 3a: Example on page 75. Then, divide the *Hypothetical Employee Monthly Contribution* in box (h) by your *Current Monthly Salary* in box (i) to determine your *Hypothetical Employee Contribution % of Salary,* which should be entered into box (j). This is the percent of your salary that you may need to contribute to your retirement plans at work after taking into account all employer contributions.

Again, this is the bottom line: It's the *percentage* your human resource department should withhold from your wages each month if you want to put a percentage of your salary into your retirement plans for the rest of your working career.

Ultimately, you also need to know how much and what percentage your employer may be putting away for you each month. Simply add the *Monthly Employer Pension Contribution Amount* in box (b) to the *Hypothetical Employer Matching Contribution* in box (g) to determine the *Hypothetical Employer Monthly Contribution* in box (k). This is the monthly amount your employer may be contributing to your retirement plans at work on your behalf.

Then, to see what percent of your salary your employer might be contributing, simply divide the *Hypothetical Employer Monthly Contribution* in box (k) by your *Current Monthly Salary* in box (i) to determine the *Hypothetical Employer Contribution % of Salary*, which should be entered in box (l). This is the percent of your salary that your employer may contribute to your retirement plans at work if you decide to use a percent-of-salary savings strategy.

After reviewing the example, use Plan Aid 42b: Your Plan now, to figure out how much you and your employer may need to put away on a percent-of-salary basis to meet your own retirement objectives.

A Few More Things to Remember

Just like in the last chapter, make sure you don't save less than you're able to save if you come up with an amount or percentage that is lower than what you're already doing. As always, you should go back and make adjustments to your plan to go after a better retirement scenario, or build in a little more conservatism. And of course, you should always contribute at least enough to get the full match.

You may also have to go back and reevaluate how much you are putting into your other savings vehicles if the amount you need to contribute at work is more than you're allowed to put in. And if you simply can't save as much as you need to, you may have to scale back your plans, reconsider your expectations, and find ways to reduce the amount you need to accumulate in the first place.

Plan Aid 42b: Your Plan
Percent of Salary Monthly Retirement Plan Contributions

MONTHLY EMPLOYER CONTRIBUTION AMOUNTS

Hypothetical Total Monthly Savings Amount ....
(a) $ _____

(From item (g), Plan Aid 41b: Your Plan on page 341)

Monthly Employer Pension Contribution Amount .....
(b) $ _____

(From item (d), Plan Aid 37b: Your Plan on page 309)

Hypothetical Net Monthly Savings Amount ....
(c) $ _____

(a) - (b)

Employer Matching Contribution Factor ....
(d) _____

(From item (j), Plan Aid 38b: Your Plan on page 313)

Preliminary Matching Contribution Amount ....
(e) $ _____

(c) x (d)

Max. Monthly Employer Matching Contribution ....
(f) $ _____

(From item (i), Plan Aid 38b: Your Plan on page 313)

Hypothetical Employer Matching Contribution ....
(g) $ _____

Smaller of (e) or (f) above

FINAL MONTHLY PERCENT CONTRIBUTION AMOUNTS

Hypothetical <u>Employee</u> Monthly Contribution ....
(h) $ _____

(c) - (g)

Current Monthly Salary ....
(i) $ _____

(From item (e), Plan Aid 3b: Your Plan on page 77)

Hypothetical <u>Employee</u> Contribution % of Salary .....
(j) _____ %

(h) ÷ (i)

Hypothetical <u>Employer</u> Monthly Contribution ....
(k) $ _____

(b) + (g)

Hypothetical <u>Employer</u> Contribution % of Salary ......
(l) _____ %

(k) ÷ (i)

Using the Worksheets and Getting Help

It's time now to go back and play around with the worksheets to try out some alternative planning scenarios. Ultimately, you should be in a much better position to talk with your advisors about what you're thinking, about what they're thinking, and about how you can work together to create a comprehensive retirement plan. Think about everything we've discussed, get some more experience with the worksheets, and call a financial professional. Or, if you're not working with a financial professional, go to our website to find someone who is "trained" in using the Grangaard Strategy® to manage money before and during retirement.

Get to It!

It's time to roll up your sleeves. *Step #25: Get Started Now* is a call to action—because it's never too early and it's never too late to create your financial plan. Remember, most people don't plan to fail, they simply fail to plan. I urge you to get started today. If you have any questions about the Grangaard Strategy®, or about choosing a financial professional, you can find more information in the appendix.

Get started now—and good luck!

APPENDIX

Selecting a Financial Advisor

Keep in mind that there are many kinds of financial professionals and they get paid in many different ways. You need to be extremely cautious in selecting your advisors, because as the old saying goes—"choose your advisor and you have chosen your advice." You need to decide who to work with and how you want to pay them. Some advisors earn commissions, some are paid based upon assets under management, and still others charge a flat hourly rate.

There are no right ways and no wrong ways to charge for financial planning services—but there are better and worse ways to create a retirement plan. Make sure you are comfortable with your advisor; make sure you are comfortable with how they are getting paid; and make sure you are comfortable with their approach to helping you accumulate money for retirement and their approach to managing it during retirement. One of the best ways to select an advisor is to talk with your friends and relatives about who they use.

Questions to Ask a Financial Professional

Most financial planning professionals agree that there are a number of questions you should ask a potential advisor. In addition to finding out whether they are familiar with the Grangaard Strategy® and if they have the tools they need to implement it, you should also go through some of these other questions when interviewing a potential advisor.

What kinds of experience do you have, and who are your typical clients?

What are your qualifications, designations, licenses, and memberships?

What did you do before you became a financial planner?

How long have you lived here?

What kinds of products and services do you offer?

What is your overall approach to financial planning before retirement?

What is your overall approach to financial planning after retirement?

Are you the only person I will be working with or do you use a team approach?

Can you work with my other advisors and can you make referrals?

How will I pay you for your services and how much do you typically charge?

Have you ever been disciplined for unlawful or unethical acts in your profession?

Have you ever been convicted of a crime?

Do you provide a written agreement and engagement letter?

How long have you been providing financial planning advice?

Resources to Check the Disciplinary History of a Financial Planner

Certified Financial Planner Board of Standards 888-CFP-MARK

North American Securities Administrators Association 888-84-NASAA

National Association of Insurance Commissioners 816-842-3600

National Association of Securities Dealers 800-289-9999

Securities and Exchange Commission 800-732-0330

Resources to Help You Find a Financial Planner

Financial Planning Association 800-647-6340

National Association of Personal Financial Advisors 888-FEE-ONLY

American Institute of Certified Public Accountants

    Personal Financial Planning Division 800-862-4272

American Society of CLU & ChFC 800-392-6900

Finding a "Trained" Grangaard Strategy® Advisor

Visit www.thegrangaardstrategy.com for a list of advisors who have attended a Grangaard Strategy® Training Program.

INDEX

INDEX